www.type

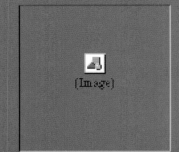
[Image]

# www.type

ROGER PRING

SERIES CONSULTANT
ALASTAIR CAMPBELL

WATSON-GUPTILL
PUBLICATIONS
*New York*

To Sarah, Sally, and Katy.

Copyright © 1999 The Ivy Press Limited and Alastair Campbell

First published in the United States in 2000 by
Watson-Guptill Publications,
a division of BPI Communications, Inc.,
1515 Broadway,
New York, NY 10036

Library of Congress Catalog Card Number: 99-68702

ISBN 0-8230-5860-3

This book was conceived, designed, and produced by
Alastair Campbell and The Ivy Press Limited
The Old Candlemakers
West Street
Lewes, East Sussex BN7 2NZ
England

Editorial Director: Sophie Collins
Art Director: Peter Bridgewater
Managing Editor: Anne Townley
Editor: Peter Leek
Designers: Roger Pring, Alastair Campbell
Special thanks to Kant Rathod for surfing far beyond the call of duty.
Additional research by Kevin Jones and Simon Phillips.

Originated and printed by Hong Kong Graphic, China

1 2 3 4 5 6 7 8 9 / 08 07 06 05 04 03 02 01 00

# INTRODUCTION

**T**his is a report, travel guide, and survival manual from a wild frontier. For every familiar fixture in this new environment there are just as many to mystify the typographic tourist. Even the underlying landscape suffers constant volcanic change. In this book I attempt to plant some markers that will help make sense of a confused situation. The method of delivering the message to the viewer has changed almost beyond recognition, but the fundamental principles that govern the manipulation of characters, words, and pages in the "old" world of print typography are still vitally important. Such a journey of discovery may lead experienced print typographers to tighten their grip still further on the familiar baggage of past practice, but there are new moves to be learned around every corner.

Web screens may blossom with movies and be garnished with soundtracks but, for the moment, type is the primary vehicle for information and persuasion. Its appearance onscreen is more crucial than ever. Intense competition for the user's attention means that words must attract and inform (and maybe seduce) as quickly as possible. Flawless delivery of the message to the screen is the goal. The road to success is very broad, but the surface rather uneven. Hold on very tight.

Roger Pring

London, April 1999

# GAINING CONTROL OF THE SHAPELESS PAGE

Designers for print have had, to date, no more than 15 years' experience of dealing with words and type in a computer-based environment. It is only a short history, but it speaks of increasing sophistication and ever-developing facilities. Though the concept of "what you see is what you get" often looks tattered around the edges, most designers have now got a working relationship with the technology. Typographic controls are expressed in thousandths of a point, and the finer points of color reproduction can, whether you approve or not, be under your personal control.

The apparent anarchy of the Web comes as a surprise to those used to the more measured environment of print. We are obliged to think differently, and to revise our expectations.

like trying to
wallpaper a room
while standing
outside the
window

This elementary sequence shows some of the differences between a conventional print-based approach and the disciplines needed for successful Web typography.

**1**
The Web page is typically crafted in a window *(left)* that bears no relationship to the format of the user's screen. This is unsurprising, since the end-user is able to change the screen format at will. Type descriptions, equally, are unlike those familiar in print-based practice.

**2 | 3 | 4**
The result: viewed in the associated browser window, the various elements shift position *(left and below)* to account for different window shapes. More work will be needed for the typographer to regain control of this situation. In a rival browser *(below left)* margins behave strangely, and the viewer's selected background makes green type disappear.

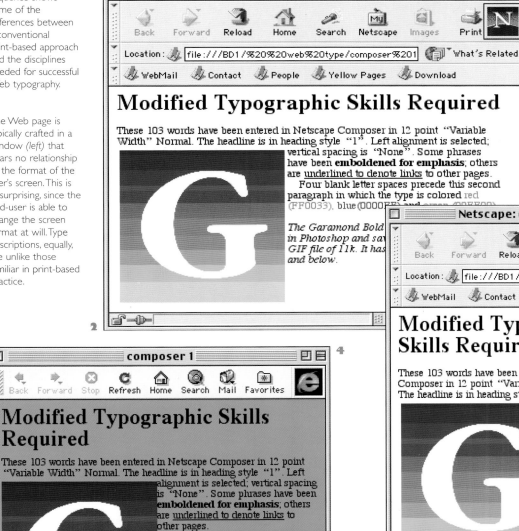

**9**

# WINNERS AND LOSERS

The examples on these two pages are intended to symbolize what has been lost and gained in the migration of the typographic design process to the Web. On the left, a homage to manuscript style and a small nod to technotype. On the right, type as it hardly ever was in a page-makeup program.

**F**OR MORE THAN FIVE YEARS, I maintained myself thus solely by the *labor of my own hands,* and found, that by working about six weeks in a year, I could meet *all the expenses of living.* HENRY DAVID THOREAU

**1**
Familiar moves in QuarkXPress *(left).* A drop capital in color, in a different face from the body text, is compressed horizontally and kerned to bring it closer to the succeeding character. The rest of the first line of text is in small caps— further emphasis is given by color and italicization. The default hyphenation and justification values have been adjusted for the whole quotation, tightening the word spacing. The author's credit is put into an anchored, colored, and baseline-shifted text box. Thick/thin rules in a tint of black top and tail the text block, which sits on a pale-colored ground.

**2**
Extremes of character compression *(right),* negative tracking, much reduced line spacing, hugely enlarged punctuation, and a ninety-degree rotation to finish. Once more in QuarkXPress.

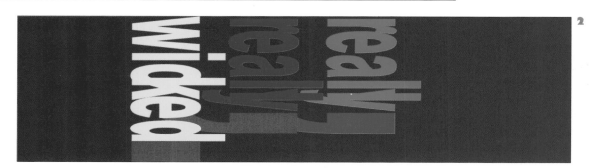

**2**

*Clockwise from top left:*

**www.absolut.com**
**www.adidas.com**
**www.cyberposium.com**
**www.desires.com**
**www.swissair.com**
**www.hillmancurtis.com**
**www.blackstarbeer.com**
**www.willoughbydesign.com**

# HOW WORDS GET TO THE SCREEN

**D**igital typographers knew that good screen display depended on having a fat folder of Type 1 printer fonts. These "outline" fonts were vital for crisp printed output, provided possibilities for type manipulation, and even do-it-yourself type design. All this still holds good for rendering type as GIFs, but there are developing, and sometimes controversial, methods for getting your chosen typeface onto the viewer's screen. The main delivery methods are shown here.

### Bitmaps and HTML

All type onscreen is by definition bitmapped. Standard HTML (Hypertext Markup Language) instructions can command a bitmapped font (if it is installed) to appear on the viewer's screen. Otherwise, either the browser's default or the user's selected font will be displayed.

### PostScript

Adobe's pioneering Page Description Language (PDL) offers scalable, therefore resolution-independent, fonts. It is the basis of the Portable Document Format (PDF), which aims to deliver high-quality printable pages to the screen, irrespective of the user's installed font set.

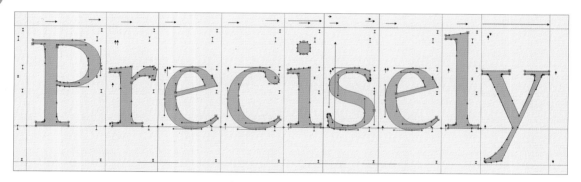

**1** The start of it all (*left,* with apologies to the original medieval punch-cutters). The Fontographer application window gives a clue to the vector-based construction of the average computer typeface (Berkeley Medium in this case).

**R** The full-resolution character as used for conventional repro-duction. The scalable outline font allows printed output at any chosen enlargement.

**e** Antialiasing averages the density of pixels around the edges of the character. These intermediate colors smooth the character's appearance onscreen.

**a** Without the benefit of antialiasing, the jagged "staircase" quality of the character's structure is clearly revealed. The effect is less marked at smaller text sizes.

**d** A historical sidelight: the absolute minimum bitmap description of the character, and for a long time the only way of getting type to the screen.

## CSS

Cascading Style Sheets add an extra dimension to basic HTML. A separate scripting language allows control of type styles, alignment, and leading. With CSS, the designer can force the browser to use a specific font if it is available on the viewer's system. A table of hierarchical values is in place to determine which instructions are to be followed in case of conflicts. Unlike plain HTML, CSS allows multilayering of elements.

## TrueDoc/WebFont

Bitstream's TrueDoc system aims to cut down on the font overhead by sending only the relevant characters and styles. The WebFont application records the shapes of the necessary characters and produces a compact data structure called a Portable Font Resource (PFR). The necessary player is built into Netscape Communicator, though Internet Explorer users need to download an ActiveX Control on first viewing a PFR-equipped site.

## OpenType/WEFT

Adobe and Microsoft have cooperated to promote OpenType, using the Web Embedding Font Tool (WEFT). The site is scanned, and compressed font files or "font objects" of the relevant characters are downloaded, just as if they were GIFs or JPEGs, then decompressed and cached by the browser in the same way. The font objects are designed for use only by the browser and cannot be accessed by other applications.

## Web Authoring

There are a number of software suites that offer a degree of insulation from the individual disciplines of HTML and CSS. Simple point-and-click programs (such as PageMill and HomeSite) and professional programs (such as CyberStudio and Dreamweaver) generate HTML behind an interface that looks more like a page-makeup application. The HTML can be edited if necessary, and the result viewed offline on any chosen browser.

13

**a**
Intentions defeated: when the browser has no Garamond Bold installed, for example, the ubiquitous Times New Roman will probably be substituted.

**b**
In extreme cases, if no proportionally spaced font is available, a fixed-width face such as Courier may appear.

**l**
A simulation to represent what may be expected from type when it appears on Web TV.

**e**
Rendered, shadowed, and shining brightly, an overenhanced escapee from the Photoshop tricks manual.

# LEGIBILITY TO THE FORE

Legibility of text onscreen is affected by a number of variables, not all of which are under the designer's control. In simple HTML text, good fortune can often assist, as in the example below. There are several tools available that can force the viewer's screen to resemble the original design more closely. Control of the color of text and background is the single most important issue, followed by an attempt to direct the browser's choice of size and style of typeface. There are monochrome screens still in use, but it is fair to assume that serious users are at least equipped with a monitor capable of showing 256 colors.

**1**

For a week after the commission of the impious and profane offence of asking for more, Oliver remained a close prisoner in the dark and solitary room to which he had been consigned by the wisdom and mercy of the board. It appears, at first sight not unreasonable to suppose, that, if he had entertained a becoming feeling of respect for the prediction of the gentleman in the white waistcoat, he would have esta prophetic character, once and for ever, by tying one end of in the wall, and attaching himself to the other. To the per there was one obstacle: namely, that pocket-handkerchief had been, for all future times and ages, removed from the order of the board, in council assembled: solemnly given a and seals. There was a still greater obstacle in Oliver's y bitterly all day; and, when the long, dismal night came on, eyes to shut out the darkness, and crouching in the corner waking with a start and tremble, and drawing himself clo feel even its cold hard surface were a protection in the gl surrounded him.

**14**

**2**

For a week after the commission of the impious and profane offence of asking for more, Oliver remained a close prisoner in the dark and solitary room to which he had been consigned by the wisdom and mercy of the board. It appears, at first sight not unreasonable to suppose, that, if he had entertained a becoming feeling of respect for the prediction of the gentleman in the white waistcoat, he would have established that sage individual's prophetic character, once and for ever, by tying one end of his pocket-handkerchief to a hook in the wall, and attaching himself to the other. To the performance of this feat, however, there was one obstacle: namely, that pocket-handkerchiefs being decided articles of luxury, had been, for all future times and ages, removed from the noses of paupers by the express order of the board, in council assembled: solemnly given and pronounced under their hands and seals. There was a still greater obstacle in Oliver's youth and childishness. He only cried bitterly all day; and, when the long, dismal night came on, spread his little hands before his eyes to shut out the darkness, and crouching in the corner, tried to sleep: ever and anon waking with a start and tremble, and drawing himself closer and closer to the wall, as if to feel even its cold hard surface were a protection in the gloom and loneliness which surrounded him.

**1 | 2**

An excerpt from *Oliver Twist (above)* as it appears in the Cyber-Studio application, with no style, size, or alignment commands invoked. The result is shown *(right)* in the Netscape Navigator 3.01 browser with standard settings. At present, the browser doesn't respond to hyphenation, giving an even more ragged appearance to the text. See "pocket-handkerchiefs," halfway down the column.

**3**

There was a rocky valley between Buxton and Bakewell, divine as the vale of Tempe; you might have seen the gods there morning and evening – Apollo and the sweet Muses of the Light. You enterprised a railroad; you blasted its rocks away. And now, every fool in Buxton can be at Bakewell in half-an-hour, and every fool in Bakewell at Buxton.

**There was a rocky valley between Buxton and Bakewell, divine as the vale of Tempe; you might have seen the gods there morning and evening — Apollo and the sweet Muses of the Light. You enterprised a railroad; you blasted its rocks away. And now, every fool in Buxton can be at Bakewell in half-an-hour, and every fool in Bakewell at Buxton.**

There was a rocky valley between Buxton and Bakewell, divine as the vale of Tempe; you might have seen the gods there morning and evening – Apollo and the sweet Muses of the Light. You enterprised a railroad; you blasted its rocks away. And now, every fool in Buxton can be at Bakewell in half-an-hour, and every fool in Bakewell at Buxton.

There was a rocky valley between Buxton and Bakewell, divine as the vale of Tempe; you might have seen the gods there morning and evening – Apollo and the sweet Muses of the Light. You enterprised a railroad; you blasted its rocks away. And now, every fool in Buxton can be at Bakewell in half-an-hour, and every fool in Bakewell at Buxton.

**There was a rocky valley between Buxton and Bakewell, divine as the vale of Tempe; you might have seen the gods there morning and evening — Apollo and the sweet Muses of the Light. You enterprised a railroad; you blasted its rocks away. And now, every fool in Buxton can be at Bakewell in half-an-hour, and every fool in Bakewell at Buxton.**

There was a rocky valley between Buxton and Bakewell, divine as the vale of Tempe; you might have seen the gods there morning and evening – Apollo and the sweet Muses of the Light. You enterprised a railroad; you blasted its rocks away. And now, every fool in Buxton can be at Bakewell in half-an-hour, and every fool in Bakewell at Buxton.

**3**

John Ruskin bemoans the pace of progress through Arcadian Derbyshire, in Arial *(far left)*, Verdana Bold *(center)*, and Goudy Old Style Medium *(near left)*. On a white ground, the two modern sans serif faces look somewhat graceless; but in the hard test of dropping out, their tougher character wins out, as the serifs get eaten away. Nevertheless, serif faces are in general easier, and therefore quicker, to read than sans faces. The serifs appear to help in forming character groups.

**15**

**4**

Legibility is not just a function of individual letter forms; it depends on the speedy recognition of the shapes made by clumps of characters. The quotations *(below)* from the Rev. Sydney Smith and Alfred Smith show that the clues reside mainly in the top half of the letter groups. Spin the page, after a decent interval, to confirm.

**4** No furniture so charming as books.

No matter how thin you slice it, it's still baloney.

Poverty is no disgrace to a man, but it is confoundedly inconvenient.

Dnamsunit witosty oleohnsen outhnn zifksotuir minutuis wi osders uttxa sjouuces.

The fourth quotation is indeed nonsense.

# PUTTING IT ALL TOGETHER

There are sites that remain static for months at a time, visit counters gathering dust—but the majority have to deal with changing content, sometimes on a minute-by-minute basis. There are many strategies for dealing with the demands of updating, but most hinge on the combination of standing type (most probably rendered as GIFs) and changing elements of HTML. This scenario is on the brink of change, but not quite yet. In any case, the decisions to be made are not so different from those that face the designer of the conventional short-deadline magazine or corporate newsletter.

**1 | 2 | 3**

The NASA Kennedy Space Center launch-information site *(below)* lays out its massive stall (one of the most complex on the entire Web), giving access to downloadable photographs and movies. A few hundred miles farther south, Malibu rum *(below right)* affects the look of a fly-posted Caribbean cabin wall—but each

scrap of type is a clickable link. In the same part of the ocean, a trawl *(below)* for information on sea-turtle nesting sites is momentarily delayed by a missing URL. However, the National Oceanic and Atmospheric Administration is a conscientious Web citizen and restores the link in short, but style-free, order.

16

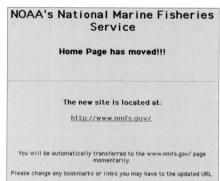

# GROUND ZERO

The hermit crab is a resourceful beast. Unwilling or unable to make the effort of growing a home of his own, he appropriates shells abandoned by his seashore neighbors. Later, when his increasing size makes the accommodation uncomfortable, he decamps to another address. Farther up the beach, and a little farther up the food chain, the average Web site typographer has to live and work in a borrowed environment, with only a faint hope of future improvement. The principal irritants are the legacy of the Web's scientific antecedents. The familiar hierarchy of heading tags was developed to facilitate the organization of scientific and technical research works. Words, lots of them, could be quickly delivered to the screen, and the viewer, or a search engine, would be assisted by the layered structure of the content. Six heading styles seemed to fill the bill, from giant, lumbering H1 all the way down to the functionally illegible H6.

18

Jill and Bob Bodoni are pleased to announce the birth of their new baby Typo.

Born at 11.59pm, 31st December 1999, she weighs eight pounds with red hair and blue eyes.

```
<html>

  <head>
    <meta http-equiv="content-type" content="text/html;charset=iso-8859-1">
    <meta name="generator" content="GoLive CyberStudio 3">
    <title>jill and bob</title>
  </head>

  <body>
    Jill and Bob Bodoni are pleased to announce the birth of their new baby Typo.
    <p><img height="125" width="125" src="media/baby.gif"></p>
    <p>Born at 11.59pm, 31st December 1999, she weighs eight pounds with red hair and blue e
    <p> 
  </body>

</html>
```

2

**1 | 2**

Infant steps in GoLive CyberStudio (*above*), with unstyled text and a GIF picture.

The underlying HTML code (*left*) is generated automatically, with syntax highlighted.

**3**

Jill and Bob Bodoni are pleased to announce the birth of their new baby Typo.

11.59pm, 31st December 1999, she ight pounds with red hair and blue eyes.

**4**

Jill d Bob Bodoni are pleased to nce the birth of their new Typo.

Born at 11.59pm, 31st December 1999, she weighs eight pounds with red hair and blue eyes.

Jill and Bob Bodoni are pleased to announce the birth of their new baby Typo.

Born at 11.59pm, 31st December 1999, she weighs eight pounds with red hair and blue eyes.

**5**

Jill and Bob Bodoni are pleased to announce the birth of their new baby Typo.

Born at 11.59pm, 31st December 1999, she weighs eight pounds with red hair and blue eyes.

**6**

**3 | 4 | 5 | 6**
The result (collapsed to show the text and image only) at 50% of actual size in four browser windows at default settings. Top to bottom: Netscape Navigator 3.0, Internet Explorer 3.0, Netscape Navigator 4.0, and Internet Explorer 4.0.

**7**
```
<h1>For oft, when on my couch I lie</h1>
<h2>In vacant or in pensive mood,</h2>
<h3>They flash upon that inward eye</h3>
<h4>Which is the bliss of solitude;</h4>
<h5>And then my heart with pleasure fills,</h5>
<h6>And dances with the daffodils.</h6>
```

**8** # For oft, when on my couch I lie

## In vacant or in pensive mood,

### They flash upon that inward eye

#### Which is the bliss of solitude;

##### And then my heart with pleasure fills,

###### And dances with the daffodils.

**7 | 8 | 9 | 10**
William Wordsworth at the hands of heading tags *(above)*, and the result on a Mac-based browser *(left)*. Individual type styles *(below and bottom)* are even less useful. Top to bottom: "no style," bold, italic, underlined, strikeout, and teletype (monospaced).

**19**

**9**
```
<body>
    For oft, when on my couch I lie
    <p><b>In vacant or in pensive mood,</b></p>
    <p><i>They flash upon that inward eye</i></p>
    <p><u>Which is the bliss of solitude;</u></p>
    <p><strike>And then my heart with pleasure f
    <p><tt>And dances with the daffodils.</tt>
</body>
```

**10** For oft, when on my couch I lie

**In vacant or in pensive mood,**

*They flash upon that inward eye*

<u>Which is the bliss of solitude;</u>

~~And then my heart with pleasure fills,~~

And dances with the daffodils.

# TURN, TURN, TURN

This page is 210mm wide by 235mm high. This paragraph, since type is more easily readable with clear margins around it, is 20mm from the left edge and 30mm from the top edge of the page. The words are ranged left (ragged right, if you prefer) to a measure of 86mm (20.5 pica ems). In scanning relatively short lines like this, the reader is not conscious of any eye or head movement to take in the information. At an average of just over nine words (just over 50 characters and spaces) to a line, this introduction contains 166 words. Onscreen, an unstyled Web paragraph could have a line length allowing up to 25 words (more than 140 characters and spaces). Pity the reader with a small monitor whose browser does not offer word-wrapping. He may have to resort to following the lines with a finger while scrolling horizontally to maintain continuity. To reinforce the point, this paragraph is tediously repeated in default text at the foot of the page.

```
<body>
    <table border="0" cellpadding="0" cellspacing="0" width="400">
        <tr>
            <td>The dark object of the conspiracy into which the chiefs of the Osborne family
        </tr>
    </table>
</body>
```

**1 | 2 | 3**

Using a 400-pixel-wide single-row single-column table (*left and below left*) controls the browser's line length (*below*). Line breaks are also preserved, but only if the browser default font is mono-spaced.

**2**

The dark object of the conspiracy into which the chiefs of the Osborne family had entered, was quite ignorant of all their plans regarding her (which, strange to say, her friend and chaperon did not divulge), and, taking all the young ladies' flattery for genuine sentiment, and being, as we have before had occasion to show, of a very warm and impetuous nature, responded to their affection with quite a tropical ardour. And if the truth may be told, I dare say that she too had some selfish attraction in the Russell Square house; and in a word, thought George Osborne a very nice young man. His whiskers had made an impression upon her, on the very first night she beheld them at the ball at Messrs. Hulkers; and, as we know, she was not the first woman who had been charmed by them. George had an air at once swaggering and melancholy, languid and fierce. He looked like a man who had passions, secrets, and private harrowing griefs and adventures. His voice was rich and deep. He would say it was a warm evening, or ask his partner to take an ice, with a tone as sad and confidential as if he were breaking her mother's death to her, or preluding a declaration of love. He trampled over all the young bucks of his father's circle, and was the hero among those third-rate men. Some few sneered at him and hated him. Some, like Dobbin, fanatically admired him. And his whiskers had begun to do their work, and to curl themselves round the affections of Miss Swartz.

**3**

The dark object of the conspiracy into which the chiefs of the Osborne family had entered, was quite ignorant of all their plans regarding her (which, strange to say, her friend and chaperon did not divulge), and, taking all the young ladies' flattery for genuine sentiment, and being, as we have before had occasion to show, of a very warm and impetuous nature, responded to their affection with quite a tropical ardour. And if the truth may be told, I dare say that she too had some selfish attraction in the Russell Square house; and in a word, thought George Osborne a very nice young man. His whiskers had made an impression upon her, on the very first night she beheld them at the ball at Messrs. Hulkers; and, as we know, she was not the first woman who had been charmed by them. George had an air at once swaggering and melancholy, languid and fierce. He looked like a man who had passions, secrets, and private harrowing griefs and adventures. His voice was rich and deep. He would say it was a warm evening, or ask his partner to take an ice, with a tone as sad and confidential as if he were breaking her mother's death to her, or preluding a declaration of love. He trampled over all the young bucks of his father's circle, and was the hero among those third-rate men. Some few sneered at him and hated him. Some, like Dobbin, fanatically admired him. And his whiskers had begun to do their work, and to curl themselves round the affections of Miss Swartz.

**5** This page is 210mm wide by 235mm high. This paragraph, since type is more easily readable with clear margins around it, is 20mm from the top edge of the page. The words are ranged left (ragged right, if you prefer) to a measure of 86mm (20.5 pica ems). In scann this, the reader is not conscious of any eye or head movement to take in the information. At an average of just over nine words (just over spaces) to a line, this introduction contains 166 words. On screen, an unstyled web paragraph could have a line length allowing up t characters and spaces). Pity the reader with a small monitor whose browser does not offer word-wrapping. He may have to resort t finger while scrolling horizontally to maintain continuity. To reinforce the point, this paragraph is tediously repeated in default text

**6**

The dark object of the conspiracy into which the chiefs of the Osborne family
had entered, was quite ignorant of all their plans regarding her (which, strange
to say, her friend and chaperon did not divulge), and, taking all the young ladies'
flattery for genuine sentiment, and being, as we have before had occasion to show,
of a very warm and impetuous nature, responded to their affection with quite a
tropical ardour. And if the truth may be told, I dare say that she too had some
selfish attraction in the Russell Square house; and in a word, thought George
Osborne a very nice young man. His whiskers had made an impression upon
her, on the very first night she beheld them at the ball at Messrs. Hulkers; and,
as we know, she was not the first woman who had been charmed by them.
George had an air at once swaggering and melancholy, languid and fierce. He
looked like a man who had passions, secrets, and private harrowing griefs and
adventures. His voice was rich and deep. He would say it was a warm evening,
or ask his partner to take an ice, with a tone as sad and confidential as if he were
breaking her mother's death to her, or preluding a declaration of love. He trampled
over all the young bucks of his father's circle, and was the hero among those
third-rate men. Some few sneered at him and hated him. Some, like Dobbin,
fanatically admired him. And his whiskers had begun to do their work, and to curl
themselves round the affections of Miss Swartz.

**4**

The same markup as
on the opposite page,
but the more usual
result (below) with a
proportionally spaced
browser font, which
produces different line
breaks. Misfortune
dictates a tragic widow
at the end. Screens on
these pages are in the
Netscape Navigator
4.0 window. The words
are from *Vanity Fair* by
William Thackeray.

**4**

The dark object of the conspiracy into which the chiefs of the Osborne family had
entered, was quite ignorant of all their plans regarding her (which, strange to say,
her friend and chaperon did not divulge), and, taking all the young ladies' flattery
for genuine sentiment, and being, as we have before had occasion to show, of a very
warm and impetuous nature, responded to their affection with quite a tropical
ardour. And if the truth may be told, I dare say that she too had some selfish
attraction in the Russell Square house; and in a word, thought George Osborne a
very nice young man. His whiskers had made an impression upon her, on the very
first night she beheld them at the ball at Messrs. Hulkers; and, as we know, she
was not the first woman who had been charmed by them. George had an air at once
swaggering and melancholy, languid and fierce. He looked like a man who had
passions, secrets, and private harrowing griefs and adventures. His voice was rich
and deep. He would say it was a warm evening, or ask his partner to take an ice,
with a tone as sad and confidential as if he were breaking her mother's death to her,
or preluding a declaration of love. He trampled over all the young bucks of his
father's circle, and was the hero among those third-rate men. Some few sneered at
him and hated him. Some, like Dobbin, fanatically admired him. And his whiskers
had begun to do their work, and to curl themselves round the affections of Miss
Swartz.

left edge and 30mm
ively short lines like
characters and
ds (more than 140
ing the lines with a
ot of the page.

**5**

Reading comfort is
not enhanced (left) by
having some of the
words in the gutter,
but it is excessive line
length that's at the
root of the problem.

**6 | 7 | 8**

A very labor-intensive
and ultimately futile
option. Putting a return
at the end of each
line (left) makes the
browser reflect the
intended line breaks
(below), but resizing the
window has painful
consequences (bottom).

**7**

ject of the conspiracy into which the chiefs of the Osborne family
was quite ignorant of all their plans regarding her (which, strange
riend and chaperon did not divulge), and, taking all the young ladies'
enuine sentiment, and being, as we have before had occasion to show,
rm and impetuous nature, responded to their affection with quite a
ur. And if the truth may be told, I dare say that she too had some
tion in the Russell Square house; and in a word, thought George
ery nice young man. His whiskers had made an impression upon
ery first night she beheld them at the ball at Messrs. Hulkers; and,
she was not the first woman who had been charmed by them.
n air at once swaggering and melancholy, languid and fierce. He
looked like a man who had passions, secrets, and private harrowing griefs and
adventures. His voice was rich and deep. He would say it was a warm evening,
or ask his partner to take an ice, with a tone as sad and confidential as if he were
breaking her mother's death to her, or preluding a declaration of love. He trampled
over all the young bucks of his father's circle, and was the hero among those
third-rate men. Some few sneered at him and hated him. Some, like Dobbin,
fanatically admired him. And his whiskers had begun to do their work, and to curl
themselves round the affections of Miss Swartz.

**21**

**8**

The dark object of the conspiracy into which the chiefs of the Osborne
family
had entered, was quite ignorant of all their plans regarding her (which,
strange
to say, her friend and chaperon did not divulge), and, taking all the young
ladies'
flattery for genuine sentiment, and being, as we have before had occasion to
show,
of a very warm and impetuous nature, responded to their affection with
quite a
tropical ardour. And if the truth may be told, I dare say that she too had
some
selfish attraction in the Russell Square house; and in a word, thought
George
Osborne a very nice young man. His whiskers had made an impression
upon
her, on the very first night she beheld them at the ball at Messrs. Hulkers;
and,
as we know, she was not the first woman who had been charmed by them.
George had an air at once swaggering and melancholy, languid and fierce. He
looked like a man who had passions, secrets, and private harrowing griefs
and
adventures. His voice was rich and deep. He would say it was a warm
evening,
or ask his partner to take an ice, with a tone as sad and confidential as if he
were
breaking her mother's death to her, or preluding a declaration of love. He
trampled
over all the young bucks of his father's circle, and was the hero among those
third-rate men. Some few sneered at him and hated him. Some, like Dobbin,
fanatically admired him. And his whiskers had begun to do their work, and
to curl
themselves round the affections of Miss Swartz.

# TIME FOR A BREAK

Long texts need to be broken into sections. There are HTML equivalents for almost all the customary typographic conventions of ordering blocks of text. Some work efficiently, others are notably inadequate.

Where there are multilayer text hierarchies, lists, and subsections, some of the old "scientific" tags can be used. There are also workarounds involving invisible spacer GIFs, though these can cause trouble when they arrive on browsers not set up for image downloading.

**1**

"We have no ballast on board; and indeed it seems to me that, if lightened, it would go much quicker."↵
"Slower."↵
"Quicker."↵
"Neither slower nor quicker," said Barbicane, wishing to make his two friends agree, "for we float in space, and must no longer consider specific weight."↵
"Very well,' cried Michel Ardan in a decided voice, "then there remains but one thing to do."↵
"What is it?" said Nicholl.↵
"Breakfast," answered the cool, audacious Frenchman, who always brought up this solution at the most difficult juncture.↵
In any case, if this operation had no influence on the projectile's course, it could at least be tried without inconvenience, and even with success from the stomachic point of view. Certainly Michel had none but good ideas.↵
[...]en at two in the morning; the hour mattered [...]his usual repast, crowned by a glorious bottle [...]te cellar. If ideas did not crowd on their [...]air of the Chambertin of 1853. The repast [...]s began again. Around the projectile, at an [...]were the objects that had been thrown out. [...]slatory motion round the moon, it had not [...]tmosphere, for the specific weight of these [...]uld have checked their relative speed.↵
[...]restrial sphere nothing was to be seen.|

**2**

"We have no ballast on board; and indeed it seems to me that, if lightened, it would go much quicker." "Slower." "Quicker." "Neither slower nor quicker," said Barbicane, wishing to make his two friends agree, "for we float in space, and must no longer consider specific weight." "Very well,' cried Michel Ardan in a decided voice, "then there remains but one thing to do." "What is it?" said Nicholl. "Breakfast," answered the cool, audacious Frenchman, who always brought up this solution at the most difficult juncture. In any case, if this operation had no influence on the projectile's course, it could at least be tried without inconvenience, and even with success from the stomachic point of view. Certainly Michel had none but good ideas. They breakfasted then at two in the morning; the hour mattered little. Michel served his usual repast, crowned by a glorious bottle drawn from his private cellar. If ideas did not crowd on their brains, we must despair of the Chambertin of 1853. The repast finished, observations began again. Around the projectile, at an invariable distance, were the objects that had been thrown out. Evidently, in its translatory motion round the moon, it had not passed through any atmosphere, for the specific weight of these different objects would have checked their relative speed. On the side of the terrestrial sphere nothing was to be seen.

**1 | 2 | 3 | 4**
Simple carriage returns *(top right)* are not enough to persuade the browser *(above)* to perform correctly. The correct style is a break `<br>` at the end of each paragraph. The addition of several nonbreaking spaces `< >` at the start of each paragraph results *(above right)* in reliable indenting. A 20-pixel-square transparent GIF at the same position also indents the line, as well as forcing additional space above it *(right)*. The text is from *Round the Moon* by Jules Verne.

**3**

"We have no ballast on board; and indeed it seems to me that, if lightened, it would go much quicker."
"Slower."
"Quicker."
"Neither slower nor quicker," said Barbicane, wishing to make his two friends agree, "for we float in space, and must no longer consider specific weight."
"Very well,' cried Michel Ardan in a decided voice, "then there remains but one thing to do."
"What is it?" said Nicholl.
"Breakfast," answered the [...] most difficult juncture.
In any case, if this operati[...] without inconvenience, and e[...] none but good ideas.
They breakfasted then at t[...] crowned by a glorious bottle [...] despair of the Chambertin of [...] at an invariable distance, were[...] round the moon, it had not pa[...] objects would have checked t[...]
On the side of the terrestri[...]

**4**

"We have no ballast on board; and indeed it seems to me that, if lightened, it would go much quicker."

"Slower."

"Quicker."

"Neither slower nor quicker," said Barbicane, wishing to make his two friends agree, "for we float in space, and must no longer consider specific weight."

"Very well,' cried Michel Ardan in a decided voice, "then there remains but one thing to do."

"What is it?" said Nicholl.

"Breakfast," answered the cool, audacious Frenchman, who always brought up this solution at the most difficult juncture.

In any case, if this operation had no influence on the projectile's course, it could at least be tried without inconvenience, and even with success from the stomachic point of view. Certainly Michel had none but good ideas.

They breakfasted then at two in the morning; the hour mattered little. Michel served his usual repast, crowned by a glorious bottle drawn from his private cellar. If ideas did not crowd on their brains, we must despair of the Chambertin of 1853. The repast finished, observations began again. Around the projectile, at an invariable distance, were the objects that had been thrown out. Evidently, in its translatory motion round the moon, it had not passed through any atmosphere, for the specific weight of these different objects would have checked their relative speed.

On the side of the terrestrial sphere nothing was to be seen.

**5 | 6**

Minimal type styling and insertion of minimum-thickness rules *(below)* help to open up formulaic text *(right)*. The default rule has a distracting shadow; `<noshade>` suppresses it.

**5**

```
<strong>VINTAGE PORT</strong>
<hr size="1" noshade>
Amazingly, Vintage Port accounts for only about one per cent of all Port
produced. Nevertheless this classic wine flies the flag for Port virtually
single-handed. The vintages can be confusing until you realise that only the best
years are &#145;declared&#146;, and that not all the shippers declare the same
vintages.
<p><strong> 1963 </strong>
<hr size="1" noshade>
This is the classic year everyone still talks about, but sadly there is not
much left. A supreme example of the staying power of Vintage Port &#150; 35 years
on they are drinking beautifully.</p>
<p><strong>1966</strong>
<hr size="1" noshade>
Initially underrated in the shadow of the &#146;63s, but well-respected by
the dawn of the 1980s. Some say they may outlive the &#146;63s. The lucky ones
can taste them side by side. </p>
```

**7 | 8**

Short subheads can be organized to align with accompanying text by using tables. The cell edges are visible in the HTML layout window *(bottom)*, but are given zero value and therefore disappear in the browser *(below)*. The `<colspan>` tag lets the intro extend across the first two cells. The text is from *The Wine & Spirit Diary*.

**23**

**6**

## VINTAGE PORT

Amazingly, Vintage Port accounts for only about one per cent of all Port produced. Nevertheless this classic wine flies the flag for Port virtually single-handed. The vintages can be confusing until you realise that only the best years are 'declared', and that not all the shippers declare the same vintages.

### 1963

This is the classic year everyone still talks about, but sadly there is not much left. A supreme example of the staying power of Vintage Port – 35 years on they are drinking beautifully.

### 1966

Initially underrated in the shadow of the '63s, but well-respected by the dawn of the 1980s. Some say they may outlive the '63s. The lucky ones can taste them side by side.

### 1970

Drinking now, but will reward the patient. Perfect weather yielded healthy grapes, which produced wonderful wines. The best will 'go' until 2020.

### 1975

23 shippers declared the '70, but only seventeen declared the '75 – probably a fair reflection of these pleasant, attractive wines which are now drinking well.

### 1977

This great vintage was born of a September heatwave. Twenty shippers declared, but many who didn't regretted it later, for the best of these wines will mature quietly until 2020.

### 1980

A small but underrated softer vintage offering good value for today. Few will develop further, so you should not feel too guilty.

### 1982

With only twelve shippers declaring, opinions differed then as now. Varying qualities mark this attractively powerful vintage. Drink up now.

### 1983

After a couple of lighter vintages, the '83 came just in time. Definitely in the 'very good' category. Giving pleasure now, the best will continue

**VINTAGE PORT**

Amazingly, Vintage Port accounts for only about one per cent of all Port produced. Nevertheless this classic wine flies the flag for Port virtually single-handed.

The vintages can be confusing until you realise that only the best years are 'declared', and that not all the shippers declare the same vintages.

| | |
|---|---|
| 1963 | This is the classic year everyone still talks about, but sadly there is not much left.. A supreme example of the staying power of Vintage Port – 35 years on they are drinking beautifully. |
| 1966 | Initially underrated in the shadow of the '63s, but well-respected by the dawn of the 1980s. Some say they may outlive the '63s. The lucky ones can taste them side by side. |
| 1970 | Drinking now, but will reward the patient. Perfect weather yielded healthier grapes, which |
| 1975 | 23 shippers declared, but only seventeen fair reflection |
| 1977 | This great vint declared, but n mature quietly |
| 1980 | A small but un develop furthe |
| 1982 | With only twe qualities mark |
| 1983 | After a couple 'very good' ca another ten to |
| 1985 | Declared unani concentrated v millennium. |

John Downes MW

**8**

**7**

VINTAGE PORT↵
Amazingly, Vintage Port accounts for only about one per cent of all Port produced. Nevertheless this classic wine flies the flag for Port virtually single-handed.↵
The vintages can be confusing until you realise that only the best years are 'declared', and that not all the shippers declare the same vintages.↵

| | |
|---|---|
| 1963 | This is the classic year everyone still talks about, but sadly there is not much left.. A supreme example of the staying power of Vintage Port - 35 years on they are drinking beautifully. |
| 1966 | Initially underrated in the shadow of the '63s, but well-respected by the dawn of the 1980s. Some say they may outlive the '63s. The lucky ones can taste them side by side. |
| 1970 | Drinking now, but will reward the patient. Perfect weather yielded healthy grapes, which produced wonderful wines. The best will 'go' until 2020. |
| 1975 | 23 shippers declared the '70, but only seventeen declared the '75 - probably a fair reflection of these pleasant, attractive wines which are now drinking well. |
| 1977 | This great vintage was born of a September heatwave. Twenty shippers declared, but many who didn't regretted it later, for the best of these wines will mature quietly until 2020. |
| 1980 | A small but underrated softer vintage offering good value for today. Few will develop further, so you should not feel too guilty. |
| 1982 | With only twelve shippers declaring, opinions differed then as now. Varying qualities mark this attractively powerful vintage. Drink up now. |
| 1983 | After a couple of lighter vintages, the '83 came just in time. Definitely in the 'very good' category. Giving pleasure now, the best will continue to do so for another ten to twenty years. |
| 1985 | Declared unanimously in Oporto - a vote of confidence heralding this heady, concentrated vintage which will sleep in your cellar until long after the millennium. |
| | |

John Downes MW

# GALLEY SLAVERY

Shorter line lengths make text more readable (your daily newspaper is the best example). On the screen, multicolumn page layouts should make for better reading, assuming the browser can accommodate them without scrolling in either axis. When HTML and tables are used, a battle must be fought to maintain equality of column depth. Cutting, pasting, recutting, and repasting of excess linage must be endured, as well as testing in different browsers. Lack of automatic or discretionary hyphenation, usually just an irritation, here becomes a real problem with these narrower measures. Some comfort may be taken in the ancient list hierarchies that have been onboard since the beginning of HTML.

**3**

In the sepulchre of Metella, the wife of Sulla, in the Roman Campagna, there is an echo which repeats five times, in five different keys, and will also give back with distinctness a hexameter line which requires two and a half seconds to utter it. On the banks of the Nahe, between Bingen and Coblentz, an echo repeats seventeen times. The speaker may scarcely be heard, and yet the responses are loud and distinct, sometimes appearing to approach, at other times to come from a great distance.

Echoes equally beautiful and romantic are to be heard in our own islands. In the cemetery of the Abercorn family, at Paisley, when the door of the chapel is closed, the reverberations are equal to the sound of thunder. If a single note of music is breathed, the tone ascends gradually with a multitude of echoes, till it dies in soft and bewitching murmurs. In this chapel is interred Margery, the daughter of Bruce, and the wife of William Wallace.

The echo at the 'Eagle's Nest', on the banks of Killarney, is renowned for its effective

repetition of a bugle-call, which seems to be repeated by a hundred instruments, until it gradually dies away in the air. At the report of a cannon, thunders reverberate from the rock, and die in seemingly endless peals along the distant mountains.

At the castle of Simonetta, a nobleman's seat about two miles from Milan, a surprising report is produced between the two wings of the building. The report of a pistol is repeated by this echo sixty times, and Addison, who visited the place on a somewhat foggy day, when the air was unfavourable to the experiment, counted fifty-six repetitions. At first they were quick, but the intervals were greater in proportion as the sound decayed. It is asserted that the sound of one musical instrument in this place resembles a great number of instruments playing in concert. The echo is occasioned by the existence of two parallel walls of considerable length, between which the wave of sound is reverberated from one to the other until it is entirely spent.

**4**

In the sepulchre of Metella, the wife of Sulla, in the Roman Campagna, there is an echo which repeats five times, in five different keys, and will also give back with distinctness a hexameter line which requires two and a half seconds to utter it. On the banks of the Nahe, between Bingen and Coblentz, an echo repeats seventeen times. The speaker may scarcely be heard, and yet the responses are loud and distinct, sometimes appearing to approach, at other times to come from a great distance.

Echoes equally beautiful and romantic are to be heard in our own islands. In the cemetery of the Abercorn family, at Paisley, when the door of the chapel is closed, the reverberations are equal to the sound of thunder. If a single note of music is breathed, the tone ascends gradually with a multitude of echoes, till it dies in soft and bewitching murmurs. In this chapel is interred Margery, the daughter of Bruce, and the wife of William Wallace.

The echo at the 'Eagle's Nest', on the banks of Killarney, is renowned for its effective

repetition of a bugle-call, which seems to be repeated by a hundred instruments, until it gradually dies away in the air. At the report of a cannon, thunders reverberate from the rock, and die in seemingly endless peals along the distant mountains.

At the castle of Simonetta, a nobleman's seat about two miles from Milan, a surprising report is produced between the two wings of the building. The report of a pistol is repeated by this echo sixty times, and Addison, who visited the place on a somewhat foggy day, when the air was unfavourable to the experiment, counted fifty-six repetitions. At first they were quick, but the intervals were greater in proportion as the sound decayed. It is asserted that the sound of one musical instrument in this place resembles a great number of instruments playing in concert. The echo is occasioned by the existence of two parallel walls of considerable length, between which the wave of sound is reverberated from one to the other until it is entirely spent.

**1**

In the sepulchre of Metella, the wife of Sulla, in the Roman Campagna, there is an echo which repeats five times, in five different keys, and will also give back with distinctness a hexameter line which requires two and a half seconds to utter it. On the banks of the Nahe, between Bingen and Coblentz, an echo repeats seventeen times. The speaker may scarcely be heard, and yet the responses are loud and distinct, sometimes appearing to approach, at other times to come from a great distance.

Echoes equally beautiful and romantic are to be heard in our own islands. In the cemetery of the Abercorn family, at Paisley, when the door of the chapel is closed, the reverberations are equal to the sound of thunder. If a single note of music is breathed, the tone ascends gradually with a multitude of echoes, till it dies in soft and bewitching murmurs. In this chapel is interred Margery, the daughter of Bruce, and the wife of William Wallace.

The echo at the 'Eagle's Nest', on the banks of Killarney, is renowned

for its effective repetition of a bugle call, which seems to be repeated by a hundred instruments, until it gradually dies away in the air. At the report of a cannon, thunders reverberate from the rock, and die in seemingly endless peals along the distant mountains.

At the castle of Simonetta, a nobleman's seat about two miles from Milan, a surprising report is produced between the two wings of the building. The report of a pistol is repeated by this echo sixty times, and Addison, who visited the place on a somewhat foggy day, when the air was unfavourable to the experiment, counted fifty-six repetitions. At first they were quick, but the intervals were greater in proportion as the sound decayed. It is asserted that the sound of one musical instrument in this place resembles a great number of instruments playing in concert. The echo is occasioned by the existence of two parallel walls of considerable length, between which the wave of sound is reverberated from one to the other until it is entirely spent.

**2**

In the sepulchre of Metella, the wife of Sulla, in the Roman Campagna, there is an echo which repeats five times, in five different keys, and will also give back with distinctness a hexameter line which requires two and a half seconds to utter it. On the banks of the Nahe, between Bingen and Coblentz, an echo repeats seventeen times. The speaker may scarcely be heard, and yet the responses are loud and distinct, sometimes appearing to approach, at other times to come from a great distance.

Echoes equally beautiful and romantic are to be heard in our own islands. In the cemetery of the Abercorn family, at Paisley, when the door of the chapel is closed, the reverberations are equal to the sound of thunder. If a single note of music is breathed, the tone ascends gradually with a multitude of echoes, till it dies in soft and bewitching murmurs. In this chapel is interred Margery, the daughter of Bruce, and the wife of William Wallace.

The echo at the 'Eagle's Nest', on the banks of Killarney, is renowned

for its effective repetition of a bugle-call, which seems to be repeated by a hundred instruments, until it gradually dies away in the air. At the report of a cannon, thunders reverberate from the rock, and die in seemingly endless peals along the distant mountains.

At the castle of Simonetta, a nobleman's seat about two miles from Milan, a surprising report is produced between the two wings of the building. The report of a pistol is repeated by this echo sixty times, and Addison, who visited the place on a somewhat foggy day, when the air was unfavourable to the experiment, counted fifty-six repetitions. At first they were quick, but the intervals were greater in proportion as the sound decayed. It is asserted that the sound of one musical instrument in this place resembles a great number of instruments playing in concert. The echo is occasioned by the existence of two parallel walls of considerable length, between which the wave of sound is reverberated from one to the other until it is entirely spent.

**1 | 2 | 3 | 4**

An apparently successful arrangement *(above)* of two equal columns in the Web-design software ends in disaster in the browser *(right)*. At the second attempt, an asymmetrical layout *(top right)* finally gets the desired result *(center right)*. The text comes from *The World of Wonders: A Record of Things Wonderful in Nature, Science and Art*.

```
<ol>
    <li>Though there may be grumblers in every voyage, they are
generally people who have never been to sea before, and who do not know
that second-class passengers now enjoy accommodation which a few years ago,
would have been unattainable even in first class.
    <li>The deck saloon of the <i>Ormuz</i> is a magnificent
apartment of 42 feet by 20 feet. It is situated on the promenade deck, as
nearly as possible in the middle of the ship. It is furnished with with
library and writing tables, and with a great wealth of comfortable lounges.
    <li>The apartment also contains a piano and an organ.
    <li>The smoking room is well aft on the same deck.
    <li type="disc">The total length of the ship is 481 feet and the
breadth 52 feet.
    <li>Her gross registered tonnage is is 6,116, and her effective
horsepower, 8,500.
    <li>The engines are constructed on the triple expansion system,
and are fitted with no fewer than seven vast boilers.|
    <li>The best run on a recent voyage was 420 knots in 24 hours.
    <li>If the term horsepower were strictly exact, all the horses
in use in the British Army, if we would compel them to join in a gigantic tug
of war with the <i>Ormuz</i>, would be pulled over.
    </ol>
```

1. The deck saloon of the *Ormuz* is a magnificent apartment of 42 feet by 20 feet. It is situated on the promenade deck, as nearly as possible in the middle of the ship. It is furnished with with library and writing tables, and with a great wealth of comfortable lounges.
2. The apartment also contains a piano and an organ. The smoking room is well aft on the same deck.
3. The total length of the ship is 481 feet and the breadth 52. Her gross registered tonnage is is 6,116, and her effective horsepower, 8,500.
4. The engines are constructed on the triple expansion system, and are fitted with no fewer than seven vast boilers. The best run on a recent voyage was 420 knots in 24 hours.
5. If the term horsepower were strictly exact, all the horses in use in the British Army, if we would compel them to join in a gigantic tug of war with the *Ormuz*, would be pulled over.

S.S. ORMUZ.

**5 | 6 | 7**

The many virtues of the steamship *Ormuz* (above) are neatly summarized with the ordered-list tag (top). Netscape Navigator 3.0x obliges (top right) in default Times New Roman. The text comes from the *Orient Line Guide: Chapters for Travellers by Sea and by Land.*

Though there may be grumblers in every voyage, ... have never been to sea before, and who do not kn... now enjoy accommodation which a few years ag... even in first class.

1. The deck saloon of the *Ormuz* is a magn... feet. It is situated on the promenade dec... middle of the ship. It is furnished with w... with a great wealth of comfortable loung...
2. The apartment also contains a piano and an organ.
3. The smoking room is well aft on the same deck.

● The total length of the ship is 481 feet and the breadth 52 feet.

Her gross registered tonnage is is 6,116, and her effective horsepower, 8,5...

The engines are constructed on the triple expansion system, and are fitted... fewer than seven vast boilers.

The best run on a recent voyage was 420 knots in 24 hours.

If the term horsepower were strictly exact, all the horses in use in the British Army, if w... compel them to join in a gigantic tug of war with the *Ormuz*, would be pulled over.

```
<html>

    <head>
        <meta http-equiv="content-type" content="text/html;charset=
iso-8859-1">
        <meta name="generator" content="GoLive CyberStudio 3">
        <title>Welcome to GoLive CyberStudio 3</title>
    </head>

    <body>
        Though there may be grumblers in every voyage, they are generally
people who have never been to sea before, and who do not know that
second-class passengers now enjoy accommodation which a few years ago,
would have been unattainable even in first class.
        <ol>
            <li>The deck saloon of the <i>Ormuz</i> is a magnificent
apartment of 42 feet by 20 feet. It is situated on the promenade deck, as
nearly as possible in the middle of the ship. It is furnished with with
library and writing tables, and with a great wealth of comfortable lounges.
            <li>The apartment also contains a piano and an organ.
            <li>The smoking room is well aft on the same deck.
        </ol>
        <ul>
            <li type="disc">The total length of the ship is 481 feet and the
breadth 52 feet.
        </ul>
        <p>Her gross registered tonnage is is 6,116, and her effective
horsepower, 8,500. </p>
        <dl>
            <dt>The engines are constructed on the triple expansion system,
and are fitted with no fewer than seven vast boilers.<br>
             
            <dt>The best run on a recent voyage was 420 knots in 24 hours.
        </dl>
        <p><sub>If the term horsepower were strictly exact, all the horses
in use in the British Army, if we would compel them to join in a gigantic
tug of war with the <i>Ormuz</i>, would be pulled over. </sub>
    </body>

</html>
```

```
  1. Arabic numbers
 II. Uppercase Roman numbers
iii. Lowercase roman numbers
  D. Uppercase alphabet
  e. Lowercase alphabet

    ● Bullet
       Circle
    ▫ Square

Term
    Definition

Decreased list level

Decreased list level x 2
```

**8 | 9 | 10**

Within the list tag there are a few, rather inflexible, styles. Used with care, some (8, 9) can be useful. The whole collection is shown (10) in Explorer 4.0x, which disregards the circle style entirely.

25

# THE PERSISTENT TYPE

There are three strategies for grasping the browser's typographic controls—politely suggestive (shown here), mildly persuasive (shown on page 27), and frankly invasive (shown on page 29). Staying within the confines of plain HTML, the insertion of font tags gives some control of typeface selection, but the hierarchy of seven type sizes allows only a broad-brush approach. The sizes are relative to one another, not absolute dimensions, and are liable to vary in the browser.

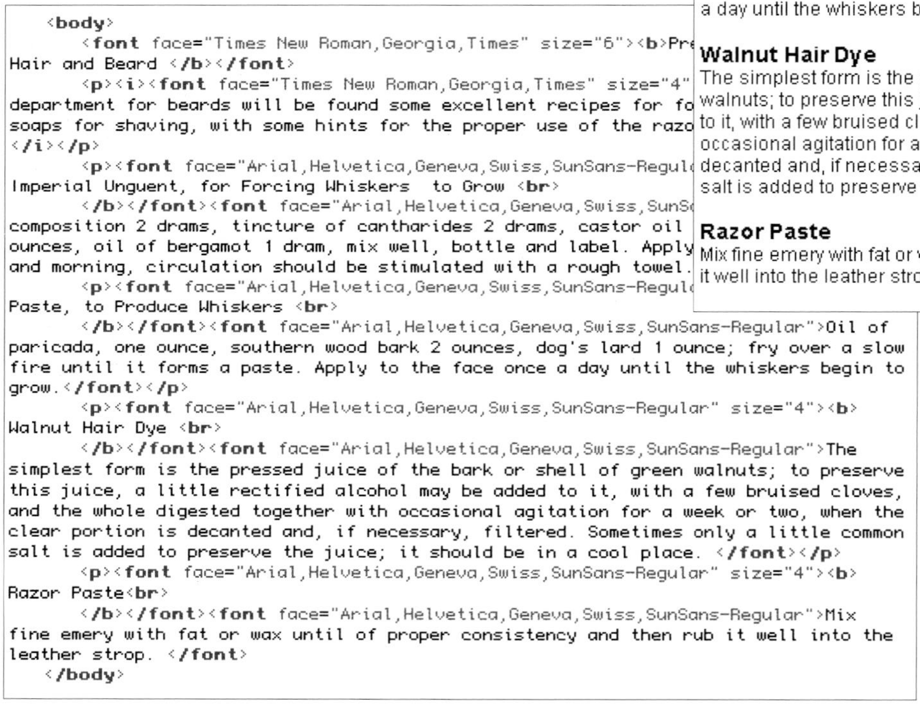

```
    <body>
        <font face="Times New Roman,Georgia,Times" size="6"><b>Pr
Hair and Beard </b></font>
            <p><i><font face="Times New Roman,Georgia,Times" size="4"
department for beards will be found some excellent recipes for fo
soaps for shaving, with some hints for the proper use of the razo
</i></p>
            <p><font face="Arial,Helvetica,Geneva,Swiss,SunSans-Regul
Imperial Unguent, for Forcing Whiskers  to Grow <br>
        </b></font><font face="Arial,Helvetica,Geneva,Swiss,SunS
composition 2 drams, tincture of cantharides 2 drams, castor oil
ounces, oil of bergamot 1 dram, mix well, bottle and label. Apply
and morning, circulation should be stimulated with a rough towel.
            <p><font face="Arial,Helvetica,Geneva,Swiss,SunSans-Regul
Paste, to Produce Whiskers <br>
        </b></font><font face="Arial,Helvetica,Geneva,Swiss,SunSans-Regular">Oil of
paricada, one ounce, southern wood bark 2 ounces, dog's lard 1 ounce; fry over a slow
fire until it forms a paste. Apply to the face once a day until the whiskers begin to
grow.</font></p>
            <p><font face="Arial,Helvetica,Geneva,Swiss,SunSans-Regular" size="4"><b>
Walnut Hair Dye <br>
        </b></font><font face="Arial,Helvetica,Geneva,Swiss,SunSans-Regular">The
simplest form is the pressed juice of the bark or shell of green walnuts; to preserve
this juice, a little rectified alcohol may be added to it, with a few bruised cloves,
and the whole digested together with occasional agitation for a week or two, when the
clear portion is decanted and, if necessary, filtered. Sometimes only a little common
salt is added to preserve the juice; it should be in a cool place. </font></p>
            <p><font face="Arial,Helvetica,Geneva,Swiss,SunSans-Regular" size="4"><b>
Razor Paste<br>
        </b></font><font face="Arial,Helvetica,Geneva,Swiss,SunSans-Regular">Mix
fine emery with fat or wax until of proper consistency and then rub it well into the
leather strop. </font>
    </body>
```

1

## Preparations for the Hair and Beard

*Included under the department for beards will be found some excellent recipes for forcing the growth, soaps for shaving, with some hints for the proper use of the razor and strop.*

**Imperial Unguent, for Forcing Whiskers to Grow**
Benzoin composition 2 drams, tincture of cantharides 2 drams, castor oil 6 ounces, alcohol 9 ounces, oil of bergamot 1 dram, mix well, bottle and label. Apply the unguent night and morning, circulation should be stimulated with a rough towel.

**Paste, to Produce Whiskers**
Oil of paricada, one ounce, southern wood bark 2 ounces, dog's lard 1 ounce; fry over a slow fire until it forms a paste. Apply to the face once a day until the whiskers begin to grow.

**Walnut Hair Dye**
The simplest form is the pressed juice of the bark or shell of green walnuts; to preserve this juice, a little rectified alcohol may be added to it, with a few bruised cloves, and the whole digested together with occasional agitation for a week or two, when the clear portion is decanted and, if necessary, filtered. Sometimes only a little common salt is added to preserve the juice; it should be in a

**Razor Paste**
Mix fine emery with fat or wax until of proper consist it well into the leather strop.

2

## Preparatio

*Included under the a recipes for forcing t proper use of the raz*

**Imperial Unguent**
Benzoin composition alcohol 9 ounces, oil o unguent night and mo

**Paste, to Produce**
Oil of paricada, one o over a slow fire until it whiskers begin to gro

**Walnut Hair Dye**
The simplest form is t preserve this juice, a l cloves, and the whole two, when the clear po a little common salt is

**Razor Paste**
Mix fine emery with fa leather strop.

3

**1 | 2 | 3**

A modest markup *(1)*, using the basic tags. Selecting the main default faces in both the Macintosh and Windows environments prompts the browser to follow the intended style. Ancient wisdom states that the same type appears bigger on a Windows screen compared to the Macintosh equivalent. The typical Macintosh screen *(2)* operates at 72 pixels per inch; the Windows screen *(3)* at 96 ppi. It looks as if the old wisdom is right. In fact, the comparison works only for monitors operating, as here, at the same resolution. Multisync monitors allow widely differing resolutions in both camps. The Windows user has the further option of redefining the relationship between pixels and points. The text is taken from *Lee's Priceless Recipes: the Standard Collection of Formulas for Every Department of Human Endeavour.*

**4**

# Preparations for the Hair and Beard

*Included under the department for beards will be found some excellent recipes for forcing the growth, soaps for shaving, with some hints for proper use of the razor and strop.*

### Imperial Unguent, for Forcing Whiskers to Grow
Benzoin composition 2 drams, tincture of cantharides 2 drams, cas alcohol 9 ounces, oil of bergamot 1 dram, mix well, bottle and label unguent night and morning, circulation should be stimulated with a r

### Paste, to Produce Whiskers
Oil of paricada, one ounce, southern wood bark 2 ounces, dog's lar over a slow fire until it forms a paste. Apply to the face once a day u whiskers begin to grow.

### Walnut Hair Dye
The simplest form is the pressed juice of the bark or shell of green preserve this juice, a little rectified alcohol may be added to it, with cloves, and the whole digested together with occasional agitation fo two, when the clear portion is decanted and, if necessary, filtered. S a little common salt is added to preserve the juice; it should be in a

**4 | 5 | 6**
Some interior décor enthusiasts *(left)* like to redecorate their browsers too. If they are also enthusiastic about type *(below)*, the designer may as well revert to more useful tasks about the studio. The preferences *(bottom, in Internet Explorer)* are proof against HTML and Cascading Style Sheets.

**5**

# Preparations for the Hair and Beard

*Included under the department for beards will be found some excellent recipes for forcing the growth, soaps for shaving, with some hints for the proper use of the razor and strop.*

### Imperial Unguent, for Forcing Whiskers to Grow
Benzoin composition 2 drams, tincture of cantharides 2 drams, castor oil 6 ounces, alcohol 9 ounces, oil of bergamot 1 dram, mix well, bottle and label. Apply the unguent night and morning, circulation should be stimulated with a rough towel.

### Paste, to Produce Whiskers
Oil of paricada, one ounce, southern wood bark 2 ounces, dog's lard 1 ounce; fry over a slow fire until it forms a paste. Apply to the face once a day until the whiskers begin to grow.

### Walnut Hair Dye
The simplest form is the pressed juice of the bark or shell of green walnuts; to preserve this juice, a little rectified alcohol may be added to it, with a few bruised cloves, and the whole digested together with occasional agitation for a week or two, when the clear portion is decanted and, if necessary, filtered. Sometimes only a little common salt is added to preserve the juice; it should be in a cool place.

### Razor Paste
Mix fine emery with fat or wax until of proper consistency and then rub it well into the leather strop.

27

# r the Hair and Beard

*nt for beards will be found some excellent h, soaps for shaving, with some hints for the trop.*

### rcing Whiskers to Grow
tincture of cantharides 2 drams, castor oil 6 ounces, ot 1 dram, mix well, bottle and label. Apply the culation should be stimulated with a rough towel.

### ers
uthern wood bark 2 ounces, dog's lard 1 ounce; fry paste. Apply to the face once a day until the

ed juice of the bark or shell of green walnuts; to fied alcohol may be added to it, with a few bruised together with occasional agitation for a week or ecanted and, if necessary, filtered. Sometimes only preserve the juice; it should be in a cool place.

ntil of proper consistency and then rub it well into the

**6**

**Fonts**          Change the fonts in your display

| For the Encoding: | Western | | |
|---|---|---|---|
| Variable Width Font: | Mistral | Size: | 16 |
| Fixed Width Font: | Courier New | Size: | 10 |

Sometimes a document will provide its own fonts.
- ● Use my default fonts, overriding document-specified fonts
- ○ Use document-specified fonts, but disable Dynamic Fonts
- ○ Use document-specified fonts, including Dynamic Fonts

# PLAYING BY THE RULES

Cascading Style Sheets offer an elegant and relatively future-proof way out of the Web's current typographic morass. CSS builds on the framework of plain HTML, but with one vital difference—the styling is applied to the document's structure, not to its content. An analogy with the style sheets used in page-makeup applications for print is valid at a basic level. Once degrees of importance have been ascribed to titles, subtitles, main and subsidiary text, and so on, global style changes can be made by amendments to the master style sheets. CSS, though its typographic controls are still crude by comparison with print-based systems, extends the style-sheet concept into unfamiliar territory.

There are three principal levels of CSS: "linked" (otherwise called "external"); next comes "embedded"; and finally, "inline." Analogy enthusiasts may like to think of a small and erratic democracy. A linked style sheet is presidential, with powers to influence all the pages—and even sites—under its command. Embedded style sheets (the national government) have authority over individual pages, but where there is a conflict with the president, the embedded sheet takes priority. In the same way, a lowly local functionary, the inline sheet, governs paragraphs or individual words. At this level, conflicting instructions from above—even from the president—are ignored in favor of the inline sheet. In the absence of any instructions at all, the downtrodden plebs take charge once more with their default settings.

As in any democracy, there are other forces at work. CSS is a feature of the more recent browsers. Very old browsers tend to reproduce the actual styling tags on screen without understanding what they mean, though the tags can be rendered invisible by enclosing them inside the "comment" convention. Newer, but still obsolescent, browsers are inconsistent in their reaction to CSS. The passage of time will heal all such divisions.

28

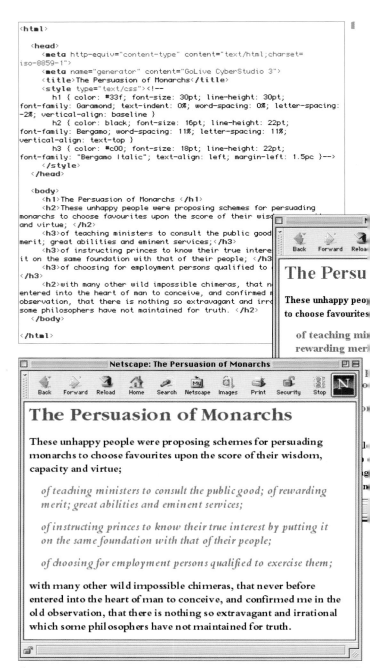

```
<html>

  <head>
    <meta http-equiv="content-type" content="text/html;charset=
iso-8859-1">
    <meta name="generator" content="GoLive CyberStudio 3">
    <title>The Persuasion of Monarchs</title>
    <style type="text/css"><!--
      h1 { color: #33f; font-size: 30pt; line-height: 30pt;
font-family: Garamond; text-indent: 0%; word-spacing: 0%; letter-spacing:
-2%; vertical-align: baseline }
      h2 { color: black; font-size: 16pt; line-height: 22pt;
font-family: Bergamo; word-spacing: 11%; letter-spacing: 11%;
vertical-align: text-top }
      h3 { color: #c00; font-size: 18pt; line-height: 22pt;
font-family: "Bergamo Italic"; text-align: left; margin-left: 1.5pc }-->
    </style>
  </head>

  <body>
    <h1>The Persuasion of Monarchs </h1>
    <h2>These unhappy people were proposing schemes for persuading
monarchs to choose favourites upon the score of their wisdom
and virtue; </h2>
    <h3>of teaching ministers to consult the public good;
merit; great abilities and eminent services;</h3>
    <h3>of instructing princes to know their true intere
it on the same foundation with that of their people; </h3
</h3>
    <h3>of choosing for employment persons qualified to
</h3>
    <h2>with many other wild impossible chimeras, that n
entered into the heart of man to conceive, and confirmed
observation, that there is nothing so extravagant and irr
some philosophers have not maintained for truth. </h2>
  </body>

</html>
```

## The Persuasion of Monarchs

These unhappy people were proposing schemes for persuading monarchs to choose favourites upon the score of their wisdom, capacity and virtue;

*of teaching ministers to consult the public good; of rewarding merit; great abilities and eminent services;*

*of instructing princes to know their true interest by putting it on the same foundation with that of their people;*

*of choosing for employment persons qualified to exercise them;*

with many other wild impossible chimeras, that never before entered into the heart of man to conceive, and confirmed me in the old observation, that there is nothing so extravagant and irrational which some philosophers have not maintained for truth.

The source code *(top)* shows the fundamental difference between Cascading Style Sheets and regular HTML styling. The armory of styles is in the head of this embedded style sheet and is applied in the body of the text by short tags. More important, there is now the possibility, dependent as always on the browser and the fonts installed, of stronger typographic control.

**5**

```
        <style type="text/css"><!--
        h3 { color: #60f; font-size: 17pt; line-height: 20pt; font-family: Palatino; margin-right: 9%;
margin-left: 2% }
        b { color: #f33; font-style: italic; font-weight: bolder; font-family: Palatino }
        h3.greencaps { color: #093; font-variant: small-caps; font-size: 175%; font-family: Palatino;
text-transform: uppercase; letter-spacing: 2mm; vertical-align: top }-->
        </style>
    </head>
    <body>
        <h3>Because <strong style="COLOR:#000">half a dozen grasshoppers </strong>under a fern make the
field ring with their importunate chink, whilst thousands of great cattle, reposed beneath the shadow of the
British oak,</h3>
        <h3 class="greencaps">chew the cud and are silent, </h3>
        <h3><b>pray do not imagine that</b> those who make the noise are are the only inhabitants of the
field; that, of course, they are many in number; or that, after all, <b>they are other than</b>the little,
shrivelled, meagre, hopping, though <b>loud and troublesome insects</b>of the hour. </h3>
    </body>
```

**5 | 6**

Occasional inline tags (like h3.greencaps, *left*) can be used to override the embedded styling. The browser's reaction *(below)* can be troublesome, with mysterious paragraph breaks.

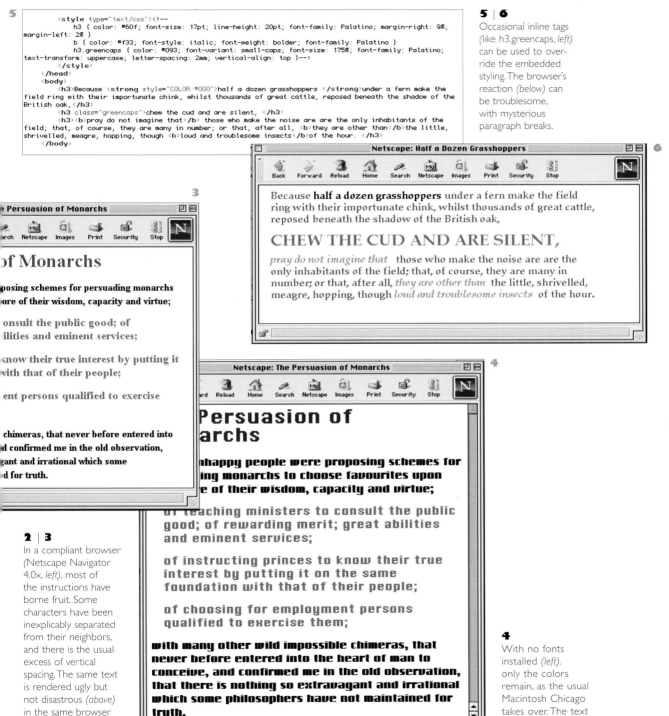

**2 | 3**

In a compliant browser (Netscape Navigator 4.0x, *left*), most of the instructions have borne fruit. Some characters have been inexplicably separated from their neighbors, and there is the usual excess of vertical spacing. The same text is rendered ugly but not disastrous *(above)* in the same browser with the user's fonts set as the default.

**4**

With no fonts installed *(left)*, only the colors remain, as the usual Macintosh Chicago takes over. The text is from *Gulliver's Travels* by Jonathan Swift.

29

# WYSIWTS

The most elegant way to ensure WYSIWTS (what you send is what they see) is to enclose the fonts along with the page. Objections both ethical and technical arise with this method. Although typeface designs are not legally copyrightable, they are nevertheless the intellectual property of the designer or typefounder. Those who continue to design good and useful type deserve the same treatment as designers of good and useful software. Their cause, and that of their predecessors, would not be well served by having their work broadcast worldwide for no recompense. The technical objections are concerned with file size, and therefore downloading speed, both of which will no doubt be overcome.

The type manufacturer Bitstream offers TrueDoc as the way forward. Under this regime, a "WebFont maker" utility built into the Web-authoring software scans the page and generates a "Portable Font Resource" (PFR),

which includes the styles and characters used in the page. The PFR accompanies the page when downloaded, and the screen image is activated by a player resource in Netscape Navigator, or by downloading an ActiveX control when first viewing the page in Internet Explorer. Microsoft aims to counter with WEFT (Web Embedding Font Tool). WEFT operates along similar lines, except that a protocol can prevent the use of the selected face(s) outside the confines of the browser.

2

**Chianti**
abcdefghij
ABCDEFGH
123456&?!

**BOLD**
abcdefghijklmnopqrstuvwxyz
ABCDEFGHIJKLMNOPQRSTUV
WXYZ 1234567890 &?!

Dennis Pasternak designed Chianti for Bitstream in 1991. He wanted to create a humanist sanserif typeface that was highly readable, no matter the size or weight. By incorporating a classical roman structure in the letterforms, humanist sanserifs improve the readability of classic sanserifs. Frutiger, Optima, and Gill Sans are examples of successful humanist designs. Well known for his keen typographic eye and meticulous workmanship, Dennis has created an elegant and functional addition to the humanist typeface group.

1

Announcement | Type over Color | Math Equations | Pi Fonts | Chianti | Eyeballs | Prima | Kanji

# TrueDoc Lets You Create Dynamic Fonts for the Web!

HOME
WHAT'S NEW
GET STARTED
EXAMPLES
PFRS
FAQS
HELP
CONTACT US
TEST DRIVE

## See the New World of Web Publishing

世界を見ます

Bitstream's award-winning TrueDoc technology lets users see the world from their desktops.

If you are a web author, you can create a home page with any font you own - including international fonts, such as Cyrillic and Kanji - without worrying if users viewing your document have the same fonts on their systems.

www.truedoc.com open 24 hours a day

Bitstream TrueDoc gives authors complete control over the look and feel of documents created for the World Wide Web. Documents retain complete font fidelity. If an author uses Kuenstler 165 or Zurich Bold Extended for a headline font, that is what readers see. With Bitstream TrueDoc, What You See Is What THEY Get.

SEE THE WORLD

**1 | 2**
Bitstream (*left*) gives Peignot an unwelcome outing in a pitch for font embedding. It's unclear whether the closing jellybean type is part of the proposition. In a more sober mood (*above*) Bitstream offers Chianti, optimized for screen display.

There is also no need for a special plug-in. Four levels of potential "embeddability" are associated with any typeface. These range from the "freely embeddable" face—which can be permanently installed on the user's system for unlimited screen display and printing—all the way down to the "restricted-license" face, which may not be embedded under any circumstances and need not detain us here. It is up to the typeface manufacturers to assign the desired level to their products, and for the buyer to choose.

The integrity of a typeface's appearance onscreen depends on tiny variations of stroke width and alignment. The square pixel is an extremely blunt instrument with which to portray shapes, especially those composed of sweeping arcs. Using conventional (Type 1) fonts, the computer system can use a built-in rasterizer, which visits the stored outline of each character to generate a screen-ready approximation. Typically, a pixel will be turned on whenever the rasterizer recognizes a positive value in more than 50% of the defined area. Serifed typefaces suffer especially from this purely mathematical approach—at small sizes, finer elements of the letterform can disappear completely. The TrueType system, originally developed by Apple and now also promoted by Microsoft, uses "hinting" to get to grips with the problem. Hinting is integral to each typeface and aims to override the gross errors of the rasterizer, thereby harmonizing stroke width and form. Each character, or "glyph," is described by a number of "control points." TrueType operates with a library of hinting "nudges," each one particular to a character, which, if necessary, shift the control points very slightly just before the rasterizer comes into operation.

At **www.microsoft.com**, a full insight into hinting is given in *The Raster Tragedy at Low Resolution* by Beat Stamm, principal developer of Visual TrueType.

**3**

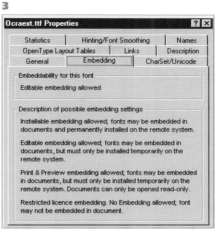

**3 | 4 | 5**
Serious in Seattle. Microsoft offers, as usual, much more information *(left)* than the average person can hope to absorb, but at least it's for a good cause. Monotype *(below)* offers second-generation hinted fonts for better display. There are some faces *(bottom)* whose charm depends on being untouched by hinting.

31

**4**

as|as
Albany (left) was designed with more open shapes to increase low resolution legibility.

Albany™  The quick brown fox jumps over the lazy dog
Arial®  The quick brown fox jumps over the lazy dog

ALBANY
The quick brown fox jumps over the lazy dog
*The quick brown fox jumps over the lazy dog*
**The quick brown fox jumps over the lazy**
***The quick brown fox jumps over the lazy***

ep|ep
Thorndale's (left) design is toned down and more open increasing low resolution legibility.

Thorndale™  The quick brown fox jumps over the lazy
Times New Roman®  The quick brown fox jumps over the lazy

THORNDALE
The quick brown fox jumps over the lazy dog
*The quick brown fox jumps over the lazy dog*
**The quick brown fox jumps over the lazy dog**
***The quick brown fox jumps over the lazy dog***

An|An
Cumberland (left) is taller and heavier to allow for better legibility at low resolutions.

Cumberland™  The quick brown fox jumps over
Courier New  The quick brown fox jumps over

CUMBERLAND
The quick brown fox jumps over
*The quick brown fox jumps over*
**The quick brown fox jumps over**
***The quick brown fox jumps over***

**5**

*Killerants*

*By Todd Dever of Cool Fonts, provided by Flashline.com*
There are two versions available, regular and bold. Regular is a very cool cracked up looking font that will be great for all kinds of stuff. Bold is one of the most distressed fonts I've ever seen - there's crap everywhere - adjust your leading (line spacing) so the grunge overlaps and you have one awesome effect. Mix 'n match letters from both versions too.

# IMAGE IS EVERYTHING

There are conflicting requirements in the multistage process of getting rendered type onto the screen. Strenuous efforts must be made to preserve the font's overall character and legibility, and to ensure that its tone and color are accurately reproduced—all this in the context of a small and economical file size. Before freezing their design in the grip of an irreversible <IMG> tag, typographers can deliberate to their hearts' content, using the skills of conventional page layout.

Without additional plug-ins, common browsers can at the moment accept only two image-file formats: GIF (Graphics Interchange File, pronounced "jif" by its inventor), and JPEG (Joint Photographic Experts Group). The former is being succeeded by PNG (Portable Network Graphics, pronounced "ping" by its inventor). Although its compressibility is not markedly superior to GIF, PNG offers 256 levels of transparency, compared with GIF's "on or off only," as well as better brightness control across different platforms. The built-in text heading should also mean an end to the tedium of inserting explanatory <ALT> text for image-disabled browsers. A companion format for animation, MNG (Multiple Image Netwrork Graphic), is on the way.

The craft of rendering type as image will one day become as rare as chimney-sweeping, and the GIF will join the 8-track cartridge in the Technology Hall of Fame. In the interim . . .

**1 | 2 | 3 | 4 | 5**

Verdana arriving at 14 on 16pt on the screen *(right)* by various routes. From the top: text keyed directly at the intended size into Photoshop with antialiasing inactive *(1)*, and active *(2)*; text entered at three times the intended size, then reduced to fit using bicubic interpolation, with antialiasing off *(3)* and on *(4)*. Finally *(5)*, text entered in a page-makeup application, exported as an EPS, rasterized in Photoshop with antialiasing on, and saved as a GIF. Type handling add-ons for Photoshop and similar image-editing applications can make bulk text entry much less arduous, but the final, rather round-about, route shown here offers the most flexibility. Editable texts can also be saved easily for the inevitable revisions. The text here is from *Les Misérables* by Victor Hugo.

1. Marius was now a fine-looking young man, of medium height, with heavy jet-black hair, a high intelligent brow, large and passionate nostrils, a frank and calm expression, and an indescribable something beaming from every feature, which was at once, lofty, thoughtful and innocent.

2. Marius was now a fine-looking young man, of medium height, with heavy jet-black hair, a high intelligent brow, large and passionate nostrils, a frank and calm expression, and an indescribable something beaming from every feature, which was at once, lofty, thoughtful and innocent.

3. Marius was now a fine-looking young man, of medium height, with heavy jet-black hair, a high intelligent brow, large and passionate nostrils, a frank and calm expression, and an indescribable something beaming from every feature, which was at once, lofty, thoughtful and innocent.

4. Marius was now a fine-looking young man, of medium height, with heavy jet-black hair, a high intelligent brow, large and passionate nostrils, a frank and calm expression, and an indescribable something beaming from every feature, which was at once, lofty, thoughtful and innocent.

5. Marius was now a fine-looking young man, of medium height, with heavy jet-black hair, a high intelligent brow, large and passionate nostrils, a frank and calm expression, and an indescribable something beaming from every feature, which was at once, lofty, thoughtful and innocent.

## SHEPHERDS BUSH GREEN TO HOUNSLOW

THE DIRECT ROUTE would be by the Goldhawk Road, Chiswick High Road, Kew Bridge and Brentford, the distance being just about 7½ miles to the *"Bell Inn"* at Hounslow. By this way, some exceedingly dangerous tramlines are encountered, especially at Kew Bridge.

### The alternative route

A better, or at any rate, a quieter, way, and one mostly free from tramlines, though not particularly easy to find, is as follows: go along the Goldhawk Road, i.e., the main road on the south side of Shepherd's Bush Green, and continue south-west about 1¼ mile to the *"Queen of England"* public house. There are trams and much traffic, but the road is fairly wide, and not specially crowded. The main road and the trams then bend suddenly to the left (S.S.W.), but we continue straight forward (W.S.W.) along Stamford Brook Road, which is tarred macadam, wide and quiet. Go on over the level crossing at Bath Road Station and along Bath Road, which is pretty quiet, with plenty of room, and then one arrives at Back Common. Here, turn to the right (leaving Turnham Green Station on the left) and take the first turn to the left, along South Parade. *(to be continued)*

**6**

The example *(left)* shows more of the advantages of a page-makeup application for text entry. Word and letter spacing can be controlled within fine limits. Tracking and discretionary hyphenation can be used to achieve better line breaks in justified setting. Drop and small caps are available, and the use of an expert set allows for proper fractions and ligatures. It's not all good, however. Franklin Gothic stands up well, but the main text (a Bembo variant) is beginning to suffer. The *Queen of England* pub is now the *Café Med*, and the trams have long gone for scrap. The left side of the page is at 300 dpi for print reproduction, the right at the equivalent of screen resolution. The text is from *Cycling: Easy Exits from London, Avoiding Traffic.*

# THE SMALL MATTER OF COLOR

Once upon a time, there were cheap international cookbooks with pictures printed in only the first three of the four process colors. The black text was applied afterward in the language of the relevant copublisher. An elegant and economical production solution, but the food looked disgusting. "Dithering" is an ugly word, with its roots in a similar economic fix. Obsolescent systems with monitors that can display only 256 colors will automatically dither colors that fall outside this narrow range, or "gamut." Speckling of this sort is no problem if you are selling oranges or illustrating the ravages of cellulite, but it wreaks havoc with everything else. The "Web-safe" palette of 216 colors (see page 170) is the key to avoiding the problem, and the type-rendering examples on the following pages all—or nearly all—follow this logic.

**1 | 2 | 3 | 4**

The original layout (1) made in QuarkXPress and exported as an EPS. Default RGB and process colors have been used to color the type. The background is a neutral gray. Opened as an antialiased Photoshop document (2), it was then changed to indexed color mode with the "Web" palette selected. A GIF89a export results (3) in a file size of only 8K using a palette of 34 colors (4). The same path (*not shown*) without antialiasing requires only a nine-color palette. The extra 25 colors are all accounted for by the edge effects of anti-aliasing. The text is from the introduction to the 1897 edition of *The Young Lady's Book*.

34

**EXTREME PAINS** have been taken to render the present edition of '*The Young Lady's Book*' as perfect **as is** within the scope of literary and commercial appliances.

1

**EXTREME PAINS** have been taken to render the present edition of '*The Young Lady's Book*' as perfect **as is** within the scope of literary and commercial appliances.

2

**EXTREME PAINS** have been taken to render the present edition of '*The Young Lady's Book*' as perfect **as is** within the scope of literary and commercial appliances.

3

4

**5**

**6**

**7**

**5 | 6 | 7**
Multicolor graduated
fills present the most
severe problem in
palette reduction. The
original artwork (5) is
reduced to a GIF using
the Web palette, first
with dithering (6) and
then, with disastrous
results, without (7).

**9 | 10 | 11**
JPEG compression,
more commonly used
on photographic
subjects, at highest (9)
and lowest (10) quality.
Finally, the end of the
road (11), a dithered
16-color GIF.

**8**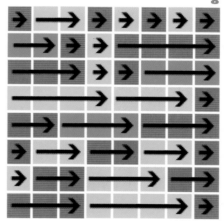

**8**
The root of the GIF
format (above)—
runlength encoding
that looks for
continuous runs of
pixels of the same
color and notes
them in short code.

**9**

**10**

**11**

35

# PRESSED FOR SPACE

In the interests of reduced file size and quicker down-loading, the humble GIF can be manipulated down to the lower limits of legibility. The images shown here all contain gradations of color that suffer under the GIF dithering regime. In the related area of managing transparency and shadows, the GIF is also a very blunt instrument. PNG, though not currently supported by all browsers, offers a way out.

**1 | 2**

The original RGB (8-bit) image *(below)* was first indexed with the 216-color "Web" palette. Returned to RGB, then reindexed with the "exact" palette

to reduce the number of necessary colors, it was subjected *(right)* to the complete range of GIF options. From the top: 8 bits (not dithered);

7 bits (128 colors); 6 bits (64 colors); 5 bits (32 colors); 4 bits (16 colors); 3 bits (8 colors); and, for old times' sake, a bitmap.

36

**3**

**3 | 4 | 5**
The irregularly shaped artwork *(3)* was exported as usual in GIF89a format. Then the separate channel masks that were used in making the artwork were recalled and merged as an overall mask *(4)*. The mask was selected *(5)* to provide transparency against the browser background.

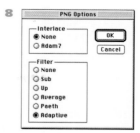

**8**

**8 | 9**
Better handling of transparency with PNG. The same artwork was saved on a black ground *(below)*, with the same mask. The dialog box *(left)* saves a single channel if one is present.

**37**

**4**

**6 | 7**
Only moderate success *(below)* in the browser window against a plain background, and none at all when seen *(bottom)* against a variegated background image.

**5**

**9**

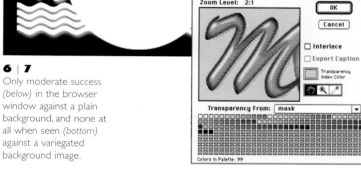

**10**

**6**

**10 | 11**
In the browser window *(above)*, the cast shadows fall convincingly across a variegated background.

Compared with the GIF example *(7)* the shadows cope well with all background colors *(11)*.

**7**

**11**

# SCRIPT EDITING

After a fruitless search through the type catalog for the perfect face in which to set a few words, what could be more rewarding than to do it yourself? The examples here were produced in Freehand, but similar results can be achieved in any of the vector-based drawing applications. There is also an opportunity for old scribbling skills to be resurrected and redundant rubber-stamp sets to be pressed into use.

**1 | 2 | 3 | 4**
The "freehand tool" in Freehand *(right)* offers useful settings for the amateur scribe. With the aid of a stylus and pressure-sensitive graphic tablet, random doodles make editable paths *(below left)* that can be filled *(below)* and revised *(lower)*.

**2**

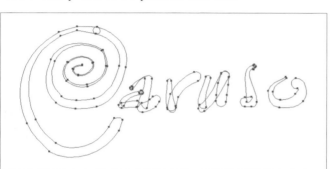

**3**

**5**
Once exported as an EPS and opened in Photoshop *(below)*, the script was filled with color. To conclude, the outline was selected, saved as a path, and stroked with the paintbrush tool set to "multiply."

**4**

**5**

FLAGSTAD

**6 | 7 | 8**
Again with the "free-hand" tool, but set to "calligraphic," frantic scratching with the stylus yields interesting results *(above right)*. Still in Freehand, brutal use of the "envelope" function *(right)* distresses the image even more *(below)*.

**9 | 10 | 11**
Old-style tracing-paper, a soft pencil, and very small handwriting *(above left)*, much enlarged and then reduced to black only *(left)*, give an abrasive effect when duplicated, colorized, and shifted a few pixels *(below)*.

**12 | 13 | 14**
Equipped with a toy printing outfit and a supply of absorbent paper *(right)*, a suitable impression is finally made. After using such crude methods, it may seem a bit perverse to then adjust the letter spacing *(far right)*. A high-contrast version, filled with color, is given a gratuitous glow *(right)*.

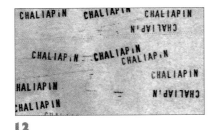

# NATURAL SELECTION

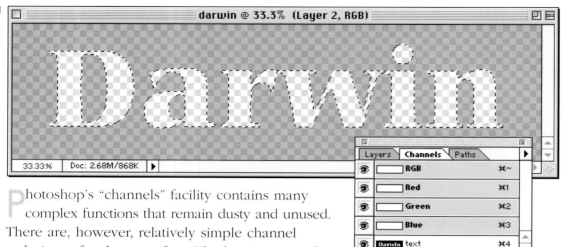

*darwin @ 33.3% (Layer 2, RGB)*

33.33%  Doc: 2.68M/868K

| Layers | Channels | Paths | |
|---|---|---|---|
| 👁 | | RGB | ⌘~ |
| 👁 | | Red | ⌘1 |
| 👁 | | Green | ⌘2 |
| 👁 | | Blue | ⌘3 |
| 👁 | Darwin | text | ⌘4 |

**1**
Once selected, imported text can be cut from the live document layer and planted in a channel *(below left)*. When needed, it can be selected and will reappear in the layer as an outline *(left)*. The color is only an indicator that the channel is active, and does not print.

**40** Photoshop's "channels" facility contains many complex functions that remain dusty and unused. There are, however, relatively simple channel techniques for the rest of us. The key is to avoid Photoshop's own typesetting facility. To input small amounts of text, use an application such as Illustrator or Freehand; for larger amounts, employ any page-makeup program that gives proper typographic control. In any event, import the result into Photoshop and bury it safely in a channel.

**7**

> " I have called this principle, by which each slight variation, if useful, is preserved, by the term of Natural Selection."

**7**
The "negative" area of the channel selection is useful as a simple template. It can be modified by adding or subtracting another selection to make edge effects *(above)*. The text is from Darwin's *The Origin of Species*.

**2 | 3 | 4 | 5 | 6**
The selection (2) is used as a mask (3 and 4). Hidden (5), but still active, it is shrunk by a few pixels to form an outline. The same mask, feathered and shifted, is employed to throw a shadow on a new lower layer (6).

**2**

**3**

**4**

**5**

**6**

## 8 | 9 | 10 | 11

Type shaping in vector-based applications offers repeatability and fine control. The Playbill setting *(above left)* was attached to an arc, reduced to outlines, and then "enveloped" in Freehand. Imported as an EPS into Photoshop, the distorted type was left in its layer and filtered with KPT Texture Explorer *(left)* and Plastic Wrap *(below left)*. The plain text, also imported as an EPS, was given a new channel, selected, feathered, and filled *(below)* to produce a soft shadow.

## 12 | 13

With the basic forms in place, the channel can be repeatedly called up for different purposes *(above)*. The layer icons *(right)* give a clue to some of the maneuvers. The first lettering fill proved far too weak, so the selection was used to make a strong blue copy layer underneath. This hard shadow was then shifted downward and rightward, and filter noise was also added. The same selection enabled the transparent effects where the two words intersect. To achieve this show-through,

fragments of the background type *(layers 6 and 7 above right)* were given different "overlay" and "screen" layer settings. Even with this small number of variables, it is easy to lose the plot. Multiple undos in recent Photoshop versions are a help.

12

13

| | | | |
|---|---|---|---|
| 👁 | | | Layer 7 |
| 👁 | | | Layer 6 |
| 👁 | | | Layer 5 |
| 👁 | | | Layer 4 |
| 👁 | | | Layer 3 |
| 👁 | ✏ | | **Layer 2** |
| 👁 | | | Layer 1 |

# A CALCULATED RESPONSE

The "calculations" dialog box has a gloomy aspect, but if you can force its powerful mysteries you will soon be cavorting on the sunlit uplands of merge. The promise is the facility to mix channel information from more than one file. The only proviso is that the chosen files be of identical size and resolution. With the basic calculation "apply image" you can make a channel created in one file act upon a channel in the other. Using the same two files with the full calculations option, you can direct the merged result to a channel in one of the existing files, or use it to create a completely new file. In all cases, all the familiar layer-merging options are available. In this example, calculations were first used in an attempt to make the type artwork act upon the tonal values in the photograph. Initial results were consigned to channels within the main document for further selection and intersection.

**1 | 2**
The starting file is set in Bremen, a suitably fat and mannered typeface *(top right)*. The companion document, at identical size and resolution, is a gray-scale scan *(above right)*.

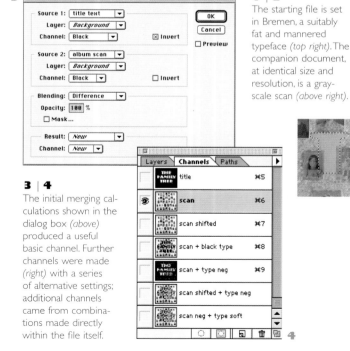

**3 | 4**
The initial merging calculations shown in the dialog box *(above)* produced a useful basic channel. Further channels were made *(right)* with a series of alternative settings; additional channels came from combinations made directly within the file itself.

**5 | 6 | 7**
The basic type channel was used extensively on a new layer to control the lettering density. The selection (5) was color-filled, shifted diagonally, and inverted to select a "shadow" edge (6). This area was colorized (7). A shift in the other direction allowed a highlight to be added in the same way.

42

**8**
Later, the same day. A wide variety of layer combinations and filter effects has been used *(left)* to modify the original image. Some moves succeeded in evoking the metallic surface of early tintype photographs (though all these images were only bromide prints). Others were less helpful, but with a full complement of saved channels, another attempt could be made on another day.

43

# DISPLACEMENT THERAPY

The panorama below is one of a series of more than 100 taken in 1920 along the French and Italian Mediterranean coast. High resolution was the watchword. Eighty years later, this tribute to pioneering photography  views the picture through the bottom of a bottle—or rather, through the window of a speeding mobile café. A little displacement is a dangerous thing.

**"VILLAINS!' I shrieked,
"dissemble no more! I
admit the deed! – tear
up the planks! here!**

2

**"VILLAINS!' I shrieked,
"dissemble no more! I
admit the deed! – tear
up the planks! here!
here! – it is the beating
of his hideous heart!"**

3

**1 | 2 | 3**
The default Photoshop displacement maps, like "pentagons" (above), are small RGB or gray-scale files that act as distorting lenses on the background image. They are apparently seamless when tiled over a large area. Low (darker) values in the maps produce the most image distortion, lighter values the least. The degree of distortion can be separately varied in both axes— in the example (top and above), there is 30% horizontal and 50% vertical distortion. The text is from The Tell-Tale Heart by Edgar Allan Poe.

## 4 | 5 | 6 | 7 | 8 | 9

The do-it-yourself displacement map operates on the same basis as the built-in version. Here the intention was to make one large "lens," rather than tiling the same effect overall. In this sequence, one letter only is used to demonstrate the technique. Imported type (4) was placed in a channel, resized, and moved to fit the background image. Additionally, the word was split to allow for the loss of image in the gutter of the book (bottom)—not a problem with a Web page. A duplicate of the type channel was created, and the image blurred (5) with Gaussian blur, set at 15 pixels in this case. A selection was then made of the original hard-edged type, inverted to select the type background (6), and used to sharpen the edge of the blurred version by filling the selected area with black (7). This channel was then copied and saved by itself as a Photoshop file for use as the displacement map. The background image (8) was treated with various strengths of the new displacement map until a satisfactory result appeared (9).

## 10

The blurred type channel was activated several times to treat different areas of the image (bottom). Various layers of color were tried in combination, and the background was finally treated with motion blur.

**4**

**5**

**6**

**7**

**8**

**9**

45

**10**

# AT THE ROCK FACE

The KPT interfaces have until recently been famous for being made of rock or futuristic metals. Though their appearance is more sober now, you can still waver indecisively between the competing attractions of "utterly shattered shutters," "liquid purplex," and "killer sweepoid." Some of these effects go way beyond the call of polite behavior. In this example, the Gradient Designer filter is used in conjunction with the channels function in Photoshop.

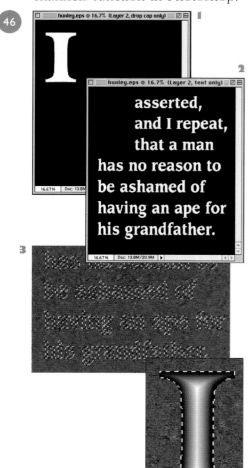

**1 | 2 | 3 | 4**
Imported from a page-makeup application, the drop cap (1) and the remaining text (2) each get a separate channel. While it might seem more reassuring to see black type on a white ground, the channels function is much more useful this way around, not least because the selected channel arrives in the working layer (3) with the type, rather than the background, active. The drop-cap channel was selected as a layer, filled, then treated with Gradient Explorer set to "circular shapeburst" (4). The selection was colorized to give the result shown on the opposite page.

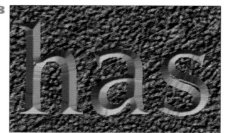

**5 | 6 | 7 | 8**
To get incised lettering, the gradient must be applied, with the type selected, to a copy of the type channel, rather than the active layer. The gradient that was used on the drop cap is reversed (left). The result (below left) shows a shadow effect in the body of the letters, but will not of itself produce the illusion. The next step is to apply the gradient as a texture, using the regular Photoshop Lighting Effects filter (below). "Chisel marks" (bottom) are a bonus.

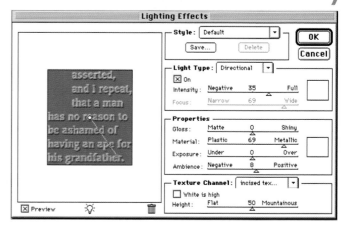

**9**
Edge effects on the result (opposite) are courtesy of the vital shareware Sucking Fish filters (DekoBoko for the bevel; Frame Curtain for the rule). The text is from a speech by T. H. Huxley.

I asserted, and I repeat, that a man has no reason to be ashamed of having an ape for his grandfather.

# ALPHABET SOUP

Eileen Caps provide the target for this scattershot tour of filters and effects. The first half of the alphabet has been treated with Photoshop's native filters, the balance largely with KPT 5.0, with some homegrown examples added for good measure.

**A** Untreated.

**B** Stylize/emboss. Angle 135°; height 7 pixels; amount 100%.

**C** Stylize/solarize.

**D** Stylize/tiles. Number of tiles 10; maximum offset 10%.

**E** Distort/ripple. Size large; amount 100%.

**F** Sketch/notepaper. Image balance 25; graininess 10; relief 10.

**G** Artistic/neon glow. Size 10; brightness 25; color blue.

**H** Sketch/bas-relief. Detail 10; smoothness 9; light direction top left.

**I** Texture/stained glass. Cell size 5; border thickness 1; light intensity 4.

**J** Stylize/plastic wrap. Highlight strength 15; detail 10; smoothness 10.

**K** Pixelate/color halftone. Dot size 8 pixels.

**L** Render/lighting effects. Spotlight; texture from red channel.

**M** Distort/glass. Tiny lens; distortion 5; smoothness 3; scale 100%.

**N-U** Using KPT 5.0 filters as follows:

**N** ShapeShifter. Shadow; glow.

**O** ShapeShifter. Bevel; shadow; glow.

**P** RadWarp. Fisheye.

**Q** Frax4D. Dust devil. Character masked and colorized.

**R** FraxPlorer. Caterpillar Freeway.

**S** FraxPlorer. Mandelbrot, basic potential. Character masked and colorized.

**T** FiberOptix. Default setting; colored light.

**U** Orb-It. Default setting; colored light.

**V** Using one channel. Character selected; area reduced and inverted. Outline colorized; area enlarged and feathered. Background colorized; noise added; blurred; rendered with lighting effects.

**W** Using one channel. KPT Texture Explorer and lighting effects to make pattern. Character cut out; outside area feathered and colorized. Background colorized; feathered channel used to make shadow.

**X** Using one channel. Character selected; color filled; selection shifted and colorized. Background textured with noise, blur, and lighting effects.

**Y** Character selected; painted with brush set to "difference"; reduced and defined as pattern.

**Z** Using Painter. Character filled with Buchanan tartan from weaves palette. Background filled with image hose set to "clover." Shadowed with ShapeShifter.

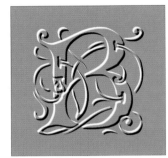

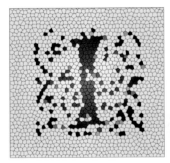

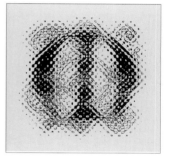

49

# REALLY REAL

Virtual reality seems to have got stuck in the traffic, and those of us who took the trouble to extend our hat racks to accommodate a shiny new helmet now look fairly foolish. Wireframe-based applications such as Strata StudioPro offer some interim therapy. Type can be either set directly in the application window or imported from outside files. At a more lowly level, there are filter packages like Andromeda that act on the two-dimensional image file.

**1**
In Strata StudioPro. "One": type extruded and given a chamfered profile, with "tootie dots" texture applied. "Two": type extruded with a straight profile and covered with a "mahogany" texture. "Three": extruded type subtracted from a solid block, and covered with "lizard skin."

"Four": extruded type combined with a sphere and then covered with "black-and-white tile." "Five": type set and "swept" 345° around an offset axis. The "brick" finish was applied radially, and additional spot lighting used to enhance the shape and texture.

50

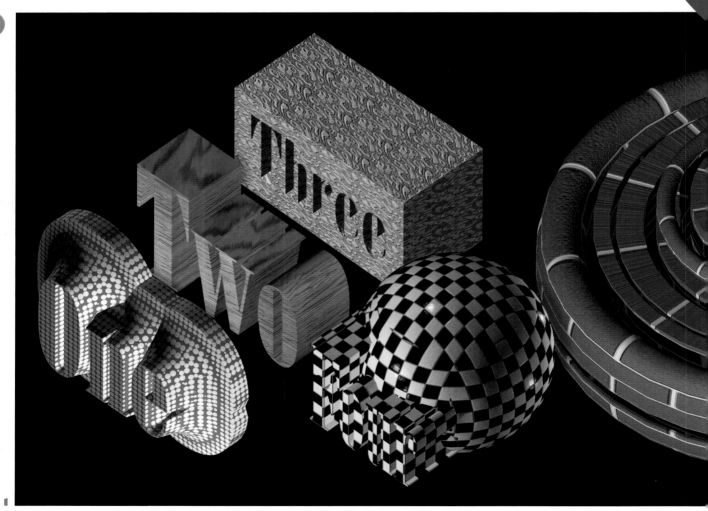

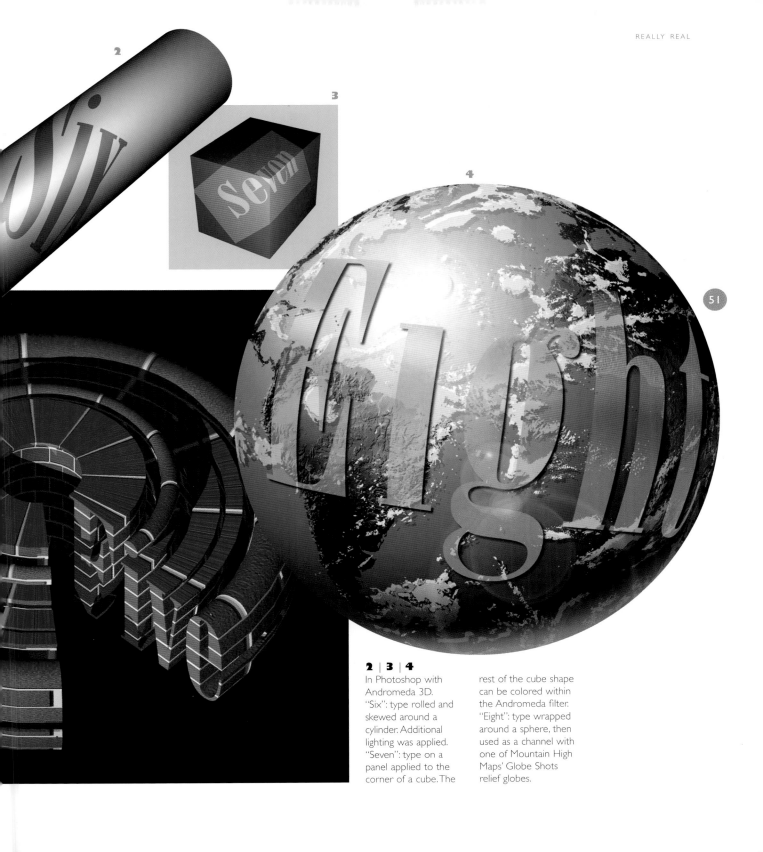

**2 | 3 | 4**

In Photoshop with Andromeda 3D. "Six": type rolled and skewed around a cylinder. Additional lighting was applied. "Seven": type on a panel applied to the corner of a cube. The rest of the cube shape can be colored within the Andromeda filter. "Eight": type wrapped around a sphere, then used as a channel with one of Mountain High Maps' Globe Shots relief globes.

# SIGNS OF MOVEMENT

The animated GIF is the mongrel dog of the Web, scruffy, scorned, but always waiting patiently in the corner for an opportunity to earn a biscuit. Its role will atrophy as Flash and its confederates gain control. For the moment, the GifBuilder application provides some basic tools to get type moving onscreen.

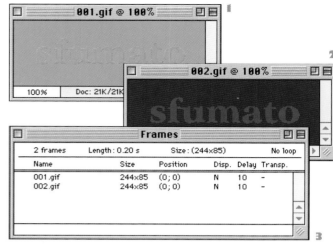

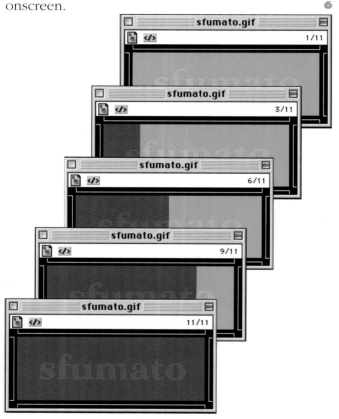

**1 | 2 | 3 | 4 | 5 | 6**
In this sequence the artwork's color values were inverted (1, 2); and both versions, saved as GIFs, dragged to the "frames" window (3). The result is a two-frame animation with a 0.1 second delay between frames. The GifBuilder filters are grouped into "static," "dynamic," and "transition" categories. With the "wipe" transition filter (4) applied to the second frame, a set of inter-mediate frames is automatically generated (5). The interframe delay was reduced to 0.05 seconds at the same time. The actual replay speed of the sequence (6) is determined by the browser—in fact, GifBuilder's instructions warn against invoking the "as fast as possible" setting, for fear of crashing the viewer's machine.

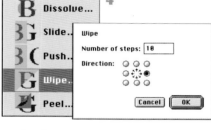

**7**
The "dynamic" filter menu offers "tiles" for progressive pixelation. With the frame sequence reversed (left), the treated image will appear to reconstruct itself.

Frames (first)

| Name | Size | Position | Disp. | Delay | Transp. |
|---|---|---|---|---|---|
| 001.gif | 244x85 | (0; 0) | N | 10 | - |
| 002.gif | 244x85 | (0; 0) | N | 10 | - |

2 frames · Length: 0.20 s · Size: (244x85) · No loop

Frames (second)

| Name | Size | Position | Disp. | Delay | Transp. |
|---|---|---|---|---|---|
| 001.gif | 244x85 | (0; 0) | N | 5 | - |
| Transition 204 | 244x85 | (0; 0) | P | 5 | - |
| Transition 205 | 244x85 | (0; 0) | P | 5 | - |
| Transition 206 | 244x85 | (0; 0) | P | 5 | - |
| Transition 207 | 244x85 | (0; 0) | P | 5 | - |
| Transition 208 | 244x85 | (0; 0) | P | 5 | - |
| Transition 209 | 244x85 | (0; 0) | P | 5 | - |
| Transition 210 | 244x85 | (0; 0) | P | 5 | - |
| Transition 211 | 244x85 | (0; 0) | P | 5 | - |
| Transition 212 | 244x85 | (0; 0) | P | 5 | - |
| 002.gif | 244x85 | (0; 0) | N | 5 | - |

11 frames · Length: 0.55 s · Size: (244x85) · No loop

**8**
Once imported into the frames window, individual images can be moved or resized independently. The sequence (right) uses four image files and a white "blank" file to progressively reveal and hide the balls. The active frame is marked by horizontal rules while stepping through the animation.

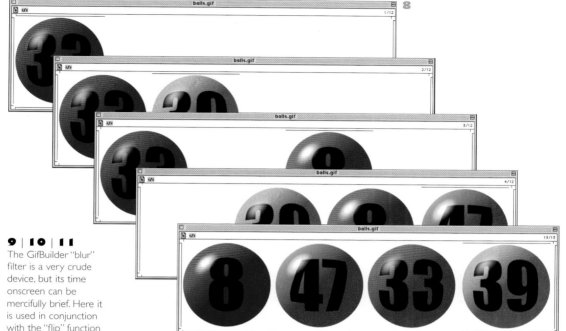

**9 | 10 | 11**
The GifBuilder "blur" filter is a very crude device, but its time onscreen can be mercifully brief. Here it is used in conjunction with the "flip" function on the artwork (9). The "push" transition finally shoves it out of the frame (10). Italic type in the frame window (11) means that a filter or movement has been applied. In this case, every frame has been treated.

## Frames

20 frames    Length: 2.00 s    Size: 255×255

| Name | Size | Position | Disp. | Delay |
|------|------|----------|-------|-------|
| *this way up* | 255×255 | (0 ; 0) | N | 10 | – |
| *this way up side* | 255×255 | (0 ; 0) | N | 10 |
| *this way up* | 255×255 | (0 ; 0) | N | 10 |
| *this way up side* | 255×255 | (0 ; 0) | N | 10 |
| *this way up* | 255×255 | (0 ; 0) | N | 10 | – |
| *Transition 20* | 255×255 | (0 ; 0) | P | 10 | – |
| *Transition 21* | 255×255 | (0 ; 0) | P | 10 |
| *Transition 22* | 255×255 | (0 ; 0) | P | 10 |
| *Transition 23* | 255×255 | (0 ; 0) | P | 10 |
| *Transition 24* | 255×255 | (0 ; 0) | P | 10 |
| *Transition 25* | 255×255 | (0 ; 0) | P | 10 |
| *Transition 26* | 255×255 | (0 ; 0) | P | 10 |
| *Transition 27* | 255×255 | (0 ; 0) | N | 10 |
| *Transition 28* | 255×255 | (0 ; 0) | P | 10 |
| *Transition 29* | 255×255 | (0 ; 0) | P | 10 |
| *Transition 30* | 255×255 | (0 ; 0) | P | 10 |
| *Transition 31* | 255×255 | (0 ; 0) | P | 10 |
| *Transition 32* | 255×255 | (0 ; 0) | P | 10 |
| *Transition 33* | 255×255 | (0 ; 0) | P | 10 |
| *this way up red* | 255×255 | (0 ; 0) | N | 10 |

# CEL DIVISION

The average animated feature film used up nearly 130,000 individual painted cels at the rate of 24 frames a second. If you need just a few frames of type manipulation, a little patience and Photoshop will suffice. All the familiar manipulations can be saved as progressive layers and exported to Adobe Première, GifBuilder and the like. Equally, sequences created originally in Première or similar applications can be taken back into Photoshop in filmstrip format for extra frame-by-frame manipulation.

54

**1**
Type abuse *(above)* using a combination of motion blur and sphereize filters, then colorized in Photoshop for export frame by frame. A violent soundtrack would be an asset.

**2 | 3**
The lighting-effects function in Photoshop, applied sequentially to static type, can give the illusion of a sweeping light beam *(left)*. Although the controls *(below)* offer fine adjustment of lights, colors, and rendering, accurate repeatable positioning of the light source is achieved only by simple hard labor.

**4 | 5 | 6 | 7**
More hard labor is required to simulate the invisible writing hand *(above)*. A stylus and pressure-sensitive tablet make life a little easier. The progressive erasing of the script must be done with great care to preserve the illusion. The final stage is to export the finished frames in reverse order.

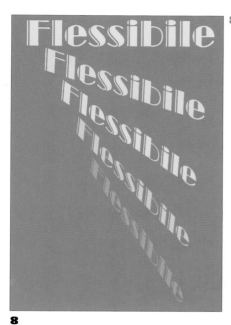

**8**

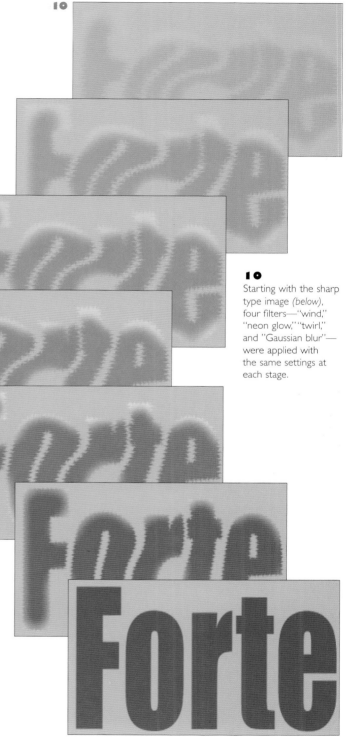

**8**

With the help of the "numeric" function in Photoshop's "transform" command, movements can be planned with absolute accuracy. In the example *(above)*, the original type has been moved, skewed, scaled, and rotated. Copied to a new layer, the same transform settings were applied. The procedure was repeated, and the resulting layers were made progressively less visible.

**10**

Starting with the sharp type image *(below)*, four filters—"wind," "neon glow," "twirl," and "Gaussian blur"— were applied with the same settings at each stage.

**9**

Progressive "uplighting" *(below)* was achieved with the "emboss" filter. In succeeding frames, a feathered selection was made, starting at the base of the image and moving upward. The type was finally colorized, and the relative brightness of the frames adjusted.

**9**

# ON THE FLY

Flash automates the repetitive labor inherent in the GIF-based animation processes shown so far. Its use of vectors recalls the logic of drawing applications like Illustrator and Freehand. Both the moving images and the paths they travel along are defined by points, rather than filled areas. This is of more than academic interest: the finished movie files are much smaller, allowing whole-screen animations and a much richer choice of controls. There is currently one proviso—the viewer's browser must be enhanced with the Shockwave plug-in. The installer for this file is free to download at the Macromedia site **www. macromedia.com**. This bit of tedium will eventually disappear when browsers get native Flash functionality.

**2 | 3**
Transformations were set up for each line as follows. Line 1: to simply move from low to high level. Line 2: to expand in from the right. Line 3: to spin and expand from the right. Line 4: to expand vertically in position. The chosen settings in the timeline *(below)* are such that each new action begins only when the previous one finishes, though it would be simple to overlap them. "Tweening" automatically inserts the necessary intermediate frames. The results *(right)* are shown in the guide colors —the actual movie shows black type only. The text is from *The Indian Serenade* by Percy Bysshe Shelley.

56

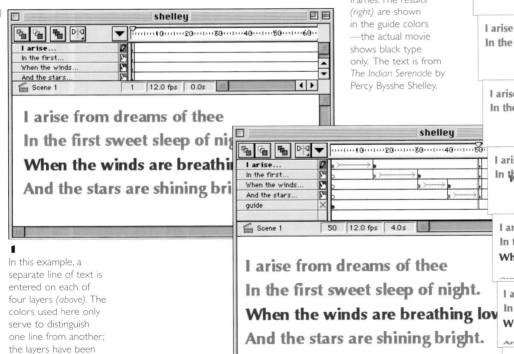

**1**
In this example, a separate line of text is entered on each of four layers *(above)*. The colors used here only serve to distinguish one line from another; the layers have been named for the same reason. The type can stay editable throughout with this simple level of animation.

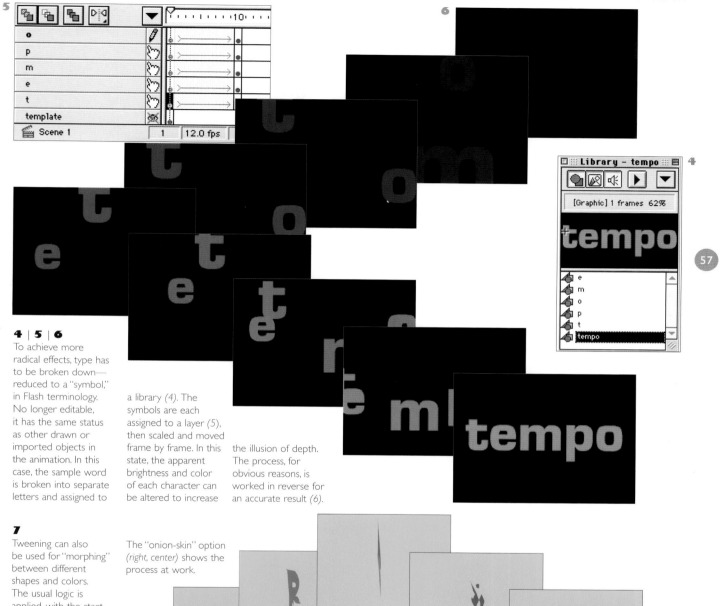

**4 | 5 | 6**

To achieve more radical effects, type has to be broken down—reduced to a "symbol," in Flash terminology. No longer editable, it has the same status as other drawn or imported objects in the animation. In this case, the sample word is broken into separate letters and assigned to a library (4). The symbols are each assigned to a layer (5), then scaled and moved frame by frame. In this state, the apparent brightness and color of each character can be altered to increase the illusion of depth. The process, for obvious reasons, is worked in reverse for an accurate result (6).

**7**

Tweening can also be used for "morphing" between different shapes and colors. The usual logic is applied, with the start and finish objects assigned to a timeline. Here the character (near right) was set to be scaled laterally to almost zero at the halfway stage, then flipped horizontally, as well as changing color by the final frame. The "onion-skin" option (right, center) shows the process at work.

# FILM FUN

Seated in a canvas-backed folding chair, the humble typographer can play movie director with chunks of type. If you can imagine the opening obelisk in *2001: A Space Odyssey* as a very large Folio Bold Condensed capital "I," you're already in the correct frame of mind. Flash borrows some of the cinematic terms (there are "stages" and "scenes") and combines them with the more familiar layers metaphor. The working file is called a "movie" even if it contains no animation, and includes one stage that is effectively the background layer. It may have any suitable number of scenes. Though these are presented in parallel in the working window to avoid long scrolling timelines,

they are actually designed to follow each other in the prescribed order. The stage level has the feel of a paint application c.1985. A small set of tools allows coloring and filling of objects drawn with a pencil. There are virtues, however. The pencil can be set to smooth faltering lines, and the charming old paint bucket can use fills with different degrees of transparency. The stage level is the destination of any items from the upper overlays that have been "broken apart" for editing. Entered text arrives on the overlay level, also the home of grouped items, symbols, and imported bitmaps. The attributes of the objects silently determine their level—there is no "stage/overlay" command.

58

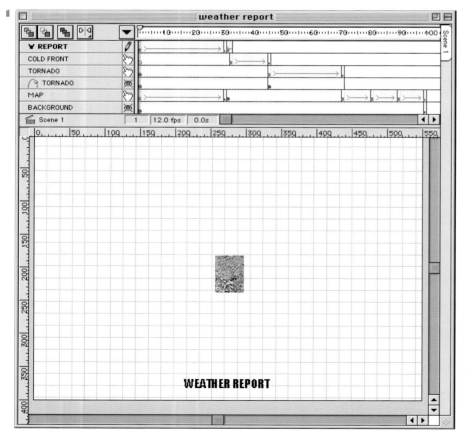

**1 | 2 | 3**
Two elements *(left)* open proceedings in this melodramatic movie. The imported relief map and directly entered text *(top and above)* are set to rotate simultaneously and in opposite directions to their final positions *(opposite, top left)*. The lowest layer (an overall yellow) is turned off here to reveal the layout grid.

**7**

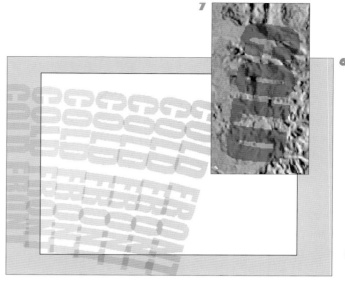

**6**

**4**

**5**

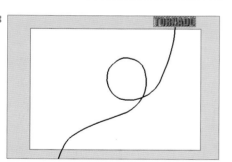

**8**

**4 | 5**
At frame 30, type and map come to rest *(left)*. Copied type is filled with white and shifted at frame 31. The progress of the map rotation is followed by an onion-skin view *(below left)*.

**6 | 7**
The workspace outside the movie frame can hold elements that will slide in from "off-stage." Here, the cold-front type *(right)* was filled with transparent blue to allow the relief map to show through *(top right)* as it passed across, scaling up at the same time.

**8 | 9**
The "motion guide" layer provides a path for any object on the layer above. The tornado path is a pencil line *(left)*, which disappears in the finished movie. The type was also set to rotate while following the path *(right, in onion-skin view)*.

**59**

**9**

**10 | 11**
Unfortunately, the shortcomings of the printed page do not allow the weather movie to see the light of day. As a substitute *(right)*, there is an onion-skin view set up to show every move of every item on every layer in every one of 70 frames. The last maneuver shows the terrain map beating a weary retreat *(far right)*.

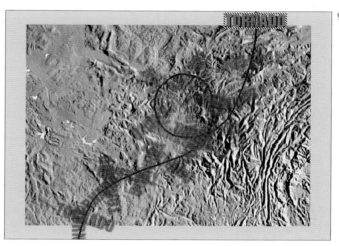

**10     11**

# ANY OTHER BUSINESS

Java is just for tacky banners, they used to say. It now seems likely that it could eventually displace the code that underpins today's mainstream page-makeup applications. Tiny Java applets already do remarkable things with type on the Web. This is not pleasant news for those who, while struggling with the banalities of HTML, skidded off the road at the learning curve, and now sit glumly in a ditch at the side of the super-highway. Remarkably, the Web throws a gossamer life-line, courtesy of the uncountable global mass of code-warriors whose greatest pleasure is to stay up late and further wear out the <, > and " buttons on their key-boards. There is Java to be plucked from overhanging boughs all over the Web. Numerous sites like Gamelan at **www.gamelan.com** *(right)* offer free and shareware applets, together with fully fledged commercial items for downloading. With good eyesight you can also find variety at **www.davecentral.com** *(far right)*. Most applets are accompanied by a user guide; some invite you to resubmit your modified version for a checkup.

**1 | 2 | 3**
Isn't it amazing how the eyes follow you around the page? The pointer-following Java applet comes free with good wishes from "Brian's Exciting Page."

60

# THE MECHANICAL APPROACH

Two essays in automotive presentation. On this page, two-wheeled and mechanically minded, *Motorcycle Online*'s www.motorcycle.com fuels the bike enthusiast —in contrast to the more leisurely, smooth, walnut-dash tones of Jaguar Cars' www.jaguar.com, opposite.

**1 | 2**

The shovel-shaped (head-shaped) layout *(left)* is not just to give the Harley-Davidson disciples a subliminal boost. Each button is generously repeated as a link at the foot of the page; with one click, you can be up to your elbows in chain oil *(below)*. With magazine-style Kabel masthead and drop shadows all over, there's plenty to attract even the laziest armchair biker.

# MOTORCYCLE ONLINE

Daily News
What's New?
Come Meet MO
Product Reviews
New Products
Bike Reviews

1999 YZF-R6

Syed Leathers

'99 Kawasakis

'99 Yamahas 1

Riding the F4

'99 Triumphs

**1**

**NO, NO, NO! What part of NO don't you understand?**

Corbin

**Daily News:**
Kelley Blue Book Adds M/C
Values to Web Site, Aprilia
Launches Green Motorcycle

EAGLERIDER
Motorcycle Rentals

| SEARCH | BREAKIN' THE LAW | OFF ROAD | MANUFACTURER'S ROW | AD INFO | MULTIMEDIA ARCHIVE | CLASSIFIED |
| RACING | PRODUCT REVIEWS | CLUBS & EVENTS | NUTS & BOLTS | ABOUT MO | VIRTUAL MUSEUM | DATABASE |

"The World's Largest and Most-Read Digital Motorcycle Magazine"
Yamaha YZF-R6 | Syed Leathers | 99 Kawasakis | Yamaha Cruisers | CBR600F4 | 99 Triumphs
Daily News | What's New | Bike Reviews | Product Reviews | Multimedia Archive | Racing
Nuts & Bolts | Touring The World | Manufacturer's Row | New-Model Database
Search | Breakin' The Law | Off-Road | Classifieds | Museum
Editorial Feedback | Advertising Inquiries | Staff
Events Calendar | New Products
© 1998 Motorcycle Online, Inc.

**2**

als
W!

- **Cutting Edge Tech**
- **Wrenching at Home**
- **How it all Works**
- **Toolbox: Dirt Tech**

the Japanese bring out their really wild stuf
al Transportation Module.

the latest in four-stroke technology.
roke in the outdoor nationals.
s down in their new ET2.
road burner, the 500 V Due.

- Two-Stroke Tech: The inner workings of Honda's ultra-clean running EXP-2
- The Future of Scooters? The Yamaha Majesty

**How it all Works**

- Chain Tech 2: Dyno results of changing a clapped-out chain.
- All About Chains: A Conversation with A Chain Legend
- Carlini's Torque Arm Does it really work?

**3**

**4**

**3 | 4**

Jaguar begins *(left)* with a polite welcome and helpfully labeled image icons for those who prefer not to download images on the fly.

The banner *(below left)* borrows from all elements of Jaguar's long-established typographic style. The hood roundel (originally designed in 1949) is modified to "read" online. Optima Bold is used for all nontrademark type.

**5 | 6**

While the North American page layout *(below left)* looks bleak and wasteful, the reason soon becomes clear *(bottom left)*.

**7**

**5**

**6**

**8**

**9**

**7 | 8 | 9**

The cars appear at last *(right)*, with Java applets animating type and pointers as the mouse runs over them. The site map *(not shown)* wearily reverts to bulleted text and a sardonic title—"You've always known where to go."

# ABSOLUTELY CLEAR

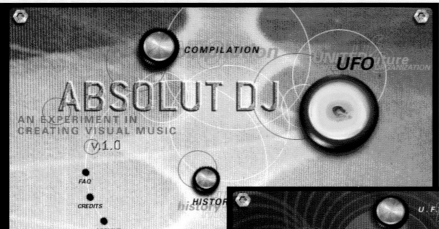

**1 | 2**

Colors and type forms are familiar from "the aliens are coming" movie and TV graphics of the 1960s. The curved UFO logo *(below)* could be formed in Freehand using distortion in the "envelope" function and then further distressed in a paint program. All type is in GIF form and benefits from the irregular colored and textured background, which disguises any ragged edges.

Old style preconceptions once demanded unflinching design allegiance to the product's brand identity. Players in the lifestyle industries, notably the international spirits suppliers, are now just as likely to adopt the graphic style of their young target market. The energizing force on this page is the music scene—in fact the main purpose of this Absolut Vodka site **www.absolutvodka.com** is to offer music and video clips of sponsored events, rather than an overt selling message. Opposite, Smirnoff **www.smirnoff.com** harnesses the more traditional attributes of barroom life and attends with great care to the stylistic nuances of history and cinema.

**3**

Just for reference, this is the actual bottle—crisp, cool Futura Bold Condensed caps.

**3**

**4 | 5 | 6 | 7**

After a little stern HTML *(4)*, a more welcoming typographic bear-hug *(5)* introduces the actual site with beaten-up Courier. All type is GIF from here on in. Java-enabled browsers can see type rollovers *(6)* in the unusually placed navigation bar. Non-Java users must be content with a rotating animated GIF logo. That false note apart, the screens are immaculate in their sensitivity to the different areas addressed—from the "heritage" ephemera of the brand's Russian ancestry to the borrowed chic *(7)* of the 007 connection. Not such good marks for spelling, however. Espionage has one "n" too many, and Miss Moneypenny has gained a surplus "e."

# GOING AROUND IN CIRCLES

Two sites that challenge the rectilinear mold. On this page Cable & Wireless **www.cwcom.co.uk** uses its globe device as the starting point. The circular layout avoids the usual hierarchical sequence in which the user subliminally assumes that the topmost choices are the more desirable or rewarding. Even so, the casual visitor seems to be warned off the probably tedious Interim Report by its six-o'clock position.

There are various national sites for Adidas—this one **www.adidas.com/global/home/mgtime.htm** celebrates Mark Gonzales, skateboard champion. The interview, opposite, closely mimics the traditional magazine inquiries as to food and literary preferences, but lays them out in an addictive circular design. Why? Why not?

66

**1 | 2 | 3**
C&W keeps it clean and simple *(left)* with flat colors and Gill Sans GIFs. The only indulgence is an animated goldfish *(bottom)*, the only jarring note the default pop-down menu.

**4 | 5**
Deeper into the site, ancient forces raise their ugly heads. A shirtsleeved executive *(below)* greets us with a cheery "hello" from his circular frame. A long swathe of HTML text and slide-show graphics follows *(left)*—it scrolls on down for 11 average screens.

6

7

**6 | 7 | 8 | 9**

Quick reactions are required to this curt inquiry *(above left)* —a negative answer consigns the viewer to a straight timeline with a fearsome row of GIFs to download *(top)*. There are no options for a down-loading trip to the Macromedia Flash site, nor even the possibility of a timid exit. More well-equipped viewers get a compendium of triumphs (including movies) and mis-adventures accessed from the zany round timeline. Now and again you'll see a shoe *(below)*; notice the faintly green tinge overall and realize the purpose of your visit.

8

9

# HOT DIESEL

**ONLINE SHOPPING**

**F/W 1998 COLLECTION**
**DIESEL KIDS** NEW
**DENIM JEANS GUIDE**
**FRAGRANCES**
**DIESEL CLUB**
**COMMUNICATE**
**COMPANY INFORMATION**

**1 | 2 | 3**
Answering "cold" to
the initial query *(top)*
gets you a thermo-
meter *(above left)*, even
a link to a temperature
converter *(above)* for
the inquisitive or
simply nervous.

From time to time, a site comes into view that successfully engages the user on a number of levels. The key at **www.diesel.com** is consistency of concept. It's simple—some clothes keep you warm, some clothes keep you very, very warm. Simplicity is in the core of the design also—Franklin Gothic is a face that looks good onscreen, both on the vast white grounds and on the hefty dark blocks employed here.

The layout and photography are familiar from fashion-magazine design, but the central idea of ascribing a "warmth factor" to each item lures the viewer into an agreeable journey through the range.

**8**
A final check *(below)* allows you to view all the images as a long scrolling contact sheet.

**4 | 5 | 6 | 7**
You can navigate between extremes *(below left and below)* —the thermometer is an animated GIF that plays in response to your mouse clicks. Your comments are very welcome *(above)*, but don't expect a reply. Credit is given where it's due *(bottom)*.

**EXIT INDEX**

**7**

**CREDITS**

**CONCEPT**
DIESEL CREATIVE TEAM

**PHOTOGRAPHY**
RANKIN

**HAIR**
ALAIN PICHON

**MAKE UP**
VAL GARLAND

**GRAPHIC DESIGN**
PRINT - ROELOF MULDER
VIRTUAL - REAL TIME STUDIO

# TRUST ME, I'M A BANKER

Personal finance is moving to the Net. The long-established financial institutions, competing for market share with upstart online bankers, must depend on their familiar imagery while also looking smart and responsive. This is a hard row to hoe. Citibank's long-standing blue identity **www.citibank.com** transfers to the screen almost intact, though the trademark's gradated horizon and italic caps suffer in the transition. Egg (a new division of the British Prudential company) shows the alternative route. Following the **www.egg.com** scenario, you have no existing corporate identity to promote, and your customers are the dominant graphics. With their faces, you define the target market, and your typographer in turn selects typefaces that reflect their lifestyle. Let the battle commence.

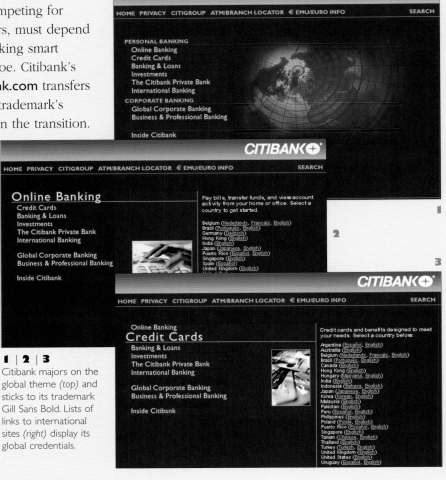

**1 | 2 | 3**
Citibank majors on the global theme *(top)* and sticks to its trademark Gill Sans Bold. Lists of links to international sites *(right)* display its global credentials.

**4**

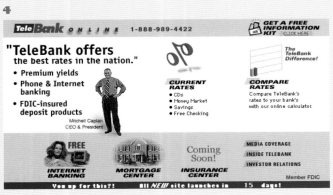

**4**
TeleBank plays it straight and hands-on-hips confident *(left).* The percent sign rotates at high speed, the bar chart increases values by the second, and the word "free" flashes in multicolor. Maybe not tasteful, but the layout and choice of type sizes and weights is assured.

**5**

Pink navigation bars *(right)* signal a site with no corporate-identity baggage, and anyone whose work involves using a PC will feel at home with the ubiquitous Verdana. Even the recurring "this site was created for . . ." refers slyly to Microsoftian phraseology.

Register | Log In | Contact Us | Send Me Info | Feedback

**egg:** Individual Money Matters

this page created for: an individual

About Egg
▸ More About Egg
Financial News
Savings
Home Finance
Loans
Info Guides
Press Releases

## About Egg

Egg exists because everyone's financial needs are different. With Egg, you'll be treated as an individual without the complications, stuffiness and small print which can be associated with managing your money.

Just take a look round our web site and see for yourself.

Whatever YOU want from YOUR finances, Egg is here to help.

**71**

**6 | 7**

A word in your ear. Some screens present the major text proposition as a GIF neatly running around the photograph; the introduction of HTML text leads to a quirk. All is well in Internet Explorer *(6)*, but Netscape Navigator *(7)* is not so tidy..

**6**

tailored for each individual customer.
Just You

What's Happening at Egg?

▸ Flexible Personal Loans
Egg personal loans allow you the flexibility to take a repayment break. If that's what you want!
▸ Mortgage rate drops again
.49 % pa
notice.
mation

**7**

tailored for each individual customer.
Just You

What's Happening at Egg?

▸**Flexible Personal Loans**
Egg personal loans allow you the flexibility to take a repayment break. If the what you want!
▸**Mortgage rate drops again**
Egg announces a 0.5% cut in its basic variable rate mortgage to 5.99% p.a. from February 22nd.
▸**A refreshing way to save**
All the interest you'd expect from a notice account, without all the notice.
▸**Current Response Times**
Click here to see our current response times for receiving an information pack and opening an account.

**8**

American Egg Board

**Welcome to the Incredible Edible Egg World Wide Web Site**

Willamette Egg Farms

**8 | 9**

Other eggs may be available *(right)* and might take precedence in an inexpert search. Script faces are evidently the norm in the real egg business.

**9**

# LIGHT AND SHADE

Two approaches to promoting art on the unforgiving monitor. Plan A: tease the viewer with tiny shards of artwork and a frantic butterfly. Plan B: offer a multi-level network of choices, accommodating even those who can't bring themselves to choose at all. First, the Remedi Project **www.theremediproject.com** uses Flash animation to great effect. The crazed insect flutters through a white Californian sky and thin skeins of tiny Helvetica. Opposite, a visit to **www.artranspennine.org.uk** reflects the grayer horizons of northern England, but shows equally fine control of type and layout.

**1 | 2**
First sighting of the unexpected butterfly *(left)*, which hovers around while you make your selection *(below)*.

**3 | 4**
Take a moment to digest the artist's statement *(above right)*, and check for missing words—but be ready for more harassment from the resident insect *(right)*.

I'm endlessly fascinated with the sky. I was initially inspired to take photos of the skyline by a cool piece of fence that was dangling off the edge a cliff

in Pacifica.

annette loudon **skyline** 04.1
**the remedi project** redesigning the medium through discovery
.1 .2 .3 .4
launch project

04. 05. 06. 07. 08. 09. 10. 11. 12. 13.

browse the artist statements below.

01.
02.
03.
14.

15.
00.

0.

matt owens **the blinders** 05.
**the remedi project** redesigning the medium through discovery
.1 .2 .3 .4
launch project

some                    he situation

04. 05. 06. 07. 08. 09. 10. 11. 12. 13.

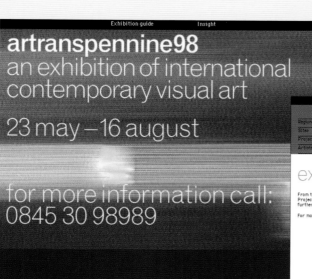

**artranspennine98**
an exhibition of international
contemporary visual art

23 may – 16 august

for more information call:
0845 30 98989

www.channel.org.uk/ofallplaces    A project by Tracy Mackenna and Edwin Janssen

News headlines    Liverpool goes bananas over its yellow sculpture
Art takes over the land in Britain's largest contemporary art exhibit

**5**

**6**

| Exhibition guide | Insight | | | |
| --- | --- | --- | --- | --- |
| | Liverpool | Manchester | Leeds | Hull | Trans-regional |
| Region | | | | | |
| Sites | | | | | |
| Projects | | | | | |
| Artists | | | | | |

exhibition guide

From the matrix, choose the category you are interested in, for example: Leeds – Artists; Leeds –
Projects; Liverpool – Sites. Roll over the index numbers which then appear and click to obtain
further information on an individual artist, site or project.

For more information call: 0845 30 98989

**5 | 6 | 7**
The opening screen
*(far left)* boldly suggests
forgetting the Web site
and picking up the
phone. Persist and the
reward is a friendly
matrix *(left)*, which
allows you to express
your preference by
region, location,
project, or artist for
the participating cities
*(below)*.

**7**

| Exhibition guide | Insight | | | |
| --- | --- | --- | --- | --- |
| | Liverpool | Manchester | Leeds | Hull | Trans-regional |
| Region | | | | | |
| Sites | | | | | |
| Projects | | | | | |
| Artists | | | | | |

| Exhibition guide | Insight | | | |
| --- | --- | --- | --- | --- |
| | Liverpool | Manchester | Leeds | Hull | Trans-regional |
| Region | | | | | |
| Sites | | | | | |
| Projects | | | | | |
| Artists | | | | | |

| Exhibition guide | Insight | | | |
| --- | --- | --- | --- | --- |
| | Liverpool | Manchester | Leeds | Hull | Trans-regional |
| Region | | | | | |
| Sites | | | | | |
| Projects | | | | | |
| Artists | | | | | |

| Exhibition guide | Insight | | | |
| --- | --- | --- | --- | --- |
| | Liverpool | Manchester | Leeds | Hull | Trans-regional |
| Region | | | | | |
| Sites | | | | | |
| Projects | | | | | |
| Artists | | | | | |

**8**

artranspennine98    Exhibition guide    Insight

| | Liverpool | Manchester | Leeds | Hull | T |
| --- | --- | --- | --- | --- | --- |
| Region | | | | | |
| Sites | | | | | |
| Projects | | | | | |
| Artists | | | | | |

Manchester Sites    Site number   1 2 3 4 5 6 7 8 9
                                   Upper Campfield Market

Museum of Science and
Industry in Manchester

Projects:          Museum of Science and Industry in Manchester
Canal              Liverpool Road
Chorus             Castlefield
Artists:           Manchester M3 4FP
Joseph Bartscherer 0161 832 1830 recorded information
Dominique Blain    0161 832 2244 Museum enquiries
                   www.edes.co.uk/mussci
                   Daily 10.00–17.00
                   £5 Adults, £3 concs, under-5s free

**8**
The end of the
quest *(above)*, with
well-organized HTML
showing precisely
what's on offer.

# A SENSE OF AUTHORITY

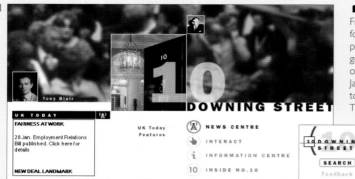

**1**
Franklin Gothic to the fore on the home page *(left)*. Leafy backgrounds stand for open government. A Java applet supplies up-to-the-minute news. This simple animation scrolls through a loop of news items—click on a topic to be taken to the full story. The color portrait of the current Prime Minister is 60 pixels tall, while previous incumbents rate only 37 pixels in grayscale. A suitably subversive applet might perhaps be programmed to activate on future election nights to downsize a defeated leader.

**74**

A surprising pair: a national-government site **www.number-10.gov.uk** that looks like a bright and friendly advertising agency, and an advertising agency **www.wpp.com** that resembles the shadowy face of some totalitarian regime (though it does sport a button labeled "fun"). The 10 Downing Street site has information on several levels—from standing material on the history of the house itself to late-breaking news. WPP has a longer history than most governments, and the self-confidence to display itself in shades of black.

**2**
[Navigation bar: 10 DOWNING STREET | SEARCH | Feedback | NEWS CENTRE — UK Today, Features | INTERACT — Email News, Live Broadcasts, Open Discussions | INFO CENTRE — The Government, Releases | INSIDE NO.10 — History, Tour, PMs in History]

Welcome to the Government News Centre. Click on UK Today for daily news direct from 10 Downing Street, or visit our Features section for a more in depth account of key Government activities.

**NEWS CENTRE**
UK TODAY FEATURES

**2 | 3 | 4 | 5**
The navigation bar remains on view throughout, and small type rollovers respond to mouse movement. The News Centre banner *(above)* owes an obvious debt to 1920s modernist typography (Herbert Bayer comes to mind) and elegantly symbolizes the concept of "spin." Deeper into the site *(left and below)*, there are solid quantities of HTML text with a few relieving GIFs. Non-ASCII characters confuse the message *(below)* when word-processed press releases get thrown into the site unedited.

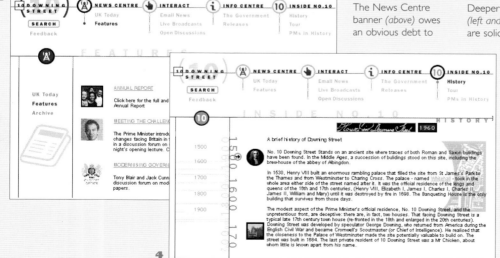

**3**
[Navigation: 10 DOWNING STREET | SEARCH | Feedback | NEWS CENTRE — UK Today, Features | INTERACT — Email News, Live Broadcasts, Open Discussions | INFO CENTRE — The Government, Releases | INSIDE NO.10 — History, Tour, PMs in History]

FEATURES
UK Today
Features
Archive

ANNUAL REPORT
Click here for the full and Annual Report

MEETING THE CHALLE...
The Prime Minister introdu... changes facing Britain in... in a discussion forum on... night's opening lecture. C...

MODERNISING GOVERN...
Tony Blair and Jack Cunn... discussion forum on mod... papers.

**4**
[Navigation: 10 DOWNING STREET | SEARCH | Feedback | NEWS CENTRE — UK Today, Features | INTERACT — Email News, Live Broadcasts, Open Discussions | INFO CENTRE — The Government, Releases | INSIDE NO.10 — History, Tour, PMs in History]

INSIDE NO.10 — HISTORY

1960

A brief history of Downing Street

No. 10 Downing Street Stands on an ancient site where traces of both Roman and Saxon buildings have been found. In the Middle Ages, a succession of buildings stood on this site, including the brew-house of the abbey of Abingdon.

In 1530, Henry VIII built an enormous rambling palace that filled the site from St James's Park to the Thames and from Westminster to Charing Cross. The palace - named Whitehall - took in the whole area either side of the street named after it. It was the official residence of the kings and queens of the 16th and 17th centuries, (Henry VIII, Elizabeth I, James I, Charles I, Charles II, James II, William and Mary) until it was destroyed by fire in 1698. The Banqueting House is the only building that survives from those days.

The modest aspect of the Prime Minister's official residence, No. 10 Downing Street, and the unpretentious front, are deceptive: there are, in fact, two houses. That facing Downing Street is a typical late 17th century town house (re-fronted in the 18th and enlarged in the 20th centuries). Downing Street was developed by speculator George Downing, who returned from America during the English Civil War and became Cromwell's Scoutmaster (or Chief of Intelligence). He realised that the closeness to the Palace of Westminster made the site potentially valuable to build on. The street was built in 1684. The last private resident of 10 Downing Street was a Mr Chicken, about whom little is known apart from his name.

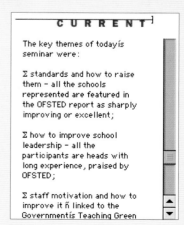

**5**
CURRENT

The key themes of today's seminar were:

Σ standards and how to raise them – all the schools represented are featured in the OFSTED report as sharply improving or excellent;

Σ how to improve school leadership – all the participants are heads with long experience, praised by OFSTED;

Σ staff motivation and how to improve it ñ linked to the Government's Teaching Green

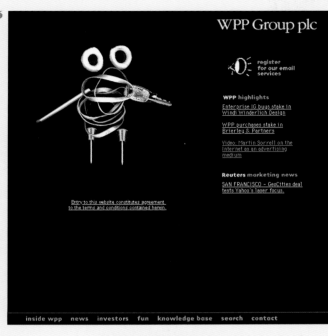

WPP Group plc

register for our email services

**WPP** highlights

Enterprise IG buys stake in Windl Winderlich Design

WPP purchases stake in Brierley & Partners

Video: Martin Sorrell on the Internet as an advertising medium

**Reuters** marketing news

SAN FRANCISCO – GeoCities deal tests Yahoo's laser focus.

Entry to this website constitutes agreement to the terms and conditions contained herein.

inside wpp   news   investors   fun   knowledge base   search   contact

WPP Group plc

investors

annual report
corporate profile
financial performance
shares
shareowners' services

**Investors**

**1998 Q3 results:** show revenues up 15% in constant currencies and up almost 14% in the first nine months. more...

*In this section...*

**Annual report**
the award-winning 1997 Annual report, with historical reports to be added shortly.

**Corporate profile**
a snapshot of WPP, its management, history and competitive positioning.

**Financial performance**
the 1997 financial summary, plus statements from December 1996.

**Shares**
the WPP share price in London and New York, plus data on WPP revenue and earnings.

**Shareowners' services**
consult our SEC filings, find our Investors Packs, see our financial calendar.

**Email services...**

subscribe to our Email services to get press releases, site updates on wpp.com or wpp.e.wire.

back to top

inside wpp   news   investors   fun   knowledge base   search   contact

**6 | 7 | 8 | 9 | 10**

The scene is set (above) with a voodoo figure animated from the debris that clutters the average desktop. A neat device, which says "We mean business, but we can be zany too." Corporate Garamond and anodyne sans-serif GIFs remain in the background. The heroes, bizarrely, are the ranks of white HTML text with discreet gray links. Artfully soft-edged images blend into the gloom—a cool and nearly flawless site.

**11 | 12 | 13**

Bad things happen . . . The "fun" section flies resolutely in the face of everything achieved in the rest of the site. Ugly type (in ugly color), then ugly misspelled type super-imposed on ugly type leading to a crude arcade-style game. Life is indeed a pitch . . .

# VORSPRUNG DURCH FLASHTECHNIK

Volkswagen led the pack in print advertising with the first "Lemon" ad. Forty years later, a picture above and copy below is not enough to sell the reborn Beetle. Here, **www.newbeetle.co.uk** draws on Flash to exhibit the new car's idiosyncratic appeal. It's a two-way process—the car's styling is heavily reflected in the layout. Volkswagen's close cousins at Audi **www.audi.co.uk** use Flash as well, with yet more lingering over their car's sculpted forms.

76

**1 | 2 | 3 | 4 | 5**
Be ready for lengthy download times. Teasing Flash movies play (right) while the "Rotascope" scenario unfolds (below). Type is all GIFs in house-style Futura Bold.

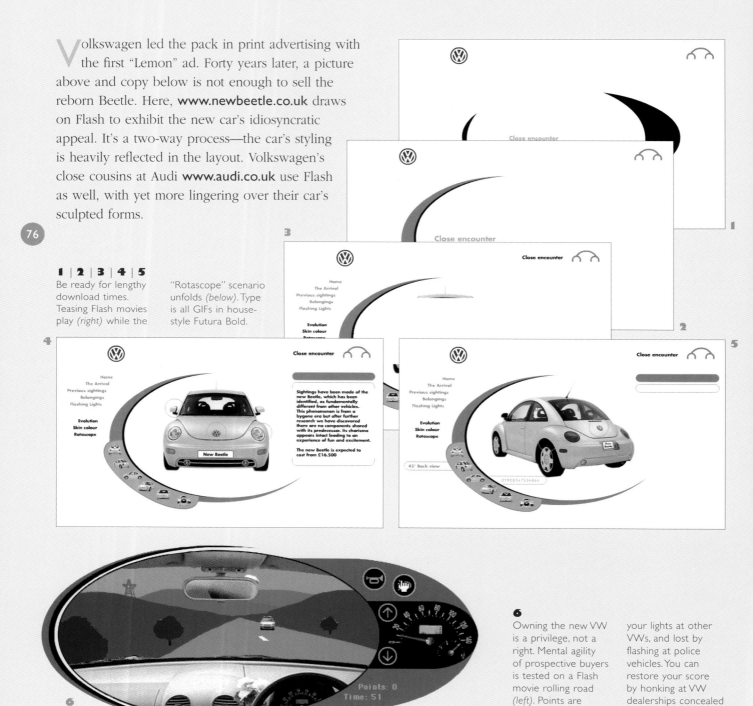

**6**
Owning the new VW is a privilege, not a right. Mental agility of prospective buyers is tested on a Flash movie rolling road (left). Points are gained by flashing your lights at other VWs, and lost by flashing at police vehicles. You can restore your score by honking at VW dealerships concealed behind curbside trees.

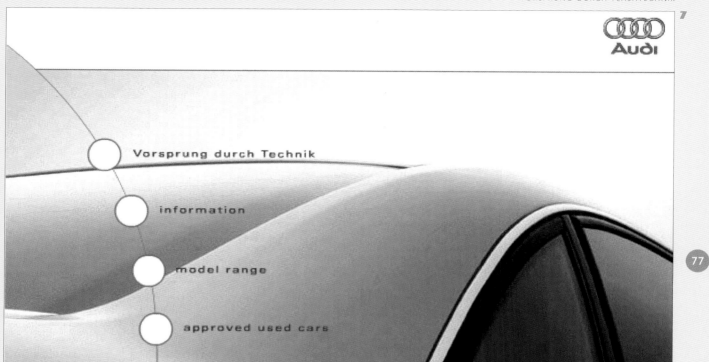

Vorsprung durch Technik

information

model range

approved used cars

contents

**7 | 8 | 9**
The home page is almost devoid of color. Clicking on a topic invokes the Flash animation—lines shoot out and subsections are revealed *(top and above)*. The "string of pearls" device acts as the navigation bar as the site gets into more detail *(right)*.

**10**
It's a rubber mirror gaiter. A debt seems due to Bill Brandt's nude photography for the closeup body shots *(above)*.

# COMPLETELY UP-TO-DATE

**M**inor stylistic differences distinguish British public service broadcasting at **www.news.bbc.co.uk** from the U.S. commercial equivalent **www.cnn.com**. Strangely, the CNN pages more closely resemble their newspaper forebears, with large mastheads and headlines. Both supplement screens with audio and video options, but only the BBC has Welsh and Mandarin Chinese sound.

**1 | 2 | 3**

The front page *(top right)* shows major stories of the day plus a series of regularly updated links. These appear as HTML text links on the left of the page. Rolling news-flashes occupy another corner. Selecting the attractions of the Euro *(right)*, for example, over those of Ms. Lewinsky, brings up a detailed story *(far right)* and further links alongside. The subject masthead GIF is repeated in a smaller version to maintain continuity.

**4 | 5**

The BBC's mandate is to cater to all ages and all sorts of people. Though the designers of the adult-oriented Darwin site *(right)* have evolved skills in making type and image GIFs, their ability to letter-space display type successfully is notice-ably inferior to that achieved *(far right)* by their Teletubby colleagues.

**6 | 7**
CNN sits at the center of a complex of commercial interests, all eager to attract the casual news enthusiast into their sites. The news content therefore has to compete *(left)* with all kinds of colorful banners and flashing devices. Big headlines can help, but it's a constant struggle. The designers finally get their chance to raid the font cupboard with "in-depth specials" *(below)*.

79

**8 | 9 | 10**
Mastheads *(foot of page)* help to distinguish the core sites among the mêlée of other elements.

# EXHIBITIONISM

The Louvre was founded in 1793, so you might have expected stylistic borrowings from an even earlier epoch—a little damaged Garamond, maybe, and a tapestry background. Current French cultural design is made of sterner stuff, however, and except for the logo *(see below)* the whole **www.mistral.culture.fr/louvre** site works on Futura Bold and HTML text. No such inhibitions exist at London's Royal Opera House **www.royalopera.org**, where stage drapes and Bembo set the scene. The Solomon R. Guggenheim Foundation site **192.215.161.38/index.html** now transcends national boundaries, but its core type style is based on the original New York building graphic. The screen layouts themselves reflect the familiar linear gallery concept.

80

**1 | 2 | 3**
The Louvre site can be viewed in several languages *(above and right)*, and the open layout easily accommodates the differences in text length. Frame-based construction allows the navigation options to remain visible while the rest of the screen updates. The background of the welcome panel is a couple of shades different from the main background. A transparent box would cure it.

**6**
Even zooming in on the VR image *(right)* reveals little of La Gioconda's smile. True high-resolution armchair gallery-going is some way off yet.

**4 | 5**
Simple color coding at the top of the screen distinguishes your chosen area and continues as you proceed through the site. It's frustrating to see a masterpiece like the *Très Riches* *Heures du Duc de Berry (above)* or the *Mona Lisa* reduced to a 20K JPEG, but at least you can take a virtual tour *(right)*. The Leonardo is on the right, behind the barrier.

**7**

**8**

## 7 | 8

Lesser mortals would have drawn a map to show the museums' geography *(above)*. Here, five little squares and some 10-pt. Trebuchet Bold do the job. The little squares are also links to the museum sites. The colored banners *(above and right)* are just for show—inactive as links, they also don't relate to the words below.

## 9 | 10

The drama of the opera is well conveyed by the pure black background *(left and below)*. The average uncultured browser, however, is likely to make a mess of the wide-measure white HTML text. And the buttons speak more of F-16 shoot'em-ups than *The Flying Dutchman*.

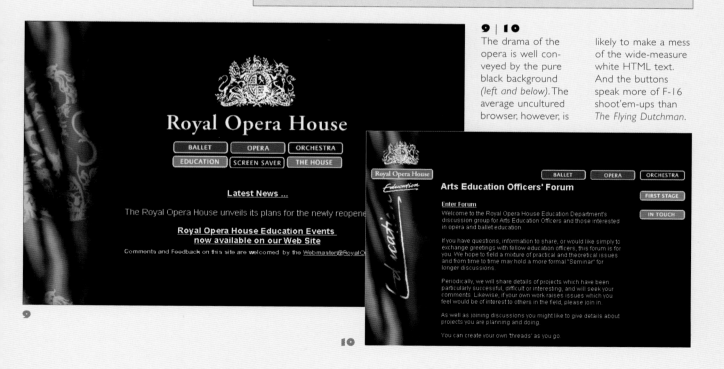

**9**

**10**

# THE SILVER SCREEN

Web site design has many resonances with the business of making movie or TV titles and credits. We are still waiting for the Web site design equivalent of Saul Bass—but, while waiting, it's interesting to observe the parallels. At the time of writing, full-motion video is out of the question for the average PC user, and at the producer's end lack of bandwidth restricts the use of anything other than short clips. Touchstone Pictures at **www.tvplex.go.com/touchstone** uses Flash to animate the conventional celebrity interview. On the big screen, the Warner Brothers site **www.warnerbros.com** employs buttons that are the modern equivalent of the Hollywood lobby card.

**3 | 4 | 5 | 6**
Rollovers on the topic disks activate leader lines to question and answer boxes *(right)* and a cast photo album *(below)*. Yellow GIF type struggles to be seen against somber backgrounds.

**1 | 2**
While the Flash movie loads, the show's script logo gradually appears *(above right)*.

*It's funny.*

**7**

Spindly HTML text only gets a bit part at Warner Bros. All the rest is rendered type here—even the drop shadows have shadows. There are a dozen links in the giant sign, and 20 more overall.

**7**

## Welcome to Warner Bros. Online

Get To Know The Ins & Out Of Your Town Here!

click here

WB ONLINE

Search | Chat | Stores | Boards | Entertaindom | Games | Hip Clips

1 Day Left Until Valentine's Day!
Find a treat for your sweet here!

Don't Blow It! Get Hot Gifts Here!

Spy On Your Free Nikita Home Page!

Score With Hot Love Coupons!

Bid On A Kiss Off From Lisa Kudrow!

Woo Her With A Musical Webcard!

**8**

Difficult choices *(below)* pop up in the Warner Bros. site from time to time.

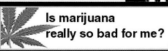

Is marijuana really so bad for me?

...lp At Jenny's Advice Column!

Escape To The Beach With Kevin Costner!

Nikita & Carmen Electra Rule Hip Clips!

Slay 'Em With A Free Buffy Home Page!

Come Find A New Valentine Here!

83

# THE SILVER SCREEN II

F ive hundred and eighty miles northeast of Holly-wood, the Sundance Film Festival **www.sundance channel.com** offers a cooler view of the cinema. In Utah, there are white backgrounds and Helvetica (and Trebuchet) in various weights. In Europe, at the British Film Institute **www.bfi.org.uk** and the Deutsches Film-museum **www.stadt-frankfurt.de/filmmuseum** there are polite buttons (and Helvetica). The Tokyo Film Festival **www.tokyo-filmfest.or.jpl** has a more frantic view.

**1 | 2 | 3**
Infoworks' design is spare and uncluttered. The home page *(above)* traces engaging loops; the schedule *(right)* organizes HTML text into GIF containers. Even HTML can be readable *(below)* if the text is absorbing. Take a moment to read the synopsis of *I Stand Alone*. Be grateful it's incomplete.

**4 | 5**
Infoworks also designed the parent Sundance TV channel site *(above)*, and switched styles to attract a quite different market sector.

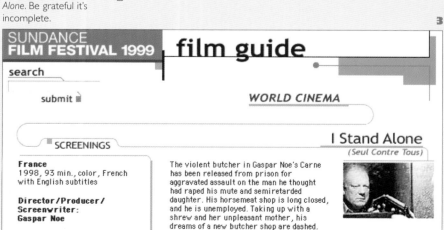

6

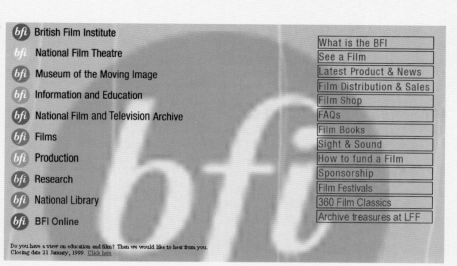

- ![bfi] **British Film Institute**
- ![bfi] **National Film Theatre**
- ![bfi] **Museum of the Moving Image**
- ![bfi] **Information and Education**
- ![bfi] **National Film and Television Archive**
- ![bfi] **Films**
- ![bfi] **Production**
- ![bfi] **Research**
- ![bfi] **National Library**
- ![bfi] **BFI Online**

| What is the BFI |
| See a Film |
| Latest Product & News |
| Film Distribution & Sales |
| Film Shop |
| FAQs |
| Film Books |
| Sight & Sound |
| How to fund a Film |
| Sponsorship |
| Film Festivals |
| 360 Film Classics |
| Archive treasures at LFF |

Do you have a view on education and film? Then we would like to hear from you.
Closing date 21 January, 1999. Click here

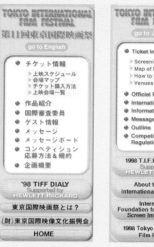

**9, 10**

**85**

**6 | 7 | 8**

The BFI's solidly organized virtues *(above)* extend down to all levels of the site. Scrolling screens *(right)* retain helpful navigation buttons at the foot. The Deutsches Filmmuseum *(far right)* revels in the historical: the logo is based on the 19th-century zoetrope, and the walking man of Muybridge stands in for the "next" button. Narrow-measure black HTML text scrolls on uncomfortably long on an overly dark background.

**9 | 10**

Button mania is absolutely rampant at the Tokyo Film Festival Web site *(above).* The background device is also worth examination.

 **Animation**

The Museum of the Moving Image is proud to present animation through a wide range of projects, screenings, events and exhibitions.

**The Animation Exhibit**

Mickey Mouse points the way to the Museum's animation exhibit. The area is designed in the shape of Reynaud's praxinoscope which, like many of the Victorian toys featured at the Museum, used animation techniques before cinema was even invented. Inside the animation area visitors are encouraged to try out their own animation skills on another early toy of visual illusion, the Zoetrope.

A whole menagerie of cartoon animals, in[...] the walls. These characters are all cel anim[...] are also explored: the cut-outs of Terry Gil[...] the puppets of East Europeans like Trnka[...] recently made so popular in Britain by Aar[...]

**Channel 4 / Museum of the Movin[...]**

The Museum encourages young British a[...] Scheme, awarding four residencies annu[...] inspired young animators win the chance[...]

![bfi Home] | Introduction | Museum Collections | Vi[...] Infor[...]
          | Education |

**7**

**deutsches filmmuseum frankfurt am main**

Home  Ausstellungen  Archive  Kino  Bibliothek  Service  Kontakt  Freunde

**8**

[ next ]

Die folgenden Seiten stellen ein Übergangslösung dar. Anfang 1999 präsentieren wir Ihnen grundsätzlich neu konzipierte Seiten in Deutsch und Englisch.

**Das Haus**

Das 1984 eröffnete Deutsche Filmmuseum hat es sich zur Aufgabe gemacht, das Filmerbe zu bewahren, Filme möglichst in ihrer Originalfassung und auf großer Leinwand zu präsentieren und zum kritischen Verständnis des Massenmediums mittels Ausstellungen, Publikationen und Veranstaltungen beizutragen. Das Haus, dessen Trägerin die Stadt

# AN INTERNATIONAL BUSINESS MACHINE

IBM is a survivor from the primordial era of the computer business. The forerunner company was established in 1911. Synonymous with profit and dependability in the 1960s and 1970s, written off wholesale in the late 1980s, the corporation now has a presence in many (and sometimes unexpected) areas of the IT world. The global site **www.ibm.com** reflects a technological confidence, as well as a necessarily more aggressive marketing posture.

**3**
The UK home page *(right)* follows the desktop metaphor of its parent. The rendered backgrounds are supplemented by HTML links to rapidly updating stories. Strangely, the "desktop" itself remains resolutely white, whatever your browser preferences. A screen of jelly beans or a tropical sunset would have made the average user feel more at home. The multiplicity of boxes can lead to problems in the download, with flaws in the delivered image *(near right)*.

**86**

**1 | 2**
The international home page *(right)* sports Paul Rand's 1952 logo—but the City Medium font he designed in 1966 has been displaced by a mixture of the ever-present Trebuchet and Verdana. Bodoni remains the corporate face of choice at larger sizes. The complex structure of these pages is revealed *(below)* as a closely interlocking series of boxes.

**3**

February | 4

IBM Global Services UK

| siness Partners | Careers | Case Studies | News | Portfolio |

**People who do.**

**Discover** the unique insight our people have to offer.

IBM Global Services UK

**Case Study - e-business Services**

How we saved ASDA £1/2 million on internal communications

**EMU Services**

Converting disruption into opportunity.

**e-business Services**

Reinventing fundamental business practices.

**Strategic Outsourcing Services**

Aligning IT with core business strategy.

**Let's Talk**

Click here to contact the people of IBM Global Services via e-mail

or

**Call Monica Hayley right now on**

**0990 454 454**

**6**

Site map

Feedback

The mark a superi e-business

About us

Archive

**5**

Countries A-Z

▶ Africa
▶ Americas
▶ Asia Pacific
▶ Europe
▶ Middle East

**7**

IBM    WorkPad

To Do List    ▼ IBM Micro

☑ Check out IBM's new copper technology   IBM

☑ See the OEM Technology Pavilion sponsored by IBM at COMDEX Fall '97   IBM

☐ Subscribe to Microelectronics Design   IBM

☐ Add IBM's Set-Top Box solutions to the design team meeting agenda   IBM

**4 | 5 | 6 | 7**

The desktop metaphor goes a bit too far sometimes. These "accessories" *(right)* have been culled (or torn off) from various different pages within the site. It's no good trying to move them onscreen—they are fixed in stone.

**Products express**

**Monster Disk Drives! Buy now**

| Hard disk drives ⬍ | Tape and Optical storage ⬍ |
| Disk storage systems ⬍ | Software products ⬍ |
| Solutions ⬍ | OEM MR heads ⬍ |

**4**

● Click once on the country name to get the contact information.

# A STUDY IN WHITE

Fitch Inc. are very long-established practitioners in the design business, and the resulting self-confidence manifests itself in a cool and deceptively simple site **www.fitch.com**. Most of what you see is white space, but it's just as vital as the minimal GIFs, industrial-grade navigation buttons, and recessive leader lines that unify the whole production.

**3 | 4 | 5**

The layout breaks out of its shackles *(right)*. The contrast is no doubt intended—the subliminal message, roughly translated, is "We have mission statements like other corporations, but we are creative and lateral-thinking too." The layout of the client list *(far right)* cleverly disguises the fact that there are few further options for explora-tion. It just looks like elegant design. The unexpected is the stock-in-trade here. The porcine salt and pepper pots *(below right)* were designed for Virgin Atlantic.

**FITCH**

*Pull our chain.*

©1998 Fitch

1

**FITCH**

*informed     creativity*

*Fitch is an international
consulting organization with
over thirty years of experience
helping companies to achieve
business success by design. We
work in partnership with our
clients to develop new products,
new forms of communication,
and new types of environments in
response to their customers' needs.*

*Push our button.*

©1998 Fitch Inc.

2

**1 | 2**

A provocative invita-tion, albeit expressed in decorous Garamond Italic, offers the visitor an interactive experi-ence *(above)*. The Fitch logo soldiers on, with its mysterious blend of Gill Bold and Medium. A mission statement *(right)* follows the stern, narrow type style of the opening screen.

**3**

 FITCH ~

what we do

focus on fitch

who we work with

how we do it

---

**4**

who

what

how

focus

FITCH ~

our international clients include:

3M
Amway
Baxter
Becton Dickinson
Blockbuster Entertainment
Boston Chicken
British Telecom
Burton Group
Caribou Coffee
Champion International
Chrysler
Comet Group
Compaq
Cybersmith
De La Rue
Digital Equipment
Disney Development
Duskin
Ellesse
First Chicago NBD
First Leisure Corporation
Fleet Financial
General Electric
GoldStar
Greenwoods
Harman Kardon
Hush Puppies
ING Bank
Iomega
JBL
Johnson Controls
Lee Company
Mallinckrodt Medical
MGM Cinemas Limited
Microsoft
Mitsubishi
Morningstar Mutual Funds
PETsMART
Procter & Gamble
Safeway Stores
Stanley
Steelcase
Svoboda
The Medicine Shoppe
Thermos
Virgin Atlantic
Warner-Lambert
Woolworth

---

**5**

back

FITCH +

Virgin Atlantic

The jet-engined pepperpot and propeller-driven salt shaker are only one-inch high and full of personality.

Virgin Atlantic Airways wanted to differentiate itself by creating a sense of fun to counter its serious business purpose.

*Attention to detail*
For Upper Class passengers, Virgin's attention to detail materializes in some surprising places. Instead of awkward little salt and pepper sachets on the meal tray, Fitch and Virgin worked together to fly in two miniature chromium-plated "airplanes."

*"Pinched from Virgin Atlantic"*
They may seem an ideal pair to smuggle home, but you are hereby warned that "Pinched from Virgin Atlantic" has been stamped firmly on each undercarriage.

# FIGURE AND GROUND

**gap** | gapkids | babygap    customer service | your info | store locator | site map

departments: men's | women's | jeans | khakis | logo | gapbody

**GAP**

shopping bag
sign in/out

## men's jeans

slim fit jeans
easy fit jeans
original fit jeans
original fit dark jeans
loose fit jeans
relaxed fit jeans
baggy fit jeans
wide leg jeans
kick plate jeans
contractor jeans
canvas contractor jeans
utility jeans
carpenter jeans
denim overalls
classic jean jacket

## women's jeans

slim fit jeans
original fit jeans
classic fit jeans
low rise jeans
flare jeans
boot cut jeans
loose fit jeans
reverse fit jeans
wide leg jeans

GAPJEANS

vintage cargo hat with a ribbed tank and carpenter jeans

Gap—something more than a pair of jeans. More like a belief system all its own. There is little preamble to the Gap site **www.gap.com**—if you need to ask what it's about, you shouldn't be here. Once you're on the site, persuasive layout makes it difficult not to buy something (orders only from mainland USA). Opposite, a rival faith is promoted at **www.dockers.com**. Strong images and layout, but not quite the missionary zeal to stick unflinchingly to one concept.

"THE DEFINITIVE GUIDE
TO EFFORTLESS STYLE"

# www.dockers.com
(pick one) [ ○ USA | ○ CANADA | ○ EUROPE ]

**DOCKERS KHAKIS**

**5 | 6 | 7**
Light-box white is
the order of the day
here *(left and below)*
with "unmounted trans-
parencies" in classic
fashion-magazine style.
Rendered and letter-
spaced Folio Light
Condensed helps the
minimalist look. The
narrow-measure HTML
looks like an unwel-
come visitor *(bottom)*.

**5**

**6**

**DOCKERS KHAKIS**

Men's Store
Women's Store
Independent Film
Membership/Promotions
Customer Service
Store Finder
Site Map

Browser Information

**7**

**DOCKERS KHAKIS** ) [ Men's Store ⬍ ]

Khakis
Shirts
Accessories
Golf
Find a Favorite

Make yourself
comfortable whether
you're @ease,
@work, @play, or
just putting around.

Mix and match some
of our most popular
colors and styles.

Special holiday
savings, featured
product and
promotions.

Fit Comparison,
Glossary of Terms
and Color Palette.

what's in store    lifestyle    changing room    hot deals    fits & fabrics

**1**
An object lesson *(left)*
in using one image,
type GIFs, towers of
HTML, and a plain
background.

**2 | 3 | 4**
The inexorable pro-
gress of the shopping
bag *(below, left to right)*.
See, try (in a virtual
kind of way), and buy.
Unlike an ordinary
store, however, there
are plenty of oppor-
tunities to change your
mind along the way.

**8**

**DOCKERS KHAKIS** ) [ Men's Store ⬍ ]

{ lifestyle } [ @EASE | @WORK | @PLAY | GOLF ]

CHOOSE ONE
A    B

# golf
Add a stroke of style to your wardrobe with our premium
gabardine khakis and golf polo shirt.

Class A Pleated Gabardine Khakis (more info)
$50.00 ( ADD TO MY BAG )

Striped Pique Polo Shirt-SALE! (more info)
$42.00 ( ADD TO MY BAG )

(Q see entire golf collection)

**8**
A slight loss of grip
leads to skewed trans-
parencies and colored
backgrounds in the golf
section *(above)*.

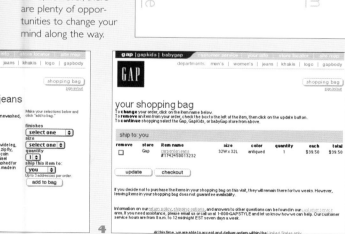

jeans

tonewashed,

Make your selections below and
click "add to bag."

finishes
[ select one ⬍ ]
size
[ select one ⬍ ]
quantity
[ 1 ⬍ ]
ship this item to:
[ you ⬍ ]
Up to 3 addresses per order.
( add to bag )

**GAP**

departments:   men's   |   women's   |   jeans   |   khakis   |   logo   |   gapbody

shopping bag
sign in/out

## your shopping bag
To **change** your order, click on the item name below.
To **remove** an item from your order, check the box to the left of the item, then click on the update button.
To **continue** shopping select the Gap, GapKids, or babyGap store from above.

ship to: you

| remove | store | item name | size | color | quantity | each | total |
|--------|-------|-----------|------|-------|----------|------|-------|
| ☐ | Gap | carpenter jeans #1742450013232 | 32W x 32L | antiqued | 1 | $39.50 | $39.50 |

( update )   ( checkout )

If you decide not to purchase the items in your shopping bag on this visit, they will remain there for two weeks. However,
leaving items in your shopping bag does not guarantee availability.

Information on our return policy, shipping options, and answers to other questions can be found in our customer service
area. If you need assistance, please email us or call us at 1-800-GAPSTYLE and let us know how we can help. Our customer
service hours are from 8 a.m. to 12 midnight EST seven days a week.

At this time, we are able to accept and deliver orders within the United States only.

**4**

# PRESSING ON REGARDLESS

Newspaper proprietors have an uncomfortable vision of the future—increasing competition from all forms of electronic media and rising costs of staffing, production and distribution. In Britain, the *Guardian*, once mostly famous for its inaccurate typesetting, now enthusiastically leads the rush to the Net. The online *Guardian* **www.guardian.co.uk** preserves onscreen many of its parent's design characteristics, while giving the assured impression that it's been onscreen forever.

**1 | 2 | 3**
The daily splash screen *(right and far right)* is supplemented by special features such as that for the London Festival of Literature *(below)*. The trademark layout of colored blocks is used through-out, with three weights of Helvetica and a scattering of HTML text.

**4 | 5**
Sports are a vital newspaper staple. Statistics are quickly provided through pull-down menus and colored links *(right)*. This is a mixed blessing for Southampton soccer supporters, whose club's appalling record is detailed here.

**6 | 7**
The use of black backgrounds with reversed-out type— possible but always scruffy in the parent paper—is employed for more drama in the online film and features pages *(right and below)*. HTML text is slotted in among the subhead GIFs.

**7**

**Past articles**

● 26.01.99
Susan Sarandon interview
Tackling Shakespeare

● 24.01.99
Observer film of the week
Other releases
Shakespeare in Love
eulogy
Philip Baker Hall
Ewan McGregor's PA
keeps mum
Multi-plexed
Recycled film music

**Films of the century**

The Marriage of Maria Braun
Derek Malcolm salutes an artistic marriage between Fassbinder and Hanna Schygulla that resulted in the director's best film.

**Film of the week**

A Fiennes romance
Jonathan Romney is only half in love with Shakespeare in Love.

**8**
Cyber-enthusiasm can bring delusion *(right)*. The lines were undoubtedly lengthy, but the *Guardian*'s virtual Monet was just a long string of small GIFs and dense text— too dull to reproduce.

8

You don't have to stand in this queue
Click here to visit the Guardian's virtual Monet exhibition instead

# A FEELING FOR HISTORY

There are many examples of advertising campaigns that have embedded themselves so deeply in the public consciousness that they have taken on some of the characteristics of art sponsorship. The advertiser may find difficulties in this unlooked-for role of patron.

The ending of the Guinness animals series in the early 1960s was certainly not popular with the British public. Nearly 40 years later, the campaign has acquired an art-historical patina and is now warmly celebrated with themes of current campaigns at **www.guinness.com**.

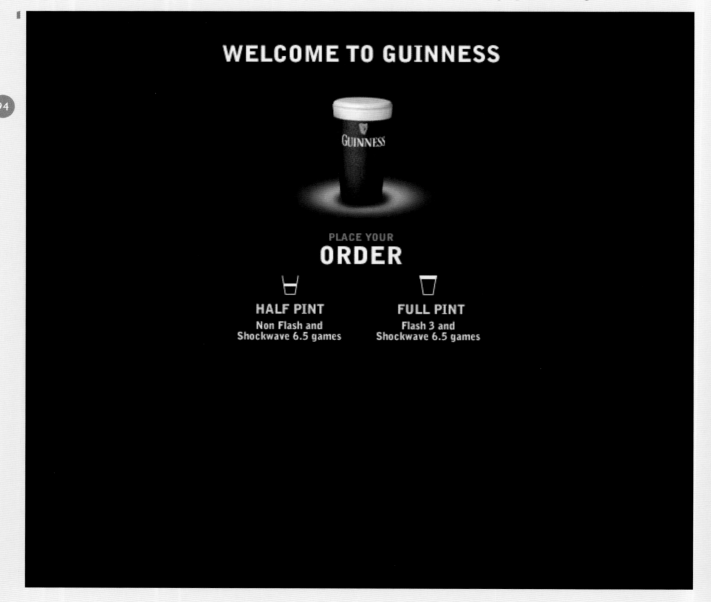

The heroic spotlit glass of stout *(left)* ushers in the first of many dry allusions. Low-level graphics are "half-pints," and the tedium of loading a Flash movie *(below)* is excused as "loading the bar." MGM's lion *(bottom)* transforms into the toucan, and their slogan "Ars, Gratia Artis" is mangled into "Taste the Drink, Live the Life, Enjoy the Art."

A salutary reminder of what's been lost in the digital revolution. The Gilroy sketches, on a lightly textured "paper," are surrounded by the Web site designer's own "pencil" notes relating to the construction of the site itself. The words themselves hover on the edge of invisibility. Very self-referential and heartening at the same time.

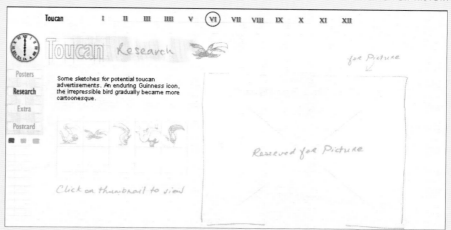

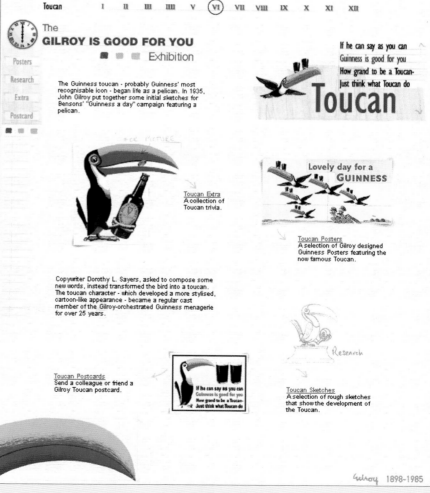

# TYPE ON THE FLY

Courtesy of Flash, type is on the move along with almost every other element of the site. Techniques that were fixtures in the TV post-production studios of 1960 are now novelties for the Web site designer. In New York, Hillman Curtis **www.hillmancurtis.com** has made a specialty of high-energy moving type. In the more esoteric field of showcasing experimental movies, the Urban Desires group at **www.desires.com** fearlessly fires giant chunks of type across a grim and axonometric city background.

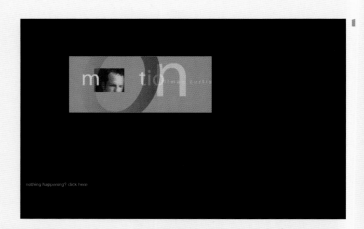

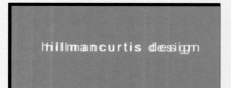

## 1 | 2 | 3 | 4

The frames on this page necessarily show only a fragment of the screen activity as the site develops. Movie sizes are limited to shorten download time. All sizes, weights, and styles of Helvetica (*small-frames sequence, above*) spin madly in concert with fragments of handwriting. The goal is the six-part window (*far right, above*) with a different movie playing in each pane. This offers links to a portfolio section (*right*). Humane help (*above*) is available in case of distress. All that's missing is the music—it's like a silent movie without even a piano accompaniment.

Title: Macromedia Online Annual Report 98 Client: Macromedia Inc.
Creative Direction: Katharine Green Art Direction: Hillman Curtis
Designers: Hillman Curtis, Buck Bito, Steven Soshea, Jeff Southard (www.415p.com)
Software: Macromedia Dreamweaver 1.02, Fireworks,
Flash 3, and Freehand 8
Description: www.macromedia.com's 1998 online annual report

Title: Macromedia Web Site Redesign '98 Client: Macromedia Inc.
Creative Direction: Katharine Green Art Direction: Hillman Curtis
Home page design: Jeremy Clark, Illene Sandler
Designers: Buck Bito, Jeremy Clark, Hillman Curtis, David Hatch,
Jacqui Maher, Matt Regan
Software: Macromedia Dreamweaver, Fireworks, Flash 3, and Freehand 8
as well as Adobe Photoshop and Allaire Homesite 3
Description: www.macromedia.com 1998 site redesign

5

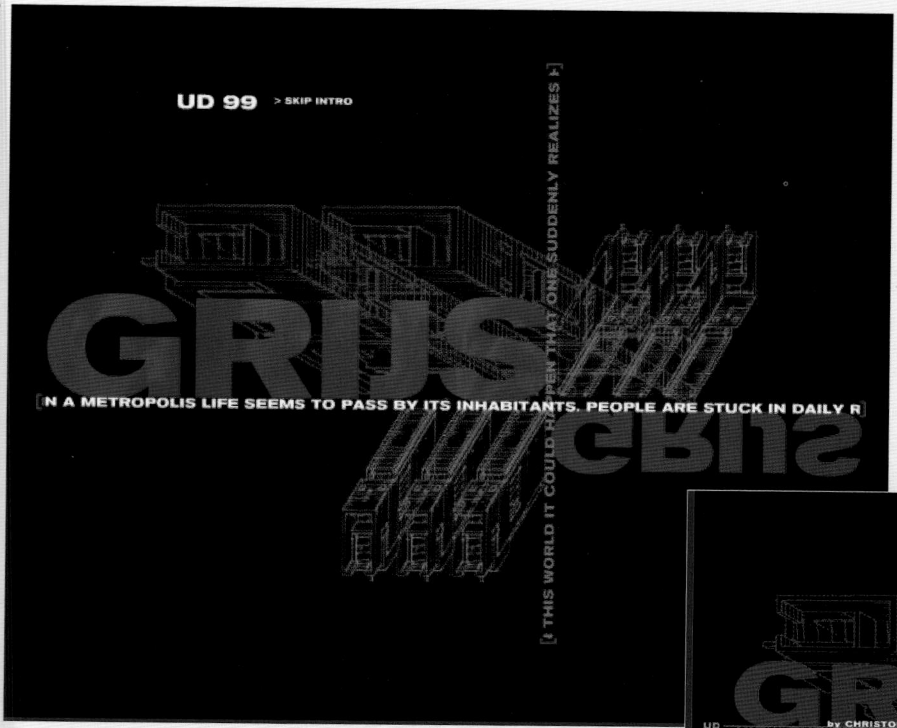

**UD 99**  > SKIP INTRO

GRIJS

[N A METROPOLIS LIFE SEEMS TO PASS BY ITS INHABITANTS. PEOPLE ARE STUCK IN DAILY R]

[‡ THIS WORLD IT COULD HAPPEN THAT ONE SUDDENLY REALIZES ⊁]

**5 | 6 | 7**
Urban Desires posts
its polemic as a moving
banner in both hori-
zontal and vertical axes
*(left)* while the title of
the featured movie
*(Gray*, in Flemish) flips
and slides by in quick
time. As for QuickTime,
the movie *(below)* is
tragically tiny. One day
the Web will be as
lavish in its possibilities
as 1960s television.

97

6

*UD99*

As an online pioneer in art and culture since 1994, we at Urban Desires
are carrying on a tradition of offering the richest content available on the
web. We are continuing to evolve along with technology to maintain an
artistic standard in our medium. 1998 proved to be an experimental time
for us as we transitioned from our traditional e-zine format, into an online
venue for moving images. Last year's award winning premiers included
the two short films from the Museum of Modern Art's permanent
collection, The Film of Her and Footprints by Bill Morrison. We had fun
with the experimental Flash animation of James Paterson, and re-visited
the art of Breakdancing in an interactive animated piece by Khoi Uong.
Other contributions to the 1998 moving image archive included a peak
from Richard Sandler's full length film, The Gods of Times Square,
and by Sandye Wilson's homage to finding a good man.
So Many Things to Consider.

Our latest and first featured film of 1999 is Grijs by Belgian Filmmaker
**by CHRISTOPHE VAN ROMPAEY**

UD  VIEW THE FILM    by CHRISTOPHE    GRIJS    VAN ROMPAEY   99

SEGMENT  1  2  3

> BACK TO INTRO

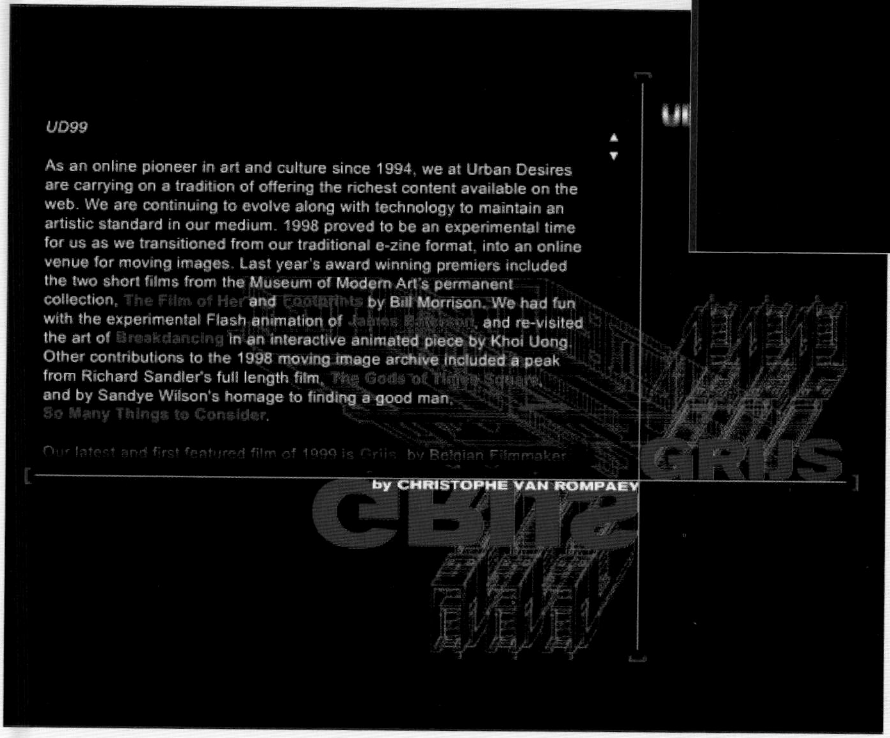

7

# COLOR IT IN

Color expressed via the glowing phosphors on even the least sophisticated monitor is infinitely more intense and alluring than the dull quartet of dots that make up the conventional four-color process. Power generators British Energy at **www. british-energy.com** have learned the lesson well, with slabs of electric blue, orange, and yellow. Opposite, the long-established

British design group HSAG **www.hsag.co.uk** uses solid blocks of color to back up a simple and dignified layout that owes nothing to current typographic trends. Meanwhile, across a wide gray ocean, Arizona designers Howalt **www.howalt.design.com** eschew the familiar palette and explore the unexpected possibilities of neglected brown.

**1 | 2**
The brisk and cheerful face of electricity generation —with purposeful buttons that click in a satisfactorily electrical way. The cozy tree-girt house *(above)* is seamlessly supplanted by a nuclear power station *(left)* as the next screen is selected.

**3** 3

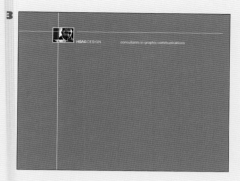

**3 | 4 | 5 | 6 | 7**
Leaving nothing to chance, HSAG's designers offer only one route out of the home page *(left)*. Clicking on the tiny animation invokes a fixed-size browser window *(below left)*, avoiding the pitfalls of erratic positioning. Simple rollovers eventually point to the portfolio section, where each category has its own submenu.

**8** 8

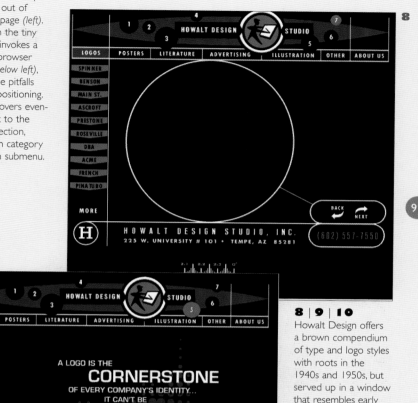

99

**4** 4

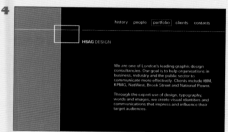

**5** 5

**8 | 9 | 10**
Howalt Design offers a brown compendium of type and logo styles with roots in the 1940s and 1950s, but served up in a window that resembles early studies for the lunar-orbiter cockpit. Tub-thumping oratory *(left)* encourages the visitor to hurry on to view the samples *(below)*.

**6** 6

**10** 10

**7** 7

**9** 9

# NOW READ ON

# BOMBSITE
## THE CONTEMPORARY CULTURE MAGAZINE

**EDITOR'S CHOICE**
**VOICES**
**FIRST PROOF**
**SUBSCRIPTION**
**PUBLICATIONS**

Current Issue

Email:
info@bombsite.com

Telephone:
1 800. 221. 3148

BOMB Magazine was founded in 1981 as a not-for-profit arts organization dedicated to publishing and promoting art and literature of the highest quality. Conceived as a forum for emerging as well as established artists and writers to discuss their work with colleagues and foster a committed dialogue. BOMB, now in its eighteenth year of publication, has continued to promote the understanding of literary, visual, and performing arts through interviews between peers as well as the presentation of fiction, poetry, and artwork. **BOMBSITE is an online companion to the magazine.**

The alternative-magazine fraternity has embraced the Web with passion. The dream of global access, unfettered by the constraints of mail or inefficient distributors, has led magazines like *Bomb*, or *Bombsite* **www.bombsite.com** in its Web version, to a lively presence onscreen. But how to make it pay? The answer is teasing—all the texts on offer come to a close just as they're getting interesting. To continue, you need to reach for a credit card and take out a subscription to the paper-based version.

# BOMBSITE
## THE CONTEMPORARY CULTURE MAGAZINE

**EDITOR'S CHOICE**
Rita McBride
Robert Lopez

**VOICES**   **FIRST PROOF**   **SUBSCRIPTION**   **PUBLICATIONS**

BOMB's contributing editors highlight the newest books, movies, music, and exhibitions of the upcoming season in Editor's Choice.

## ART: KATHY O' DELL
*Contract With the Skin: Masochism, Performance Art and the 1970s*

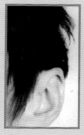

The fact that many contemporary artists are returning to performance video as well as video and film installations is testimony to the lasting impact of earlier, albeit ephemeral, works. Kathy O' Dell's study, *Contract With the Skin*, focuses on a handful of now-legendary body-art pieces from the early '70s that were tinged with violence against the self. In her astute analysis, O' Dell untangles the social, psychological and legal implications of such infamous creative acts as Chris Burden shooting himself, Vito Acconci biting his arm and filling the teeth marks with ink, Gina Payne slitting her lip with a razor blade, and Ulay sewing his mouth shut while Marian Abramovic attempted to articulate his thoughts. **Cont. on page 10, BOMB Fall 98**

Cont. on page 10, BOMB Fall 98

## MUSIC
### LUCINDA WILLIAMS
*Car Wheels on a Gravel Road*

Once you've listened to Lucinda Williams a few hundred times, she begins to seem like the older sister (or girlfriend) you always wanted- tough, traveled, knowing about unknowable things, out there. You also come to realize that for twenty years now she's been plowing the same rocky fields worked so brillantly by John Prine, Emmylou Harris, Iris Dement, Steve Earle (who here plays a fine supporting role) or even the sadly retired David Bromberg: genuine innovators in white and/or country blues. This roots music borrows from and recombines strains from the Delta, Appalachia and wherever you'd locate the oeuvre of Hank Williams. **Cont. on page 14, BOMB Fall 98**

Cont. on page 14, BOMB Fall 98

## NEW WRITING
### MURRAY BAIL
*Eucalyptus*

Murray Bail's *Eucalyptus* spins a people's history and landscape through fairy tale. In a remote property in New South Wales, Australis, a widower promises his only daughter ,a young woman of renowned beauty, to any suitor who can name every species of eucalyptus tree on his sprawling ranch. There are many suitors, and many more eucalyptus: *E. desertorum, E. maidenii, E signata, E. fruticosa, E. foecunda*... It's an ancient tale: the beautiful maiden, the unsuitable suitors, the ultimate test. **Cont. on page 16, BOMB Fall 98**

Cont. on page 16, BOMB Fall 98

## THEATER + FILM
### JOHN MAYBURY
*Love is the Devil*

Falling through the skylight of Francis Bacon's studio, petty criminal and thug-about-town George Dyer (Daniel Craig) falls into the arms of his future. "Come to bed with me, and you can have anything you like," Bacon (Derek Jacobi) promises the bewildered burglar, who is both cowed by and attracted to the artists aristocratic demeanor. Director John Maybury chronicles the glorious downward spiral that ensues in his masterful *Love is the Devil*, a "study for a portrait of Francis Bacon." **Cont. on page 22, BOMB Fall 98**

Cont. on page 22, BOMB Fall 98

**1 | 2**
Economical table-based design characterizes the *Bombsite* site. The fat black rules *(left)* are 582 × 7 pixel GIFs; all the text is HTML, except for the headings. On the "cover" *(opposite page)* the apparently complex mosaic is made of just five aligning vertical blocks.

101

**3**

**3 | 4**
Alfred E. Newman's organ *(above)* side-steps the humorless business of HTML and presents a giant GIF instead. It's interesting to note that, in the context of the Web, Newman's famous gap tooth is neatly represented *(below)* by an absent pixel.

**4**

Talk to us | Index | Search

## Ciba

Value beyond chemistry

What´s new
Corporate profile
Divisions
Local markets
Business and markets
Shareholders and investors
Employment strategy
Publications
Contacts
Guided tours

**News Highlights**

01/21/99
**Ciba Water Treatments to be combined with Ci[ba]
Additives**

click here for English
click here for German

Home / Index / Search

Shareholders and investor[s]

Financial informatio[n]
Shareholder informatio[n]
Current share pric[e]
How to inves[t]

Last updated
21 January 1999

Ciba Specialty Chemicals is a global leader in the discovery,
manufacture and marketing of innovative specialty chemicals. Our
products hold leading positions in their chosen markets.
We add value beyond chemistry for our customers, employees and
shareholders through our state-of-the-art environmentally
compatible technologies and proven international marketing expertise.
Our focused product offering provides colour, performance and care for
plastics, coatings, fibres, fabrics and other materials, improving
process economies and the quality of final products.

The chemical industry remains largely unloved. Even benevolent pharmaceuticals sometimes raise suspicions. Ciba **www.cibasc.com** offers an open-faced image and spacious layout for its specialty-chemicals site. There's more human interest at Unimed **www.unimed.com** and Pfizer **www.pfizer.com**, as well as more conventional "Web-type" graphics.

**Ciba**

**Welcome shareholders and investors**

Welcome to that part of the Ciba Specialty Chemicals web site designed for shareholders and investors. Here you will find information about our company's finances, its governance, how to contact us with questions about the company...

**1 | 2**
Trademark Frutiger to the fore, and native Swiss precision in the handling of type size, color, and weight *(opposite page and left)*. The better it gets, the worse the HTML looks—especially on these rolling white Alpine pastures.

**3 | 4**
Complex multilayer structures at Pfizer *(left and below)*. A curving cutout follows the mouse pointer, revealing a synopsis of the selected topic. The related shadows obediently shift as well.

**3**

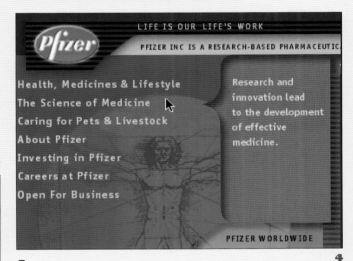

LIFE IS OUR LIFE'S WORK

PFIZER INC IS A RESEARCH-BASED PHARMACEUTIC...

Health, Medicines & Lifestyle
The Science of Medicine
Caring for Pets & Livestock
About Pfizer
Investing in Pfizer
Careers at Pfizer
Open For Business

Research and innovation lead to the development of effective medicine.

PFIZER WORLDWIDE

**4**

Corporate **Overview**

Unimed **Products**

Unimed **News**

Corporate Overview | Unimed Products | Unimed News | Clinical Trials

If you have any questions or comments, contact marissa_weber@edelman.com

**5**
Stock shots are handled with skill at Unimed *(left)*—but it's a hefty GIF to download, and disappointing that only the typeset squares respond to clicking.

**6**

SOME people still think we SELL *medicines*.

Actually, our job is to OPTIMIZE their *value* for your PATIENTS.

**6**
Very faint echoes of quality typography can be heard at the Glaxo Wellcome site *(right)*. *But* THEY are very FAINT.

# UPWARDLY MOBILE

Orange mobile phones **www.uk.orange.net** are network-service providers (the phones themselves are made by other suppliers). The competition have broadly similar services to offer. The problem of recognition is addressed here with simple graphics and a consistent type style. The Web site complements press and other media activity intended to distinguish Orange from the other more institutional and longer-established players. As the market moves toward apparent saturation in Europe, Orange holds its own.

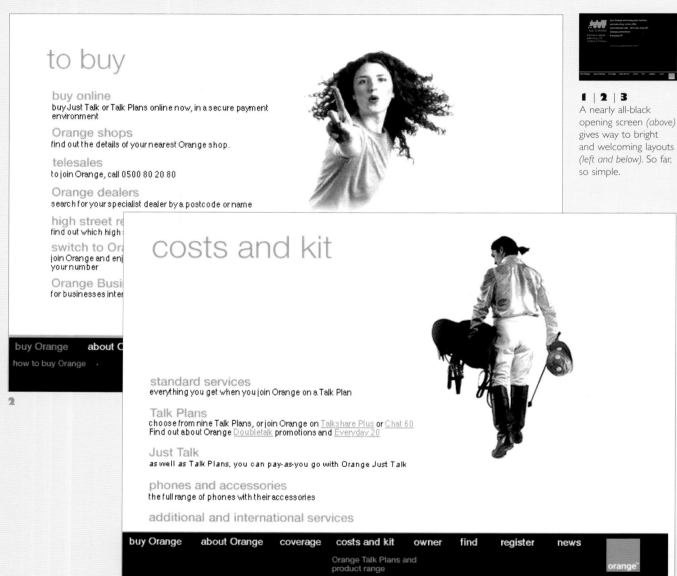

**1 | 2 | 3**
A nearly all-black opening screen *(above)* gives way to bright and welcoming layouts *(left and below)*. So far, so simple.

**to buy**

**buy online**
buy Just Talk or Talk Plans online now, in a secure payment environment

**Orange shops**
find out the details of your nearest Orange shop.

**telesales**
to join Orange, call 0500 80 20 80

**Orange dealers**
search for your specialist dealer by a postcode or name

**high street re**
find out which high

**switch to Or**
join Orange and enj
your number

**Orange Busi**
for businesses inter

buy Orange        about O
how to buy Orange    ·

2

**costs and kit**

**standard services**
everything you get when you join Orange on a Talk Plan

**Talk Plans**
choose from nine Talk Plans, or join Orange on Talkshare Plus or Chat 60.
Find out about Orange Doubletalk promotions and Everyday 20

**Just Talk**
as well as Talk Plans, you can pay-as-you go with Orange Just Talk

**phones and accessories**
the full range of phones with their accessories

**additional and international services**

buy Orange     about Orange     coverage     costs and kit     owner     find     register     news

Orange Talk Plans and product range

orange

3

## phones and accessories

To view full specifications and accessories click on your chosen phone

justtalk™
Motorola c520

dual band
Nokia 6150e

dual band
Mitsubishi mt401

buy Orange   about Orange   coverage   costs and kit   owner   find   register   news

orange

**4 | 5**
Orange links *(left)* lead on to the decisive moment. A barrage of technical data *(below left)* is accommodated in HTML text and continued in the ugly default scroll box.

105

## Mitsubishi mt401

The Mitsubishi Orange mt401 is the first phone to benefit from an exclusive Orange design with its striking matt silver styling. It also includes a portable Handsfree Kit as standard. In addition, the mt401 is a highly featured handset, supporting all Orange network services, such as EFR technology, enabling even clearer call quality, Fax and Data, Line Two, Conference Calling, and text messaging. It is also the first dual band phone from Mitsubishi with roaming capabilities allowing you to make and receive calls on 152 networks in 82 countries throughout the UK, Europe and beyond. The battery will give up to 2.5 hours of talktime and 5 days standby time under optimum conditions. This phone with a combination of looks and performance appeals to both the fashion conscious as well as the business user.
Recommended retail price: £24.99 (inc. VAT).

Until 30 April 1999 Doubletalk promotion applies.

Select a Talk Plan
Buy now

Exclusive buy online offer.

### main features

- International Dual Band Roaming capability

- EFR technology enables even clearer call quality

- up to 2.5 hours talk time or up to 5 days on standby (under optimum conditions)

- unique and fashionable 170g overall slimline design

- four-line screen for ease of viewing.

specifications   accessories

Note: Some of these services may not be available when you roam. These services are available on the Orange network. Please check with your Service Provider for further information

how to buy   about Orange   coverage   costs and kit   owner   find   register   news

orange

Flymo

product orange lawnmower & gardencare 98

Home
Non-collecting
Grass-collecting
Wheeled Rotary
Hedge Trimmers
Grass Trimmers
GARDENVAC
Power Hoe

GARDENVAC

Wheeled Rotary Mowers

Electric & Cordless Trimmers

Grass-collecting Hover Mowers

Non-collecting Hover Mowers

Power Hoe

Hedge Trimmers

**Europe's** leading powered garden equip

**6**
Flymo **www.flymo.com** follow a more curvaceous route *(above)* to sell their orange products. Their site is equipped, moreover, with a live hedgehog that leaves a scrolling message in his wake.

# TAKE A LETTER

The grisly typographic limitations of the Web at the end of the 20th century have fostered renewed enthusiasm for the history of type design. It may look like sentimentality for a lost age, but Tiro Typeworks **www.tiro.com** and their fellows are owed a debt of gratitude for keeping fine letter design on the agenda until the current compromises and endless workarounds are swept away. Watch this hairspace.

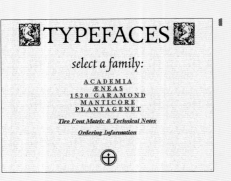

**1**

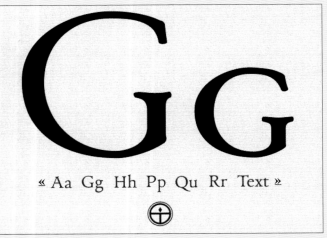

**2**

**3**

JOURNAL

JOURNAL CONTENTS

An Address to the American Historical Printing Association
*W. Thomas Taylor*

**4**

AN ADDRESS TO THE
AMERICAN PRINTING HISTORICAL
ASSOCIATION

W. THOMAS TAYLOR

TEN YEARS AGO, in a moment of exuberant optimism, I decided to open a printing shop. I bought from a friend a 20 x15-inch Heidelberg cylinder press, part of the agreement being that my friend would teach me how to run it. Unfortunately, I have never been on good terms with machinery. To that time I had been strictly a hobby printer, with a Vandercook proof press and some foundry type in my garage, used mostly for cards and a few pamphlets. A Vandercook is forgiving of fear and ineptitude, but a Heidelberg, like a well-bred horse, is not, and it was soon apparent that if I was going to do any serious printing, I needed help. It arrived in the form of Bradley Hutchinson, whose mastery of printing techniques ranges from flawless impression on a handpress to the manipulation of photographs in Adobe Photoshop. At the time, however, it was the middle ground of technology - Monotype - that interested us. Faced with a declining number of sources of type, and increasing costs of composition from those, we decided to set up our own typecasting operation. I should have known better. When I told Henry Morris about our first large

1.
«TURN»

**5**

acquisition, an entire shop in Indianapolis, he asked if the truck had arrived. When I said no, he suggested that when it did, I should direct the driver to proceed to the Gulf Coast, position the truck at the head of a pier, put a brick on the accelerator, and consign the whole load to a watery grave. Instead of heeding his timely warning, we unloaded and set up several tons of equipment and continued to buy a caster here, some matrices there, assembling a motley collection raked up from the detritus of a dying industry. I even constructed a building to house the foundry and the expanding pressroom, for some reason confident that we could spit into the powerful technological winds that were and are transforming the printing industry. I was, of course, wrong. In the crucibles of the Monotype casters I discovered a new alchemy that transformed gold into lead. ¶ We did manage to get the shop up and running, and produced a fair amount of type for a few years. I employed a casterman who came complete with yet another shop full of equipment. After two years this casterman went on his way, so Bradley cheerfully added typecasting to his already formidable range of skills. Things began to run more smoothly, and I began to hold out some hope that the Monotype operation might finally begin to earn back our considerable investment of time, energy, and money. Thus it was hard for me, very hard indeed, to be enthusiastic when the combination of an old technology - photopolymer printing plates - and a brand new technology - computer-generated digital negatives - offered the possibility of continuing to print letterpress without the quagmire of problems associated with Monotype equipment. It took Bradley over a year to convince me to get a platemaker and a while longer to persuade me to learn how to turn on a computer. But the economic logic was compelling, and within a year of acquiring the platemaker

2.
«TURN»

## 1 | 2 | 3 | 4 | 5

A featured typeface *(above)* is 1530 Garamond. Type scholarship is not cast in stone, however. A tiny note reveals that it was previously known as 1520 Garamond.

Wide-measure, uncompromising ranks of HTML size 2, plus microscopic "turn" marks, characterize W. Thomas Taylor's recollections *(right)* of getting into print.

# ⊕ TIRO TYPEWORKS

**TIRO TYPEWORKS** is an independent digital type foundry developing & marketing high quality Postscript typeface families for PC and Mac platforms. Our commitment is to continuing the independent tradition of typography, as it has existed for more than five hundred years, free from the influence of fashion and novelty. Our type is designed with the professional typographer in mind, but it is hoped that these web pages will interest, educate and inspire anyone who is interested in type, lettering and printing. ¶ Our web pages are divided into two main sections. In the first, we present our current catalogue, which will be updated as new faces and families are developed. As well as displaying a number of samples of each typeface and its variants, the catalogue includes a form which you can use to order a printed catalogue and/or text samples of specific faces. The catalogue also contains information about the Tiro Type Matrix, our new standard character sets, which have been carefully designed to maximise ease and efficiency in text typesetting. ¶ The second section contains the *Journal* ; this is an online anthology of essays and articles relating to type design, typography, lettering & calligraphy and letterpress printing. Many of the articles will directly relate to the design and use of typefaces offered for sale by Tiro Typeworks, while others will discuss aspects of typographic practice, both current and historical, and others will be purely whimsical. We will also reprint and repost articles from other sources which we feel will be of interest to readers.

# CATALOGUE

# JOURNAL

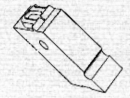

# Ordering Information

107

**6**
Tiro's opening page
*(left)* is sage enough
to recall the priorities.
Read the catalog and
browse the journal—
but don't forget to
order the fonts.

# PAPER MONEY

Information is power—and nowhere more so than in the financial markets. The average investor now has the opportunity to play the market with almost as much confidence as his or her professional counterpart. Almost. The online *Financial Times* **www.ft.com** and *Wall Street Journal* **www.wsj.com** offer a constant deluge of news and comment, though the stock prices are generally subject to a 20-minute delay.

Distinctions between daily newspapers and weekly magazines are no longer of any significance—*Fortune* **www.fortune.com** and *Forbes* **www.forbes.com** are now just as quick with the numbers and the surefire opportunities as their competitors.

**1 | 2 | 3**
The *Financial Times* nods to its paper parent *(top)* and continues to be pink all over. The home page *(above)* has Javascript rollover links to other sections. Subsection panels *(right)*, composed entirely of HTML text, lead to more specialized areas.

**4**
Familiar Bodoni Condensed carries *The Wall Street Journal* onto the Web *(above)*, but sits strangely with a companion slug of Garamond Bold Italic. Still, it's easier to read than the "real" newspaper.

**5 | 6**
There is no preamble with magazine heavyweights *Fortune* and *Forbes (opposite)*. They just jump in with massive scrolling screens and multicolored links. Time online is money, even if the call is free—so the philosophy in both cases is to spread the goods out as fast as possible.

For a chance to win a Lightware VP800 projector → SHOOT THE DUCK. 🦆

Asian flu affecting your business? ASIAWEEK

**5**

## FORTUNE.com

VALLEY TALK
with Melanie Warner

February 20, 1999
news

### IPO First, Product Launch Later?

A look at Internet stock mania on a whole new order of magnitude.

- Home
- News
- Investor
- Careers
- Technology
- Business Life
- Company Lists
- Fortune 500
- Small Business
- Magazine
- Free Trial Issues
- Subscriptions

Stock/Fund Quotes:
[ ] Go

### PATHFINDER
20 TOP NEWS SITES

SEARCH:
[ ] Go

**MONEY.com**
> Fund Manager's Pulpit is the Web

**YOUR COMPANY**
> Burned by NAFTA and Keeping Score

**TIME.com**
> Was the Scandal Good for America?

**TIME DIGITAL.com**
> Web Gives Disabled Genius a Voice

**ENTERTAINMENT WEEKLY.com**
> Rose McGowan Talks About Being Nasty

MORE:
[CNN ▾]

### FORTUNE
Business Resources
- Easy shopping at the Giftfinder
- Business Books @barnesandnoble
- Tax Software at Outpost.com
- Office Products @officedepot.com
- Free Trial Money Magazine
- Fortune Education Program
- Fortune Conferences

Instant Download:
- The Fortune 500
- New for 1999!
- Most Admired List
- NEW for 1999! Asiaweek Datastore

### Get 3 FREE TRIAL ISSUES!
CLICK HERE

**careers**
### Ask Annie: Office Romances
"A co-worker and I recently started dating, and I couldn't be happier. But my boss recently cautioned me that getting involved with a colleague could be bad for my career...."

**web exclusive**
### Extended Interview with Seagram's Edgar Bronfman, Jr.
Here, Bronfman explains his radical revamping of Seagram -- starting in 1995, when, with chemicals rebounding and DuPont poised for a turnaround, Seagram negotiated an $8.8 billion buyback and used the proceeds to go into show business via MCA.

**technology**
### Kim Polese: The Beauty of Hype
Tech startup Marimba promoted its gorgeous CEO more than its product. The result: a public relations bonanza--and a marketing nightmare.

**business life**
### Top Ten Cars for the Millennium
Nostalgia-drunk, luxury-drenched models stole the show in Detroit. Herewith, Fortune's countdown of the top ten vehicles for 2000.

**road warrior**
### Havin' an Ice Time
The world's coolest hotel is also the backdrop for some of Sweden's hottest brands. It's the perfect place to chill out--considering that it's made completely from ice.

**magazine**
### Microsoft Diary: Witnesses in Wonderland
On trial in Washington, Microsoft saw its witnesses get skewered, its video crash, and its prospects for victory take a serious turn for the worse.

**feedback**
### Contact Fortune.com
Comments? Complaints? Compliments? Write to the staff of Fortune.com.

**forum**
### The Boards: America's Most Admired Companies
Agree with the rankings? Disagree? Join the discussion in FORTUNE's Companies Forum.

**company lists**
### America's Most Admired Companies
The corporations that rise to the top exemplify ingenuity and other admirable qualities. Plus: Rank the companies by your own criteria.

**companies**
### Best Companies to Work For
The 100 companies on our list offer such perks as on-site swimming pools, stock options, and free breakfasts daily. See which employers appeal to you.

**investor**
### Portfolio Tracker
Track and analyze up to 150 stocks in a free portfolio.

### More Business Information

**small business**
### FORTUNE's Your Company
Practical advice on finance and strategy.

**MONEY**
### MarketRap
Daily market news with FORTUNE's Bethany McLean.

**tv**
### CNN/Fortune Newsstand
Wednesdays, 10 p.m. ET

---

### Investor
DJIA
+0   9339.95
NASDAQ
+23.05   2283.60
S&P 500
+1.91   1239.19

**street life**
### Internet Stocks Rise Across the Board
We continued the long unabated rally Friday, although techs overall were kind of mixed.

### Search Fortune
[ ] Go
Help

**investor**
### Fortune/Money Stock Tournament
Put your inner Warren Buffett to the test. Sign up now and try to create a portfolio that beats other contestants' stock picks.

---

[ Pull down for more FORTUNE.com ▾]

Search Fortune [ ] Go  Help

Top of Page

---

**6**

## Forbes Digital Tool

February 20, 1999

The three grand essentials of happiness are: something to do, someone to love, and something to hope for.
- ALEXANDER CHALMERS

[Digital Tool Home ▾]

Subscribe Now!

Toolbox

Search Engine
[ ] Go
Advanced search

Quick Quotes
[ ] Go

$StockPlayer
FREE

Tool Newsletter
[e-mail ▾] Go

**Departments**
Technology
Convergence
Startups
Companies
E-Business
Personal Finance

**Publications**
Archives
Forbes
Forbes Global
ASAP
FYI
American Heritage

**Centers**
Career Center
Small Business
Mutual Funds
Buyer's Guide

**Forums**
Forbes Forum
On My Mind

**Streaming Media**
Conferences
Audio Series
Media Center
Management Forum

**Services**
Subscriptions
Archives
Sitemap
Employment
Editorial Calendar
Contact Us
Reprints
Masthead
Help

Letters to the Editor

Special Sections

Conferences

Digital Feedback

Subsc

Forbes Digital Tool is sponsored by:
clique  BRIDGE  Gateway  ORACLE  Microsoft  Stock Player

All index quotes are delayed 20 minutes
| Technology | Convergence | Startups | Companies | E-Business | PersonalFinance |

DJIA  9340.00  +41.00  +0.44%  NASDAQ  2283.6  +23.05  +1.02%  S&P 500  1239.19  +1.91  +0.15%
February 19, 1999  5:00 PM

**E-BUSINESS**
### Searching in Dolby
Direct Hit is good news for netizens who still haven't found what they're looking for.
By Penelope Patsuris
Sponsored by Microsoft

**TODAY @ FORBES**
### Table of Contents

### Seeing green
Al Gore and his eco-advisers show their antibusiness bias.
By Pranay Gupte and Bonner R. Cohen

### Departments: Flashbacks
By Dolores Lataniotis

### Departments: Thoughts

### Now you see it...
Magician Ricky Jay does his best tricks with words.
By Adam Bresnick

### Sold! To the Internet
First came Beanie Baby auctions. Now come Picassos.
By Robert Goff

### Bourgeoisie boxes
Why lovebirds and collectors are enamored of enamels.
By Ashlea Ebeling

**sponsored by**
PRICEWATERHOUSECOOPERS

**FORBES PUBLICATIONS**
### Forbes Global:
The newest publication from Forbes, covering the rise of capitalism around the world.

### ASAP
Big Iron. Supercomputers are back and changing business, science, and soon even you.

### FYI Winter Issue now online
The guide to living the good life. Not available on the newsstand.

### American Heritage
The current issues of American Heritage, American Legacy, and Invention & Technology.

**DIGITAL TOOLS**
### Corporate America's Most Powerful People
1997 Executive Compensation. The 25 bosses listed pulled in $2.5 billion among them over the past five years. Are they worth it?

### The World's Richest People
Including home country, net worth, source of income and thumbnail biographies.

Be sure to visit the Toolbox for more.

**†Forbes News Wire**
Market Update (02/19) - 6:30 PM
### Techs get a break
By Marius Meland
### HotBot switches primary search
By Penelope Patsuris
### WebTrends' IPO success is short-lived
By Michele Rosen
### Total eclipse of Purple Moon
By Regina Joseph
### Vignette up sharply on first day of trading
By Michele Rosen
### Linux momentum grows with Big Blue alliance
By Michele Rosen
### Ciena beats the analysts, but problems abound
By Vicki Contavespi

**FORBES COVER STORY**
### Gerry-built TV
With Oxygen Media, Gerry Laybourne treads where bigger players failed: the brave new world of convergence.
By Tom Post

**FORBES COLUMNS ONLINE**
### Side Lines
By William Baldwin

Kenneth L. Fisher
Jerry Flint
Steve H. Hanke
Stephen Manes
Adam L. Penenberg
Thomas Sowell

### Streetwalker

**ON MY MIND FORUM**
### Executive bookmarks

**MEDIA CENTER**
### The Forbes 1999 Economic Panel Webcast
Watch and Listen to Rich Karlgaard, publisher of FORBES magazine, and others as they discuss the state of Japan and other Asian economies and how they will impact Silicon Valley's export market.

### The Forbes ASAP Online Roundtable
Forbes ASAP presents an evening with Stanley Crouch, Mark Helprin,

(109)

---

**7**

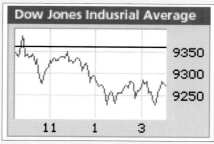

Dow Jones Indusrial Average
9350
9300
9250
11   1   3

**7**

Spelling is on the slide as well in the world's most respected economic indicator *(left)*. Eagle eyes at *The Wall Street Journal* must have been looking elsewhere when this graphic rolled by.

# PLEASE REMAIN SEATED

Soon, the air traveler will be able to click on a favorite seat, select conversation or no conversation, swipe a card through a reader, and see the free miles rack up. The only inconvenience will be getting to the airport. Until that day dawns, we must pick our way carefully through screens of varying degrees of sophistication in order to obtain our ideal, keenly priced flight. Here is a selection of the crucially seductive starting screens—United Airlines **www.ual.com**, British Airways **www.british-airways.com**, Swissair **www.swissair.com**, American Airlines **www.americanair.com**, Air Canada **www.aircanada.ca**, and KLM **www.klm.nl**.

110

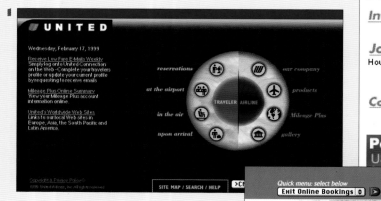

**1 | 2 | 3**
Maximum interface but no romance at UAL *(above)*, with retro-style telephone dial and Bodoni Bold Italic to match. Flying is still exotic for the Europeans *(right and above right)*. Swissair's coy graphic uses artful haiku-style Times; the rest is trademark Futura with HTML links slotted in. BA has its indecisive ribbon, drop-shadowed Friz Quadrata, and extra women.

**4**

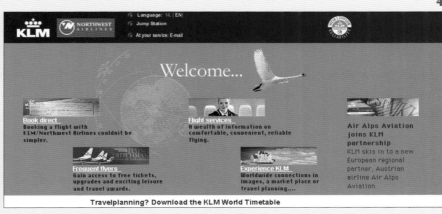

**4 | 5**
F. H. K. Henrion's 1970 KLM logo *(above)* holds up better as a little GIF than that of Northwest, KLM's affiliate. The panoramic layout takes a risk with the average browser. In "the most popular site on the Web" *(left)*, except for the upswept shadows, American Airlines plays it straight, with striking red links and color-coded pop-down menus.

**7**
At ground (or, rather, water) level, a snippet of seaborne technology *(below)* from P&O European Ferries.

**5**

**6**
Striking layout, moody lighting, and a novelty mouse from Air Canada *(left)*—but a rather disorganized array of clickable options.

**7**

# ECO WARRIORS

In Germany, the Green Party (literally "The Greens") is part of the coalition government. Their home-page sunflower is the only reference to a previous, more sandaled, way of life. The site **www.gruene-fraktion.de** offers an overview of the German political scene.

Monsanto **www.monsanto.com** shares the imagery, but has a totally different agenda. They find themselves at loggerheads with green activist groups worldwide. Consequently, forces are being gathered in all media for the public-relations battle for hearts and minds.

112

**1**
All discreetly sized Verdana on the home page *(left)*, with assured handling of transparent images, and an ironic funny-face icon for the link to the party line *(far left)*.

**4**
Monsanto's panorama *(below)* downloads in sedate style. The discreet arrows are not for pressing—use the banal old scroll bar to get around.

4

**2 | 3**

Diagonal type prompts a selection *(right)*. The relevant colored box clears and the subsequent choices are revealed. Clicking on "world politics," for example, spins the button and shows the text. It's hard to imagine getting lost with the ever-present navigation bar, but there's a clear site map *(below)* for the unwary.

**2**

Home  Aktuell  Unsere Themen  Publikationen  Archiv  Über uns      Suche  Site-Map  Info-Abo  Dialog  Drucksachen  Links

BÜNDNIS 90
DIE GRÜNEN

Bundestagsfraktion

Zur Partei

**Unsere Themen**

- Außenpolitik
- Innenpolitik
- Frauen
- Wirtschaft & Finanzen
- Jugend
- Sozialpolitik
- Arbeit
- Umwelt

### Moderne Umweltpolitik im Dialog mit der Gesellschaft

Wirksame Umweltpolitik ist keine Ressortaufgabe mehr sondern muß zugleich Wirtschafts- und Finanzpolitik, Arbeitsmarkt- und Sozialpolitik, Forschungs- und Bildungspolitik, Industrie, Verkehrs- und Entwicklungspolitik sein. Es geht uns um die Ökologisierung aller Politikbereiche. Die ökologische Steuerreform ist z. B. nicht nur umweltpolitisch wirksam sondern ein Schritt zu einer ökologischen Finanz- und Wirtschaftspolitik., mit Anreizen zum Energiesparen, zu Innovationen und zur Schaffung von Arbeitsplätzen.

Eine umfassend verstandene Umweltpolitik unter dem Leitbild des nachhaltigen Wirtschaftens begünstigt die Entwicklung neuer Produkte, ressourcenschonender Produktionsverfahren und Dienstleistungen. Ihnen gehören die Zukunftsmärkte, nicht dem bislang vorherrschenden teuren nachsorgenden Umweltschutz mit Filtern und Materialrecycling. Im Ergebnis schafft diese Entwicklung sogar Standortvorteile. Denn nur Länder, die selbst Vorreiter im Umweltschutz sind, können auch international den Umweltschutz vorantreiben und Zukunftsmärkte bedienen. Eine solche Entwicklung können wir nur mit einem neuen dialogorientierten Politikstil voranbringen: Wir wollen z. B. mit der Industrie, Gewerkschaften und Kirchen, Wirtschafts- und Bauernverbänden zu einer kritischen Partnerschaft kommen, um zentrale Reformprojekte voranzutreiben, wie den flächendeckende Naturschutz durch naturangepaßte Wirtschaftsweisen und Landnutzungen, den Einstieg in das Solarzeitalter oder die Entwicklung ökologisch verträglicher Mobilität.

Anfang der Seite

113

**3**

## Home

| Aktuell | Unsere Themen | Publikationen | Archiv | Über uns |
|---|---|---|---|---|
| In der Debatte | Außenpolitik | Schlagwortliste | Schlagwortliste | Unsere Abgeordneten |
| Beschlossene Sache | Innenpolitik | Neue Publikationen (14. WP) | Pressemitteilungen | Fraktionsvorstand |
| 100 Tage Rot-Grün | Frauen | grün & bündig | Bundestagsreden | Die Grüne Tulpe |
| Bundestagsreden | Wirtschaft und Finanzen | kurz & knapp | Parlamentarische Initiativen | Impressum |
| Pressemitteilungen | Jugend | kompakt & griffig | | |
| grün & bündig | Sozialpolitik | kompakt & fündig | | |
| | Arbeitslosigkeit | lang & schlüssig | | |
| | Umwelt | Bestellung | | |

Anfang der Seite

THERE'S A FAMILY THAT LIVES HERE..

A FAMILY OF SIX BILLION, EACH WITH THE POSSIBILITY OF LIVING LONGER AND HEALTHIER THROUGH THE DISCOVERY WE, THE PEOPLE OF MONSANTO, HAVE JUST BEGUN...

MONSANTO
Food · Health · Hope™

A FAMILY WITH HOPE - FOR TODAY AND FOR THE FUTURE ▶

# COME ON IN

Sharing a name and quantities of confidence, two sites that approach the business of self-promotion from opposite corners. Deep in the heart of London's ancient printing quarter, the 55 Web site designers of **www.deepend.co.uk** are tricky, with scrolling Java windows. Somewhere in Sonoma, a more wide-ranging proposition comes at you from **www.deepend.com**.

114

**1 | 2**
After a short wait for loading *(above)* the Alka-Seltzer metaphor splashes down on the main screen *(left)*.

**3 | 4**
Java-enabled browsers will see a discreet slider bar *(below)*— push it along to roll through the window, or click on the text links. With no Java, the old-style scroll *(below left)* lumbers into view.

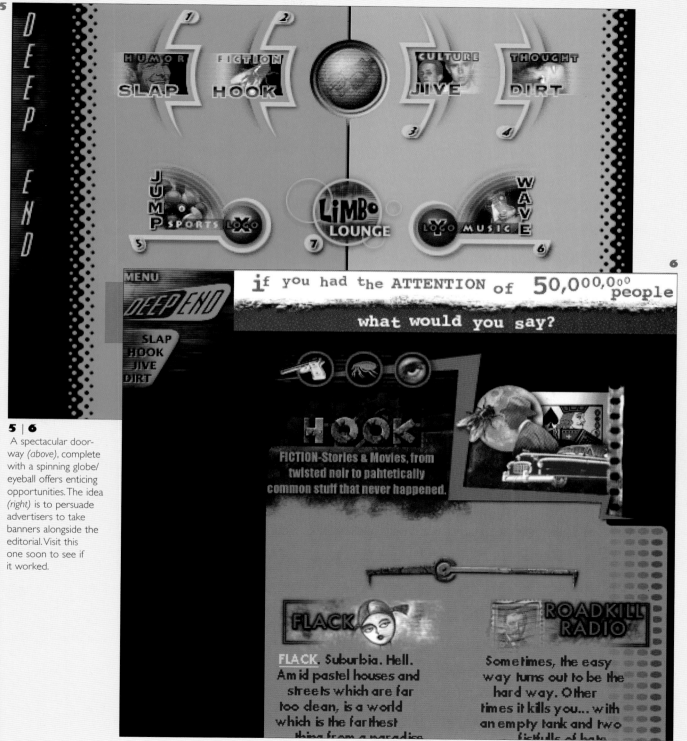

DEEP END

MENU
DEEP END
SLAP
HOOK
JIVE
DIRT

if you had the ATTENTION of 50,000,000 people

what would you say?

HOOK
FICTION-Stories & Movies, from twisted noir to pahtetically common stuff that never happened.

FLACK

ROADKILL RADIO

FLACK. Suburbia. Hell.
Amid pastel houses and
streets which are far
too clean, is a world
which is the farthest
thing from a paradise

Sometimes, the easy
way turns out to be the
hard way. Other
times it kills you... with
an empty tank and two
fistfulls of hate

**5 | 6**
A spectacular door-
way *(above)*, complete
with a spinning globe/
eyeball offers enticing
opportunities. The idea
*(right)* is to persuade
advertisers to take
banners alongside the
editorial. Visit this
one soon to see if
it worked.

6

115

# MARKET FORCES

Information is power, and especially so in the financial markets. The online annual report is now a commonplace. Chemicals group Zeneca, for example, publish their results on the Net at **www.zeneca.com**. A less passive role is available for the online shareholder. At **money.go.com** and **www.etrade.com** a complete information service is available, with access to almost real-time stock quotes.

**1**
HTML and tables, the unforgiving discipline *(below)* of the balance sheet. Frame-based design helps out with the inevitably lengthy scrolling.

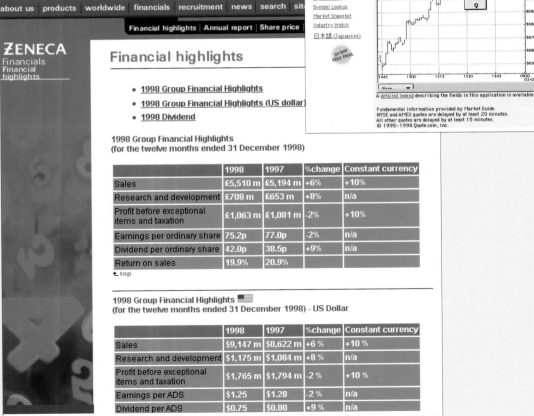

**2 | 3**
Old armchair-based investors had to wait for the daily paper before launching into the market. Now there are detailed charts *(above)* with an option to view a longer period *(top)*.

*Welcome to E*TRADE*

Home | Portfolio & Markets | Stocks & Options | Mutual Funds | Trading | My Accounts | Community | Marketplace

> LOG ON

**Customer Support**

Welcome
About E*TRADE
International Sites
Business Solutions
Investor Relations
Contact Us
Play the E*TRADE Game
Open an Account

My Profile | Set Alerts
Stock Quote(s):
Index | Site Map
> Learning Center
> Service Center
E*TRADE Mail

Graphics  ⊙On ○Off

No fees. No minimums.
Roth
Traditional
Education
Open your E*TRADE IRA today! GO

**Account Sign-up Bonus**
Get up to **10,000 United Mileage Plus miles** when you open an E*TRADE account by March 19, 1999! **Apply now** ➤

**E*TRADE Highlights**

**Free Membership**
Not ready to trade? Get free real-time quotes, personal portfolios, and more. **Go now** ➤

**Catch the Tour**
New to E*TRADE? Jump on-board and we'll show you around.
**Go now** ➤

**Million Mile Challenge**
Play the Game for a chance to win United Mileage Plus miles!
**Go now** ➤

**New! E*TRADE Funds**
Introducing the first mutual funds built for the
**Go now** ➤

Someday, we'll all invest this way. ⊗
Securities protected to $50 million

E*TRADE rated #1 online investing site in the w
by the Lafferty Group in its Web-based
Financial Services Report (4Q98).

**Market View**

Free Real-time Quotes
Enter Symbol:
[ GO ]  Look Up Symbol

**NASDAQ COMP**  03.05.1999
4:15 PM ET

| | | +45.38 |
| --- | --- | --- |
| NASDAQ | 2338.27 | +45.38 |
| DJIA | 9736.08 | +268.68 |
| S&P | 1275.46 | +28.82 |

● **In Play**
● **Stock Discussion**
● **Professional Edge**

E*TRADE | E*STATION  Your 24-hour online assistant
> CONTACT US

Learning Center | Service Center | **Tour**
MAIN | OPEN AN ACCOUNT
◄ BACK  FORWARD ►

**WELCOME to the TOUR.**
There's no time like the present—so tour the future of online investing now.

**The Next Generation of Online Investing!**
Our new Web site gives you more power, more tools, and more real-time research than ever before. And almost all of it is FREE.

For a taste of some of the features and services available through E*TRADE, click on any of the links below or click the FORWARD button above to get started right now.

**Tour Areas**

| | |
| --- | --- |
| Portfolio & Markets | Tells you what's happening in the markets. Your way. |
| Stocks & Options | Resources to make you a smarter, better-informed investor. |
| Mutual Funds | Mutual fund research and screening tools. |
| Trading | Fast, easy, online. From $14.95 a trade. |
| My Accounts | Cash management made easy. |
| Community | Exchange ideas with other E*TRADE members. |
| Marketplace | Shop 'till you drop. Then refinance your mortgage. |
| Professional Edge | Real-time analyst reports and recommendations. |
| Other Account Benefits | Even more reasons to choose E*TRADE. |

**4 | 5**
The tools of the trade
are all at hand *(above)*.
An online assistant
is available *(right)*.
What could possibly
go wrong.?

5

117

# SPEAKING VOLUMES

2

1

Music sleeves and inlays looked like Web sites long before the Net was thought of. Quick-reaction graphics were needed to detain the browsing customer in the record store, against an energetic background of competing designs. British remix specialists Massive Attack are well to the fore with a corporate identity of the hot-chili school at **www.massiveattack.com**. Their record label **www.virgin.com** takes a more sedate line.

**1 | 2 | 3 | 4**

A two-pronged attack begins *(opposite)*. Monochrome graphics download quickly, and strongly reinforce the familiar "corporate" branding. Select a sound clip *(below and right)* and you can join in the sampling fun.

CD#9 1 Teardrop (LP Version) 5.29 2 Teardrop (Scream Team Remix) 6.44 3 Teardrop (Mad Professor Mazaruni Mix) 6.06 4 Teardrop (Mad Professor Mazaruni Mix Instrumental) 6.23 5 Euro Zero Zero 4.24

"Teardrop" is the ninth single and contains the Scream Team Remix, by Brendan Lynch and Primal Scream, the Mad Professor Mazaruni mixes (vocal and instrumental) and an additional track, Euro Zero Zero, a version of Eurochild for the millenium.

BOXSET  ALBUM  VIDEO

Daydreaming · Unfinished sympathy · Safe from harm · Sly · Protection · Karmacoma · Risingson · Teardrop · Inertia creeps

BOXSET  ALBUM  VIDEO

**5**

search     home     e-mail     help

info
clips
tour
links

virgin records

## Massive Attack

"...strange, startling and seductive..."

### info

ORDER ONLINE

When the dominant trend was overloaded techno trickery, Massive Attack released the debut album, "Blue Lines" and completely redefined the boundaries of dance based pop. They were the quintessential 90's pop group, a collective inspired by rap, dub, and club culture, taking all those reference points and forging a music that opened up a whole new range of aural possibilities.
Based in Bristol, England, Massive Attack today continues to thrive as a fluid, ever-evolving aggregation of musicians orbiting around core members 3-D, Mushroom, and Daddy G. Protection, Massive Attack's second album, is as strange, startling, and seductive in its own way as its predecessor. Produced by longtime friend of the band, Nellee Hooper, it features vocal contributions from Tracey Thorn, Horace Andy, Nicolette, and Tricky.

Although Massive Attack released their first single, "Daydreaming," in 1990, they have been in existence since 1987. Their musical roots stretch back even further to the embryonic days of the British rap scene when, as The Wild Bunch -- also featuring Nellee Hooper -- they were one of the first homegrown crews to merge rap and graffiti art, rocking the scene in their Bristol hometown.

**6**

NEW RELEASES FEBRUARY/MARCH

THE COLOUR OF CLASSICS

Celibidache Edition launch!

20/21 : Music of our Time: launch of an innovative product line

Gil Shaham and Pierre Boulez perform Bartok

Pierre Boulez continues his Mahler series

Paul McCreesh's Solomon

CD NEWS
100 YEARS
ARTISTS
IN THE STUDIO
INSIGHTS

THE COLOUR OF CLASSICS

Deutsche Grammophon

HEADLINE NEWS

5 Grammy Awards for Deutsche Grammophon !

Interview with Serge Celibidachi about the Celibidache Edition

1999: Johann Strauss year with the Wiener Philharmoniker

**5 | 6**

Echoes of old-style music journalism *(left)* at Virgin Records site, **www.virginrecords.com**. Tall columns of HTML text soberly dissect all the label's bands.

Deutsche Grammophon addresses a different constituency *(above)* at **www.dgclassics.com**. Undersized type and faded GIFs teeter on the edge of invisibility.

While newspaper journalists famously ran up enormous restaurant expenses in pursuit of a story, international-fashion-magazine typographers were indulging themselves in display typesetting studios. Today, with an unlocked font CD-ROM and plenty of RAM, the overheads are lower and the possibilities limitless. *Elle International,* for example, has a corporate site **www.elle.com** as well as an online version of the magazine at **www.ellemag.com.**

**1**
Beginning with a tight-rope tour through the type-specimen book *(above),* the corporate site strings its links on a clothesline.

ELLE ONLINE

model gallery

fashion

model gallery

beauty

health &fitness

numerology &beyond

christy turlington

Alek Wek

Annie Morton

Astrid Munõz

Brandon Merrill

Charlotte

Christy Turlington

Cindy Crawford

Elsa Benitez

Erika Stromqvist

Erin O'Connor

Esther Cañadas

4

121

ELLE ONLINE

search | site map | contact

fashion

model gallery

beauty

health &fitness

numerology &beyond

designs that define our style

fashionbeautyhealthfitness

this week **online**

**fashion**stories
Yard upon yard of tulle and lace -- this is the stuff of fairy tales.

trends from the **street**
Serious fashionistas carefully consider the form and function of bags when making their purchases.

**health**newsletter
Susan Blumenthal, MD, one of the nation's top doctors for women, makes sense of the latest medical news

**fast track** trends
For spring designers have returned to celebrating the sweet side of femininity.

ELLE ONLINE

2

**2 | 3 | 4**
The online version starts *(left)* with GIFs reflecting its parent's look and layout. Subsequent pages offer textbook instruction in type manipulation.

Gigantic reversed-out Helvetica is used to erode the background image *(above)*. A similar technique modulates the restricted-palette GIF *(top)*.

3

# SHARPLY DEFINED

122

Shadowed type cuts into the tundra *(left)*, underlined with a Gallic flourish. The navigation device *(below)* sprouts confirming icons as required.

At the end of the third millennium there will be retrospectives of graphic design from the end of the 20th century. We now reflect rather smugly on the perceived decorative excesses of our 19th-century forebears—but it is impossible to imagine how we shall be judged. The analysts of the future might commend the minimalism of spectacle makers Alain Mikli of Paris **www.mikli.fr** and their German rivals Freudenhaus at **www.freudenhaus.com.** The virtue in both cases is in directness of layout and stern adherence to a grid.

**3**
Dutch bankers ING start with a clean slate *(below)*, but there's soon a committee-led jumble of debris.

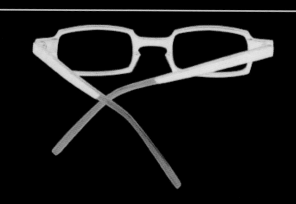

# F R E U D E N H A U S®
## EYEWEAR

**DAS FREUDENHAUS**
the flagship store

DIALOG

EYEWEAR

PRESS

SHOP

WE DESIGN FOR YOUR PLEASURE

HOME          MAIL          © 1998 FreudenHaus Optik Vertriebs GmbH. All Rights Reserved.

**4 | 5 | 6**
Almost a negative
image of the site
opposite, Freudenhaus
sticks rigidly to
sans serif and black
backgrounds.

# F R E U D E N H A U S®
## EYEWEAR

GET SHOCKWAVE

GET SHOCKWAVE FLASH

N Netscape NOW!

WE DESIGN FOR YOUR PLEASURE

© 1998 FreudenHaus Optik Vertriebs GmbH. All Rights Reserved.
info@freudenhaus.com

**DAS FREUDENHAUS**

DATA & FACTS

THE CONCEPT

SPECIALS

EVENTS

HOME          MAIL          © 1998 FreudenHaus Optik Vertriebs GmbH. All Rights Reserved.

4

# EXTENDING THE LIMITS

Experimentation one day becomes the mainstream. At MIT, the agenda at the media laboratory Aesthetics and Computation Group **acg.media.mit.edu** is wide open. Professor John Maeda directs a program of courses that bear some strange typographic fruit. The scene is set in the faculty foyer with an interactive stream of watery type (see description opposite). Most of these examples are applets that react, sometimes apparently randomly, to mouse or keyboard activity.

**1**
The sequence *(right)* is John Maeda's own work for the Tokyo Type Directors Club. The characters follow the mouse pointer in unwilling delayed fashion. Stir the mouse around and chaos results; keep the button pressed to reverse it all out.

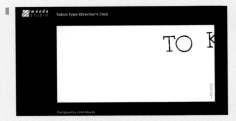

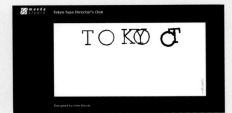

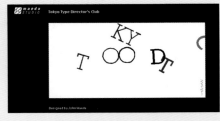

124

**MAS 962**

**6** Unstable Type
Design a parameterized typeface with inherently unstable properties.

**Brad Geilfuss**
**Peter Cho**
**Interval**

principles ▶

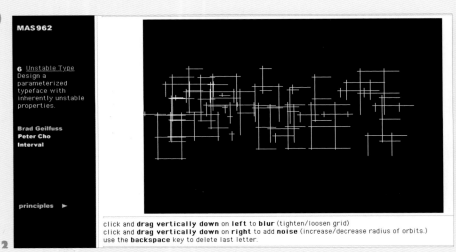

click and **drag vertically down** on **left** to **blur** (tighten/loosen grid)
click and **drag vertically down** on **right** to add **noise** (increase/decrease radius of orbits.)
use the **backspace** key to delete last letter.

**MAS 962**

**9** RSVP
Use Rapid Serial Visual Perception to play a stream of text.

**Reed Kram**
**Matt Grenby**
**Tara Rosenberger**

principles ▶

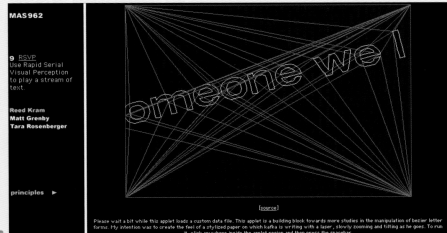

[source]

Please wait a bit while this applet loads a custom data file. This applet is a building block towards more studies in the manipulation of bezier letter forms. My intention was to create the feel of a stylized paper on which kafka is writing with a laser, slowly zooming and tilting as he goes. To run it, click anywhere inside the applet region and then press the spacebar.

**4**

The secret of the stream *(right)* is an overhead video projector that responds to sensors fitted in the watercourse.

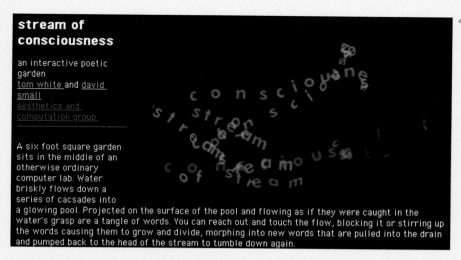

# stream of consciousness

an interactive poetic garden
<u>tom white</u> and <u>david small</u>
<u>aesthetics and computation group</u>

A six foot square garden sits in the middle of an otherwise ordinary computer lab. Water briskly flows down a series of cacsades into a glowing pool. Projected on the surface of the pool and flowing as if they were caught in the water's grasp are a tangle of words. You can reach out and touch the flow, blocking it or stirring up the words causing them to grow and divide, morphing into new words that are pulled into the drain and pumped back to the head of the stream to tumble down again.

**5**

A flavor of the MIT research is given *(right)* in the description of the Gradus project.

**2 | 3**

Typing generates moving horizontal and vertical white lines *(opposite, center)*, which gradually coalesce into near-characters. The sliders *(not seen here)* allow the user to disturb the equilibrium still further. The Kafka project *(opposite, bottom)* is much less demanding of the operator—it will run almost unattended.

## EXPLORING AN ORGANIC INFORMATION ARCHITECTURE

matt grenby, john maeda
aesthetics & computation group
mit media lab
grenby@media.mit.edu
617.253.1821

[fig.1] data bloom

[fig.1] <u>gradus</u>

## RESEARCH

In your mind's eye, consider an ancient oak tree, solitary on the crest of a hill in an open field. From a distance you can appreciate the over-all form of the tree: the strange symmetries of the branch network, the shape and color of the canopy. As you come nearer, you notice the leaves rustling in the breeze. Strong winds have torn certain branches away from the trunk. You see faint traces of charred bark, indicating that at one point this tree survived a fire in the field. The tree is teeming with life, from the birds which temporarily alight on a branch to rest, to the ants and grubs which make a meal of leaves. We know a significant amount about this particular tree. No text. No numbers. All this information has been gleaned from a quick examination of only the formal qualities of an object: its shape, not its numbers.

Now consider the stock pages of the Wall Street Journal. Columns and columns of miniscule sans-serif type, accurately detailing the smallest fluctuation in price, volume and thereby intrinsic value of any particular security you care to track. Step back from the page. Observe the larger structures: line-spacing, margins, column width, the dimensions of the pages. These pages are the picture of refinement: carefully managed, rational, terminally specialized. Unlike the tree, separate representations are required to meaningfully express the micro and the macro. The listings are the micro view of a particular exchange; separate graphs and charts are used to communicate the macro: trends in the over-all market, the state of national economies.

In our research, we strive to create representations of information that incorporate the qualities of natural expectation and familiarity usually found in organic systems with the efficacy and focus of traditional alphanumeric descriptions. Gradus, a conceptual visualization of the English language was, the first step in this direction. Headwords from the dictionary were plotted along three axes (time, alphabetic, frequency) and then packed along their vector to the origin. The resulting, tornado-like form reveals features of the history of English. For instance, a bulge halfway up the structure represents the burgeoning of words entering the language around the time of the Renaissance. In this case, rational categorization coupled with a shape-based representation serve to give an understanding of the underlying body of information which traditional structures, such as books, could never afford.

Our most recent research expands on the ideas presented in gradus, with an emphasis on increasing the sophistication of the atomic unit of

**5**

# CARRY ON REGARDLESS

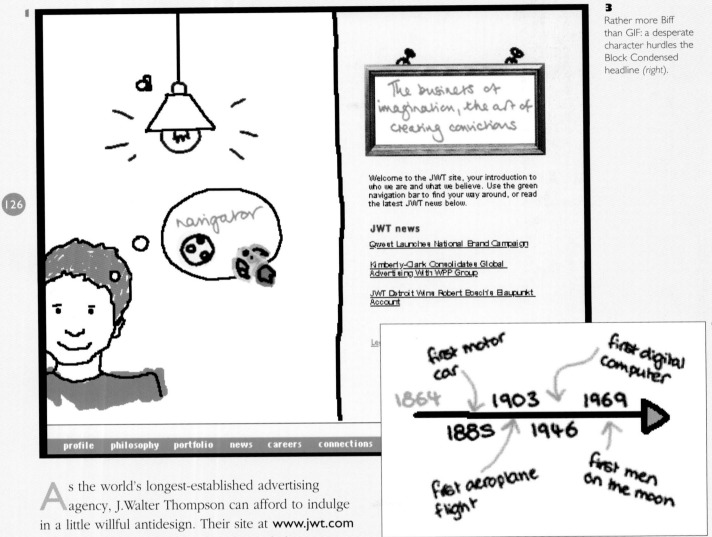

**3**
Rather more Biff than GIF: a desperate character hurdles the Block Condensed headline *(right)*.

**1 | 2**
The site appears to be directed *(top)* by an elementary-school child with moderate handwriting skills. Light bulbs and insects animate the scene. The same hand condenses 135 years of history *(above)*.

As the world's longest-established advertising agency, J. Walter Thompson can afford to indulge in a little willful antidesign. Their site at **www.jwt.com** sports clichés in abundance, but the underlying animations reinforce the idea that there are powerful forces at work behind the scenes. More sophisticated drawing skills and just as much self-confidence are on view at **www.kitchensink.com**, repository of comic requirements of every kind. The coarse demands of designing for newsprint are very close to the disciplines of image-making and type selection for the Web.

3

**SEE ART. BUY STUFF. HAVE FUN.**

· MAILING LIST · SINK LINKS · SITE MAP · SEARCH

KitchenSink.com

100's of great images, more every day! Dozens of the world's best comics artists! New books, comics, and new stuff all the time!

127

ART GALLERY

SPOTLIGHT ON: CRUMB

STRIP MALL™ FEATURING "STEVEN" UPDATED WEEKLY

CATALOG

CAPITALISM GOES ON-LINE!

**Meanwhile, back at the store...**

CAGES

Order online now and save 10%

Dave McKean's acclaimed series now in a stunning 500-page Hardcover Collection!

CAGES as it was meant to be seen and read: a true novel in visual form. Eight years in the making.

BUY

**STAY TUNED!**

More changes, updates and additions to the site are coming soon!

# LET'S GO SHOPPING

Neiman Marcus

MARCH 1999

Neiman M

MARCH

THE BO
STORE IN
SERVIC
ようこ

As seen in W magazi

Neiman Marcus 1.800.36

Y ou may be able to get through St. Patrick's Day
without the aid of a $175,000 ring—but visit the
Neiman Marcus site at **www.neimanmarcus.com**,
in any case. The discreet charm of the bourgeoisie is
reflected in measured layout, controlled choice of type,
and impeccable picture handling.

**1 | 2 | 3**
The front page
*(above)* doesn't jump
around, and the home
page *(right)* stands
squarely still. Only on
the "Notebook" entry
page *(above right)* is
there any sign of Web
designer's whimsy.
There's a white pixel
below the word
"enter."

2

**3**

# NM NOTEBOOK
The who, what, when, where, and why.

ENTER

**4 | 5**

Ten cents' worth of HTML text *(below)* describes a bauble costing the equivalent of ten reasonably good family cars. Let us be content with the book *(bottom)* for only $5.

129

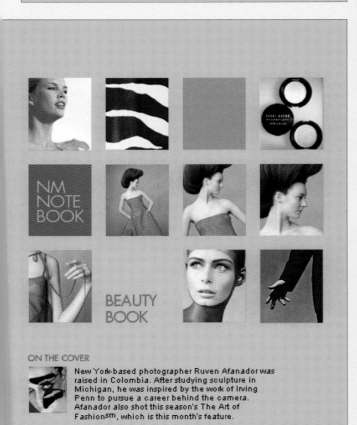

## ON THE COVER

New York-based photographer Ruven Afanador was raised in Colombia. After studying sculpture in Michigan, he was inspired by the work of Irving Penn to pursue a career behind the camera. Afanador also shot this season's The Art of Fashion℠, which is this month's feature.

---

NM NOTEBOOK

In Focus
NM Service
Who's News
Tailoring
Gift Cards
NM Credit Card
The Galleries
Horoscope
*the book*
InCircle®

Neiman Marcus
CLOSE

## PICK-ME-UP
THE WEARING O' THE GREEN

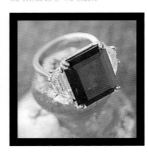

Avoid a pinch this St. Patrick's Day by donning this exquisite emerald ring. Consider it your well-deserved treasure at the end of the rainbow.

26. Emerald ring set in 18-karat gold with two diamond trillions. 175,000.00. Precious Jewels Salon in selected stores.

**4**

---

**5**

NM NOTEBOOK

In Focus
NM Service
Who's News
Tailoring
Gift Cards
NM Credit Card
The Galleries
Horoscope
*the book*
InCircle®

Neiman Marcus
CLOSE

## *the book*
OF THE MONTH

A subscription to *the book*, our award-winning publication, is available for $50.00 for ten issues ($75.00 U.S. for foreign subscriptions). *The book* is published monthly March through July and September through December.

Call 1.888.888.2880 to order. Foreign subscriptions can fax their orders to 1.972.401.6306. Or send the subscription amount with your name and address to:

# THE MARCH OF PROGRESS

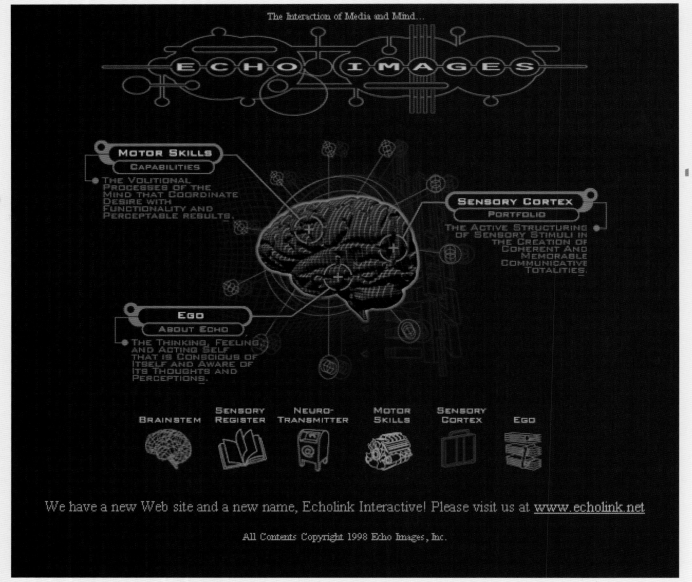

The original portfolio site of Echo Images Inc. neatly exemplifies one of the driving forces of the Web—the need to reinvent and upgrade. Their admired "brain" site **www.echoimages.com** took the cerebral metaphor, mixed in a measure of willful typography, and leavened it with glowing sci-fi monitor colors. All that is history. The current site is retro jukebox machine-worship; only little Flash screens of frantic type echo the past.

**1 | 2 | 3**

The old home page *(left)* presents the brain as circuit diagram. The strokes under the final letter of each paragraph ape the flashing cursor of old word-processor screen conventions. On the new site, a chrome-plated beast *(below)* gives shiny birth to twin columns of gleaming type. On the left is a fixed site map, with a sliding cursor; on the right, HTML text offers the late-breaking news. The zany client list *(bottom)* scrolls sideways for half a dozen screen widths.

**2**

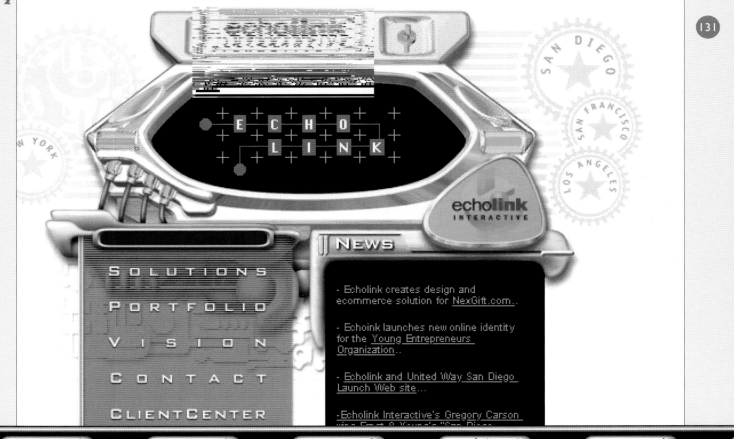

SOLUTIONS

PORTFOLIO

VISION

CONTACT

CLIENTCENTER

**NEWS**

- Echolink creates design and ecommerce solution for NexGift.com..

- Echoink launches new online identity for the Young Entrepreneurs Organization..

- Echolink and United Way San Diego Launch Web site...

-Echolink Interactive's Gregory Carson wins Ernst & Young's "San Diego

echolink
INTERACTIVE

131

- Echolink puts Brownells in its sights.

ERNST & YOUNG LLP

- EchoLink's new personal reminder software, "NeverForget" receives a

# . . . ACTUALLY SLATE UNDER A FAUX FINISH

In 1900, Jerome J. Smucker was making apple butter in Orrville, Ohio. His successors have got the wholesome look one hundred years later at **www.smucker.com**. The 216 colors of the Web are not kind to the muted tones of old artifacts, but astute palette management makes all the difference. A marbled navigation bar helps at **www.oldhousejournal.com**. Typeface selection, however, is the principal key to turning the clock back.

3

**OLDHOUSE**
*Journal Online*
HBRnet
Monday, March 01, 1999

Home | The Magazine | New Products | Old-House Notebook | Historic House Plans | Talk | Swaps & Sales | The Store | Restoration Directory | Find-A-Pro

### Quick Notes

**Find-A-Pro**
Now, you can find that help -- both remodelers and contractors -- through Find-a-Pro, a joint venture of HBRnet and ImproveNet, America's Home Improvement Network.

**Classifieds**
Find or sell anything from old houses to old radiators in our free, online classifieds.

**The Bulletin Boards**
Readers share tips about restoring windows, stripping old woodwork and scores of other subjects in our chat rooms.

Become a charter sponsor of Old-House Journal Online. Click here for details

### Slate Pretenders

Before you next kindle the coals in your dining room fireplace, take a good look at your mantel. Maybe it's not a richly veined stone or rare tropical wood, after all. If your house was built between the 1850s and 1900s or so, there's a good chance the mantel is actually slate under a faux finish.

### Kitchens of the Bungalow Era
This budget-minded restoration expert re-creates authentic bungalow kitchens that supply all the modern amenities and still look like they belong in the house. The price tag? Usually about $6,000 to $7,000.

### Historic Hardware
Where do you find historical architectural hardware — that is, products that work with the mechanics and aesthetics of an old house? Start right here.

**IRONWOOD**® ℮
View
US$25.99

**JUNIPER**® ℮
View
US$25.99

**Madrone**
View
US$25.99

**MESQUITE**® ℮
View
US$25.99

**PEPPERWOOD**® ℮
View
US$25.99 [3 fonts]

**PONDEROSA**¹ ℮
View
US$25.99

*Buy This Online Now—* just add it to your shopping cart!
Select a Platform | Add
view your shopping cart

**1 | 2**
A home page with a decidedly in-progress look (left), but alive with useful content. A visit to the grimly vulgar Adobe online type shop (above) might open a few typographic doors.

**3**

A glorious evocation of Charles Rennie Mackintosh *(opposite)* as a totem for a West Coast furniture store. The faint wallpaper background belongs to Britain's William Morris site.

**4 | 5 | 6**

Swashes and curlicues evoke transatlantic Victorian values in Smucker's home page *(right)*. The recipe for almond-dusted strawberry-balsamic chicken breasts is reproduced in full *(below)* to show that if the content is sufficiently riveting, fine typesetting can be superfluous.

Within these pages we have attempted to share some of the "flavor" of Smucker's® – including our Company's history, its products, and its principles. We appreciate your interest in our company and THANK YOU for taking the time to visit our site.

133

Smucker's is proud to be the presenting sponsor of Discover Stars on Ice. Click here for games, recipes, puzzles, videos, and more.

**Main Dish**
Oriental Chicken
Pineapple Spareribs
Porkchops with Apricot Mustard Gl
Apple-Glazed Pork Chops
Cherry Glazed Ham
Sweet & Sour Chicken Stir Fry
Pineapple Chicken
Strawberry-Glazed Ham
Sautéed Swordfish With Cherry Sals
Almond-Dusted Strawberry Balsamic

**ALMOND-DUSTED STRAWBERRY-BALSAMIC CHICKEN BREASTS**

Vegetable cooking spray (butter-flavored)
1 tablespoon extra-light olive oil or canola oil
4 boneless, skinless chicken breast halves (about 5 oz. each)
1/2 teaspoon salt
1/4 teaspoon black pepper
1/3 cup very finely chopped unblanched almonds
1/4 cup minced shallots or green onions
1/3 cup chicken broth
1/3 cup **Smucker's Strawberry Preserves**
3 tablespoons balsamic vinegar
1 tablespoon minced fresh rosemary or 1 teaspoon dried rosemary, crumbled
1 10 oz. bag ready-to-serve fresh spinach, cooked just until tender
    and kept warm
finely chopped fresh parsley for garnish, if desired

Coat a large non-stick skillet with cooking spray, add oil and heat over medium-high heat. Sprinkle chicken with salt and pepper, dredge in almonds. Place chicken in skillet; sauté 4 minutes on each side, turning once. Remove from pan and keep warm.

Reduce heat to low; add green onions to skillet and sauté 1 minute. Add chicken broth, Smucker's strawberry preserves, vinegar and rosemary; simmer until slightly thickened, about 2-3 minutes.

Place spinach on heated serving platter; top with chicken breasts and pour sauce over top. If desired, sprinkle finely chopped parsley over chicken. *Serves 4.*

# SLIDE THAT BY ME ONE MORE TIME

The stock photo agencies were early enthusiasts of computerized databases, barcode scanning, and picture distribution by CD-ROM. The Net is now their province too, with an audience that has been obliged to learn the search skills that are second nature to a picture researcher. The Stock Market, however, treats the timid client kindly at **www.stockmarketphoto.com**. You have a choice of visual and word-based searches, and a "simple" payment procedure—"only" eight steps.

**134**

**3**
The combination of "free" and an exclamation mark (above) forces the choice, though the whole site can still be accessed from here via the navigation bar.

**1 | 2**
All black to begin with (above), the site steps up a gear with color coding, shadowed button GIFs, and seductive TV screens (right).

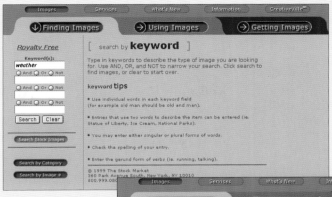

**4 | 5**
Keyword searching is explained *(left)* with a clarity that shames many mainline search engines. The old card-index metaphor looks the part for once. The results of a one-field search arrive on screen *(below)*.

**6 | 7 | 8**
Searching by image *(below)* follows the same logic as the keyword search. The required bug is soon pinned down *(bottom)*. A diversion can be made to a magnifying "light box" *(right)* for closer examination.

135

**9 | 10**
Both trophies now appear in the shopping cart *(left)* and payment channel *(below)*. High-resolution online delivery follows successful negotiation of the Eight Steps.

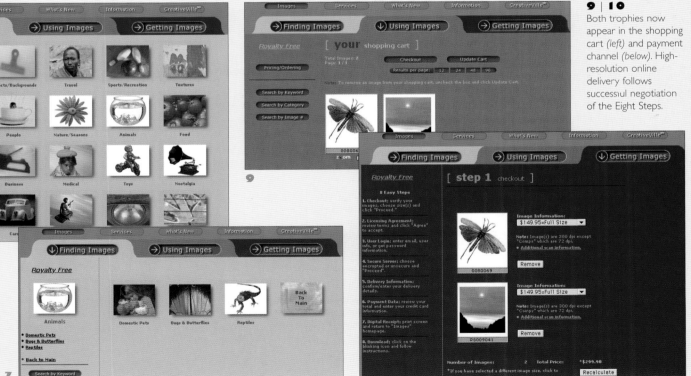

# DO NOT ADJUST YOUR BROWSER

Every system has its critics. Some, like gentlemanly polemicist Michael Sippey at **www.theobvious.com**, deal with the broad issues of Web usage and etiquette, barracking idle or greedy manufacturers, scam artists, and assorted flotsam. The intricacies of Web design itself are the preserve of Bud Uglly and his Chicago screen police at **www.wwwvoice.com/bud**. Connoisseurs of code, they know exactly where to touch the exposed nerves of HTML. They'll even design your site.

## stating the obvious

### Information

Stating the Obvious is recurring commentary on web technology, business and culture. It is the creation of Michael Sippey, and has been online since August 1, 1995.

The Internet is chock-full of news bulletins about itself; sites like News.com and Wired News are particularly adept at circulating news about the web via the web. Stating the Obvious is an attempt to provide something beyond self-referential newsbites; it's technology with a point of view.

You can have Stating the Obvious delivered right to your inbox. Simply send email to majordomo@theobvious.com with the phrase "subscribe retro-push" (without the quotes) in the body of the message.

Submissions are encouraged. Send plain ASCII email to editorial@theobvious.com.

Stating the Obvious is copyright 1995 - 1999 by Michael Sippey. All rights reserved.

## stating the obvious

1/25/99

### Welcome to "My" Parlor

Harkening back to the classic "electronic newspaper" conceit dreamed up at the beginning of the network revolution, a centerpiece of any portal worth half its market cap is news personalization (you can usually recognize it by the annoying prefix "my"). You provide some demographic data and check some preference boxes, they serve up your customized set of linked headlines.

In an effort to achieve what pundits and analysts call "stickiness," the links are nearly always limited to the news portals can co-brand or host on their servers, which typically means bland reporting from Reuters. By confining you within their castle walls and placating you with whatever content gruel they've managed to hoard, they baldly flout this technology called the "Web," which is explicitly designed to leverage the power of interconnectedness.

**out there:**
Need another free email account? Of course you do.

Bucking the trend, however, are Snap and MSN. These two forgo the Roach Motel model by being so bold as to feature links to content and news all over the web -- instead of just to stories housed in their own databases -- and in the process provide a superior content experience. With their rotating lists of external headlines, Snap and MSN essentially offer smart, updated bookmark pages. Business news from my.yahoo.com means factoid reporting from a wire feed; at Snap it means linked headlines to news, analysis and opinion from Business Week, CBS Marketwatch, Bloomberg and others.

A friend at Excite scoffed at this model, noting that they tried outside linking once, only to discover that Wall Street cares about two key portal statistics: page views, and the length of time users spend at the site. Snap sees things differently, of course. "We like stickiness as much as the next portal," explained Andrew Hyde, Snap's CFO, "but we don't want to rein in our users. We would rather make our service so relevant that they don't need to use other portals and keep coming back to use Snap as their window to the web."

Hyde explains Snap's policy as "putting the users first." And for good reason. The Web is bigger than any one site can ever hope to be (yes, even Yahoo!), and it doesn't take long for users to learn that. When offered the choice, whom would you rather be -- the spider traversing her own strands on the web, or the fly stuck in it?

-- a *Brand Peter Me* thought product

**1 | 2**
Unassuming and elegant layout *(above and left)* often conceals a barb. The archive is worth a visit.

**3 | 4**
Accurate spelling, attention to broken links, correct use of frames and repeating backgrounds, sensitivity to type color and contrast, elegant interface design, good use of HTML heading styles—all these issues are routinely ignored *(above right)*. Background patterning *(right)* is a lifetime's study in itself.

2

3

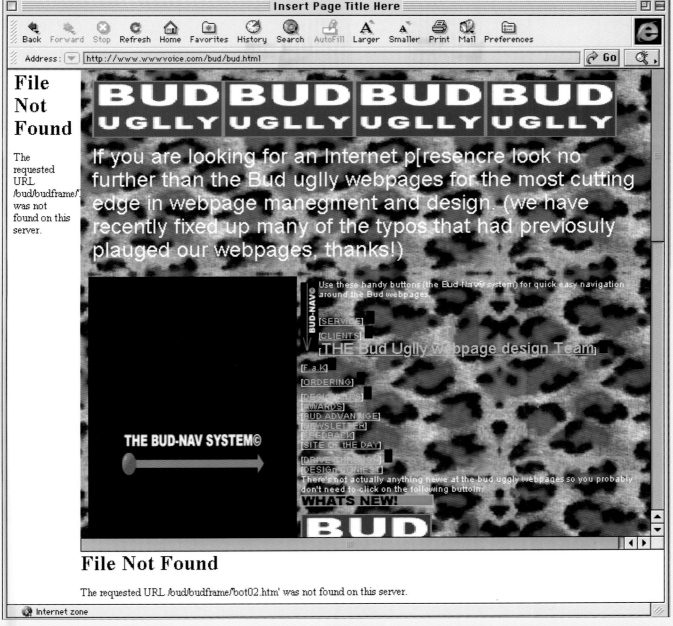

**Insert Page Title Here**

Back  Forward  Stop  Refresh  Home  Favorites  History  Search  AutoFill  Larger  Smaller  Print  Mail  Preferences

Address: http://www.wwwvoice.com/bud/bud.html   Go

# File Not Found

The requested URL /bud/budframe/1 was not found on this server.

**BUD UGLLY   BUD UGLLY   BUD UGLLY   BUD UGLLY**

If you are looking for an Internet p[resencre look no further than the Bud uglly webpages for the most cutting edge in webpage manegment and design. (we have recently fixed up many of the typos that had previosuly plauged our webpages, thanks!)

THE BUD-NAV SYSTEM©

BUD-NAV®

Use these handy buttons (the Bud-Nav® system) for quick easy navigation around the Bud webpages.

[SERVICE]
[CLIENTS]
[THE Bud Uglly webpage design Team]
[F.a.K]
[ORDERING]
[DESIGNERS]
[AWARDS]
[BUD ADVANTAGE]
[NEWSLETTER]
[FEEDBACK]
[SITE OF tHE DAY]
[DRIVE THROUGH]
[DESIGN CONTEST]

There's not actually anything newe at the bud uglly webpages so you probably don't need to click on the following buttoin.

**WHATS NEW!**

**BUD**

## File Not Found

The requested URL /bud/budframe/bot02.htm' was not found on this server.

Internet zone

137

4

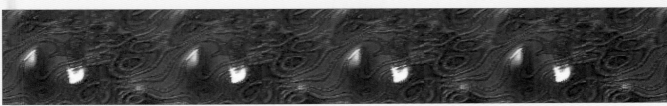

# NEW ARCHITECTURAL MOVEMENT

**A**rchitects like letters. Almost any architect's drawing that predates the age of the digital plotter shows a mannered lettering hand at work. Look for clues: the uppercase "A" with its horizontal stroke almost dragging along the ground, very compressed letterforms in combination with very large amounts of letter and word spacing. Call it enthusiasm rather than addiction. Type mania surfaces in spectacular style at Lundstrom & Associates Architects site at **www.lundstromarch.com**.

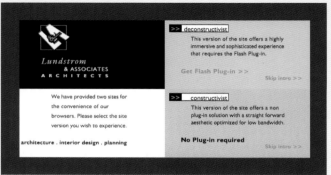

**1**
Gill Light and Medium, very sternly square in design (above), but cutting-edge cool in expression. Typeface creator Eric Gill began work in an architect's office in 1904.

**2 | 3 | 4 | 5 | 6**
Flash powers the type as it scoots around the introductory screens (left). The trademark Flash circles and arcs are in evidence as well.

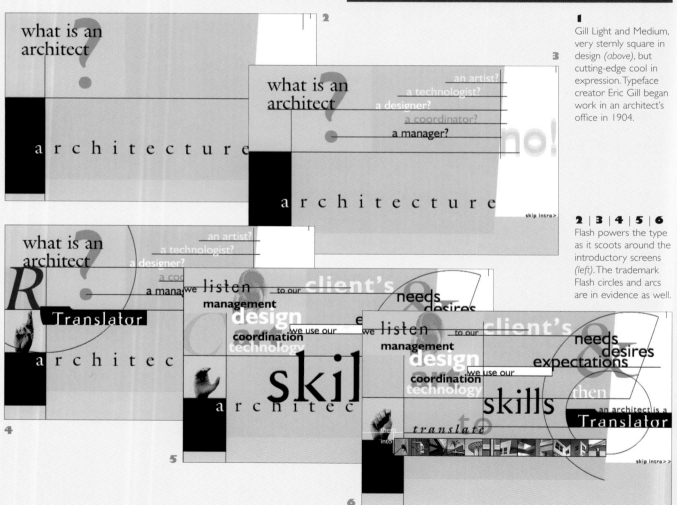

138

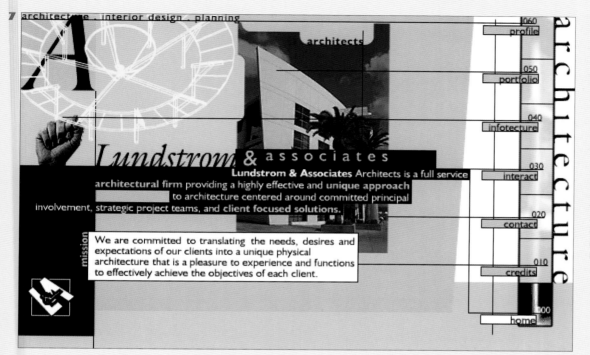

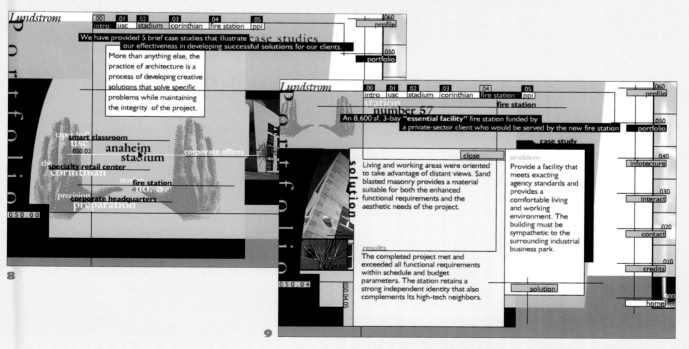

**7 | 8 | 9**

A pause for breath *(left)* and a mission statement. A little self-referential deconstructivism goes a long way: the numerals on the vertical navigation bar are taken from the site's source code location references. There are many potential typographic irritations here, especially as the portfolio section unwinds *(below)*. The crucial and redeeming ingredient is plenty of Chutzpah Bold.

# LITERARY PURSUITS

join now!

## after Dinner 16

G. Johnson
There's Nothing to See

Michael Zacks
Coffee Mug

R.K. Puma
Hers

Tony Steidler-Dennison
The Sponsor

other issues

submit a story

**1 | 2**
Understated type and soft colors lend the air of a literary salon *(left)*. Stronger stuff *(below)* with electric-blue drop shadows and leaping letters. Strangely, there are no links between these two sites.

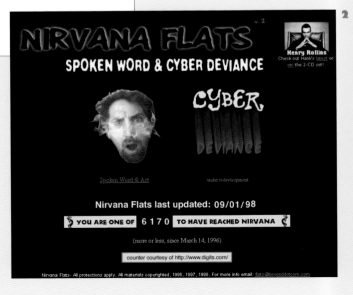

The book is dead, a British multimedia publisher once famously proclaimed. Pockets of bookishness live on, however. Visits to **www.afterdinner.com** and **www.beyonddotcom.com** offer opportunities to read new works and submit your own. Internet bookselling is hot—Barnes & Noble **www.barnesandnoble.com** slug it out with Amazon and others. Even the dusty old book collector is catered to with out-of-print services.

3

**Books** Home | Software | Magazines | Bargain Books | ▶Shopping Cart | ▶Your Account | ▶Help Desk

Search | Browse Subjects | Recommended | Gifts | Computer Books | Kids | Bestsellers | Out of Print

March 7, 1999

**The World at a Click**
Need books *en français*?
Try bol.fr.
Want a good read *auf Deutsch*?
Visit bol.de.

**Quick Search**
Title ▾
[ ] GO!
Power Search: Books

**Browse Subjects**
Africana ▾
GO!

🏫 **Buy Starbucks® Coffee**

**Oprah's Book Club™**
Set in postwar Germany, THE READER tells the deeply moving tale of a young boy's erotic awakening.

Dell Computer and IBM have announced a $16 billion partnership.

More Books in the News

**Frequent Flyer Miles** with your purchase! GO

**Preorder Bill Gates's book now!** CLICK HERE

**All Things Oprah!**

**Find a B&N Store**
ZIP your way to the B&N store nearest you:

ZIP [ ] GO!

✓ **Visit the Tax Answer Center**

**Sell Books on Your Site and Earn Commissions!** BECOME AN AFFILIATE

**Who's Online?**
Click here now to find out!

## barnesandnoble.com
### IF WE DON'T HAVE YOUR BOOK, NOBODY DOES

Ships in 24 hours! The orders for MONICA'S STORY are coming in fast and furiously. The world's most famous intern caused a sensation when she gabbed with Barbara Walters, but she saved her juiciest stuff for bestselling Princess Di biographer Andrew Morton. Read the preface. Also published simultaneously in RocketEdition format. More Monica

**DISCOVER** GREAT NEW WRITERS
And the winner is: Carrie Brown's moving and lyrical ROSE'S GARDEN takes home the 1998 Barnes & Noble Discover Great New Writers Award for the year's best first novel. Discover your own inner author, and write a review! More Fiction

**CELEBRATE WOMEN'S HISTORY MONTH**
**SILENT SPRING**
**Women's Works** Rachel Carson's SILENT SPRING -- the cautionary book that launched the modern environmental movement -- has never been out of print since its publication in 1962. And the new edition of this influential and (sadly) still relevant classic has an introduction by Vice President Al Gore, who explains that his mother emphasized the book's importance to him in a way that quite literally changed his life.

▶ Find out how Julie Grau and Cindy Spiegel became the visionary literary editors behind Suze Orman's inspiring THE COURAGE TO BE RICH in our exclusive bn interview!

**AUTHORS ONLINE**
photo: John Greene
If you caught PBS's "The Charlie Rose Show" yesterday, you witnessed something pretty cool -- author interviews taped at a B&N Manhattan bookstore. Charlie's guests included Patricia Cornwell, Elizabeth Strout, and New York Times Book Review editor Charles McGrath. If you missed the show, though, not to worry -- you can listen to it in our special audio feature "Behind the Scenes with Charlie Rose."

**Don't Miss...**
**Events and Contests** Surprises -- and prizes

**Disney Books** More Mulan mania

**Blue Mountain Arts®** Email cards and books

**Dummies Books™** Tackle any topic

**The New Yorker** Cartoon of the Week

**Reader's Catalog** The best books in print

**The New York Times** Book Review highlights

**Quarterly Black Review** The Black Book Review

**The New York Review of Books** Books for the

▶**First-Time Buyers:** Top Ten Reasons to buy your books from us!

▶**Our Music Store Is Coming Soon!** Enter your email address below, and we'll let you know about our grand opening.
[ ] Sign Up!

▶**Not in Print? Not a Problem** We have over 6 million out-of-print, used, and rare books! Start your treasure hunt here.

▶**Online Gift Certificates** Buy now -- they're fast, easy, and always fit. Redeem now -- if you received an email gift certificate.

**IN OUR SOFTWARE STORE**
**Stay Fiscally Fit** Don't feel taxed! TURBOTAX interviews you, completes your forms, and prints them out ready to file -- all while helping you pay the lowest legal taxes you can. Now get a $5 mail-in rebate and $50 credit toward setting up your own e*trade account!

**IN COMPUTER BOOKS**
**You Say You Want a Revolution** Take a look into the future of operating systems with internationally known software developer Ari Kaplan, whose NT 5: THE NEXT REVOLUTION offers an in-depth, independent perspective. Now 40% off!

**THIS WEEK'S FEATURES**
▶ The AHS GREAT PLANT GUIDE is a treasure trove of gardening info -- and it's small enough to take with you when you're plant shopping or just digging in your backyard. ( Home and Garden)

▶ Meet 60 women who dared to dream and make a living doing what they love -- be it making furniture or jewelry or restoring historic inns -- in the inspiring, practical, and gorgeously illustrated THE BUSINESS OF BLISS. (Small Business)

**NPR's Selected Shorts** Great actors reading short stories

**Electronic Books** The Rocket eBook™

**Northern Light** Over five million articles First $25 free

**textbooks.com** Buy college textbooks online!

---

## barnesandnoble.com

**Out-of-Print and Used Search Results**

**around the world on a bicycle**

We found 1 matching titles.
1 - 1 are displayed below in **alphabetical order.**

**Around The World On A Bicycle.**
Birchmore, Fred A.
**Condition:** First Edition. Hardcover. Good in Good Dustjacket. Wear to edges of dustjacket. Illustrated with b&w photographs. Peddle the planet and relive history with Fred Birchmore, the first person to circle the globe on a bicycle on the eve of World War II. ISBN: 1-887813-12-8.
**Format:** Hardcover / First Edition / Dust Jacket
**Associated Dealer:** Academy Street Books     Lincolnton, NC
**Our Price:** $15.00
▶ Buy this book or read more about it

▶ Refine Search
▶ Search Tips

141

**3**
A cornucopia of new titles clamors for attention *(left).* Books sell better with covers facing out on conventional shelving. The thin blue link is the equivalent of just a visible spine.

**4 | 5**
The Net might have been made for searching for out-of-print books. And it often works. This 1888 copy of *Around the World on a Bicycle (right)* is short of its companion volume, which begins the circumnavigation. This time, the search sadly produced only a later impostor *(top).*

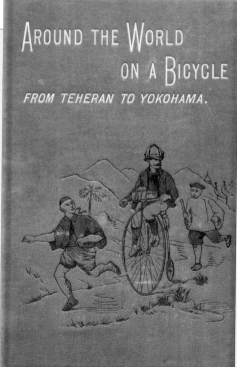

# TYPOGRAPHIC SOURCES

**At** the site maintained by the custodians of Basque typography, **www.visite-online.tm.fr/basqueletter**, it is advised that the traditional hand-cut letters should be used only as drop capitals in conjunction with serifed setting. The Basques were given the basics of letter design in stone by the occupying Romans, but not the tools with which to incise them. Over time, a simpler reductive technique was developed, resulting in characters that stand in relief of the surface. This, unfortunately, does not make for longevity—almost all pre-16th-century inscriptions are now illegible.

Celtic letterforms are preserved and developed by Michael Everson at **www.indigo.ie**. More general typographic enthusiasm is at **www.subnetwork.com**.

**1**

TOUƟES LES
LETTRES BASQUES

LISTE NON-EXHAUSTIVE
DES DIFFERENTS
TYPES DE LETTRES BASQUES
CONNUES À CE JOUR

PRIX DE CES ALPHABETS

Cliquez sur l'alphabet de votre choix...

CLASSIC

Modern

KARITZAGA

EMAKHOR

ETXEAK

FERRUS

OSƟƟA

GERNIKA

iROULeGUiA

KARAKO

KAXKO

(KUTXAS)

SCVLPTVRES

**2**

LA ƟOMBE BASQUE

LIVRE EDITE
A COMPTE D'AUTEUR
PAR
LOUIS COLAS

**1 | 2 | 3**
Fonts are available for downloading *(far left)*, and they are based on scholarly research *(left)*. The Chino, California, site of the Basque Dance Group **www.gaudenbat.com** follows style *(below)* with rendered GIFs, and invites you to conversation in the TXAT room.

HOME • CONVERSATION • DISCUSSION • LINKS
INTERNET CONTACT BOOK • PICTURE GALLERY
BASQUE CLUBS • BASQUE RESTAURANTS
GAUDEN BAT HISTORY • TXAT ROOM
UPDATES • E-MAIL • NEWS
NEW!! ORRIALDEA ELKARRIZKETAKO EUSKERAN

**3**

4

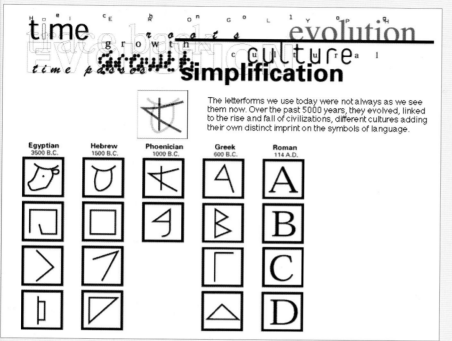

**simplification**

The letterforms we use today were not always as we see them now. Over the past 5000 years, they evolved, linked to the rise and fall of civilizations, different cultures adding their own distinct imprint on the symbols of language.

| Egyptian | Hebrew | Phoenician | Greek | Roman |
| 3500 B.C. | 1500 B.C. | 1000 B.C. | 600 B.C. | 114 A.D. |

143

5

**4 | 5**
Character analysis *(above)* is backed up with interactive Flash animations explaining the structure of letterforms and type terminology.

**6**
The generic term for these Celtic scripts *(right)* is "Ogham." Michael Everson's interests also include Unicode, the universal keyboard system.

6

**EVERSON TYPOGRAPHY**

**CeltScript**

**Everson Mono**

Member of **typeright**

Member of **TYPO-L**

*Ceanannas*

aábḃcċdḋeéfḟ
gġhiíjklmṁnoó
pṗqrsṡtṫuú
vwŵxyŷz
aábḃcċdḋeéfḟ
gġhiíjklmṁnoó
pṗqrnsſṡſṫtċuú
vwŵxyŷz
1234567890ȝȝſ

# SOMEDAY, ALL SITES WILL BE MADE THIS WAY

## < typospace >

Welcome to <typospace>, the award-winning site on Dynamic Information on the World Wide Web. Please take a quick moment to review your options:

**<typospace> 2.0 ✱**
is the latest iteration of <typospace>. A single-page "weblication" that makes extensive use of cutting-edge Dynamic HTML features allowing you to fully customise information and content. Dynamically scroll through texts, use contextual menus and your keyboard to navigate through an immersive and application-like information space.

**<typospace> 2.0 Webtop**
Will display the site as the background of your desktop, without any browser "chrome". You need to allow Netscape 4 to handle a secure script if you want to see this option.

**<typospace>**
is the slightly modified version of the original released in 1996. Similar content as above, not quite as fancy. Viewable with all browsers.

<typospace> 2.0 and <typospace> are copyright <u>Thomas Noller</u> 1996 – 98.
Last updated: May 98. ✱ requires Netscape 4+ browser. MSIE version is under development.

Thomas Noller, Dynamic HTML enthusiast and minimalist typographer, demonstrates the multilayered possibilities of DHTML at **typospace.drikka.net**. The promise is to give the user (Netscape only, for now) interactivity in the fullest sense, thereby making the experience more akin to using a sophisticated software application than just watching TV.

**1 | 2**
Sedate HTML explanations *(above)* precede the innovations, but somebody has to suffer *(right)* to make it all work.

Loading ...

July 9. Too little time to work on it...
tnoller@typospace.de

**4**
A leafy diversion
*(below)*—before falling
into the Stygian gloom.

4

< typospace > 2.0

Comments, bugs, improvements, critique.

This presentation works somewhat like an application. To toggle the main menu
hold down CTRL and click anywhere on the empty black area down here. To toggle
a submenu press CTRL again and click on the respective container. You can open
as many containers as you wish at one time. Follow the online tips in the status bar
(to the upper left) for more navigation short-cuts.

Introduction
Examples
Tutorials
Links
Resources
Opinions
Feedback

5

< typospace > 2.0

1 | 1998

Control-click a section for the contextual submenu.

**5 | 6 | 7**
A few moments of
instruction *(above)*,
and you are at the
wheel. Active screens
*(left and below)* show a
panel of information
being dragged under
the viewer's control,
then receding into the
background in favor of
a newly selected topic.
Discreet gridlines
follow the action.

Introduction In only a couple of years the World Wide Web has transformed from an
initially text based medium to a full-fledged multi-media universe.
This quantum jump comes at a price: it is getting ever more difficult to
find a specific piece of information.

Looking at timespans it took analog media to reach their formal climax
-- centuries in case of the book, decades in case of the moving image
-- the 4 or 5 years the graphical appearance of the World Wide Web is
around may only be the tiny tip of a gigantic iceberg to be revealed.
With this exponentially growing mass in mind one has to think about
new concepts of organizing and navigating this digital sprawl.

The core idea of web navigation is still based on the the hyperlink. In
earlier text-based definitions of the internet the hyperlink made
perfect sense. It was adding to the mediums depth by connecting sites
in a non-sequential, cross referencing manner. Since then, however,
the media has grown up and incorporated sophisticated technology such

6

< typospace > 2.0

Control-click a section for the contextual submenu.

<< prev  next >>

Examples

no one

[ 220 K ]

**Gif Animations**  No plug-in required.
Animated gifs are meanwhile the standard for animated
content on the web, especially in form of annoying
advertising banners or rotating logotypes. Their
biggest asset is that they are absolutely
cross-browser compatible and that they do not require
any plug-in extension. They also "stream" to the page
which means they start being displayed immediately
regardless if the whole information has been
downloaded or not.
As information carriers however, they are less suited
as they allow only little interaction other than being
clickable. A rather interesting effect is the
transformation of digital movies into animated gifs: Gif
Builder for example, the program usually used to
create these files, is able to read QuickTime file

7

Metallic effects are the DNA fingerprint of digital typography—to such an extent that the real world seems oddly flat after a hard day at the screen. In France, the rock and media magazine *Les Inrockuptibles* lays out its ironmongery with no inhibitions at **www.europline.com**. In Britain, the chocolate and soft-drinks conglomerate Cadbury Schweppes benefits from more malleable ingredients at **www.cadburyschweppes.com**.

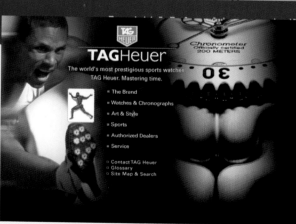

**1**
Stove doors and antique letterboxes provide the raw materials for *Les Inrockuptibles (left)*.

**2**
If your product is already metallic, like TAGHeuer's watches *(left)*, then it's more amusing to make them look like skin.

**3**
The old proud logos sit a little oddly in tandem, with their differing degrees of italicization *(above)*. Little chocolate disks are reused as buttons all over the site.

# MAD SCIENCE DIVISION

The monitor screen is not like the printed page. The intense black of the Oakley site **www.oakley.com** cannot be faithfully reproduced by lithography. Equally, the screen has an elusive quality of depth. Small type, which appears to float, and careful image preparation help maintain the desired extraterrestrial illusion.

**1 | 2**
By turns curt *(below)* and wide-measure verbose *(opposite)*, the screens insist that these are no ordinary consumer durables.

148

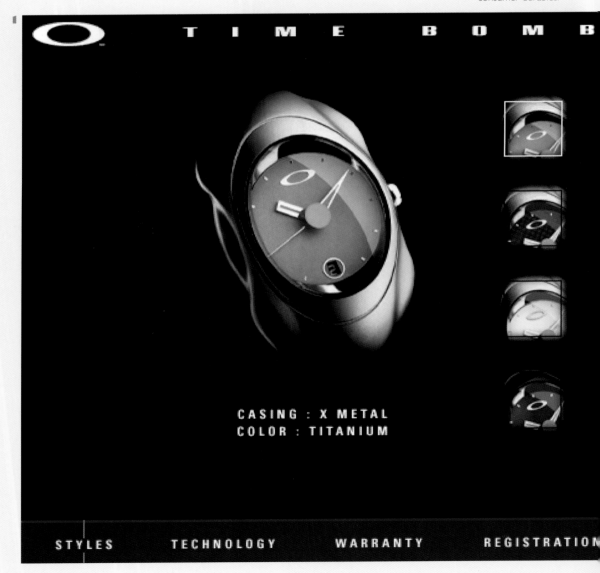

2

**3 | 4**
A relief *(below)* to
discover that even the
manufacturers are not
entirely serious. Just
time for one more
lecture *(bottom)*.

## LARIC ELLIPSOID™

ented POLARIC ELLIPSOID lens geometry is that it minimizes
s of vision. Through a highly advanced process we guard with our
ulti-radial lens geometry. It's an exponential evolution from the
hield technology. And it's vastly superior. The unprecedented
rgonomically engineered to the shape of your face. For maximum
n. And wicked sharp optics. Patent #4,867,550.

MAD SCIENCE DIVISION

3

4

## TIME BOMB™

Cradled in a sculptural metal casing, the
Oakley™ Inertial Generator™ converts human
motion into electrical current. The spin of a
precision flywheel mechanism, the O Engine™,
charges a lithium capacitor that powers the
chronometer. Proprietary World Movement™
assimilates critical technologies on a global
level, combining innovations in gearing, bearings
and microcircuitry to produce a time machine
that dismisses springs and batteries with each
flick of the wrist.

1

2

3

4

# A FACE IN THE CROWD

Old-style type designers: always middle-aged, and personally unstylish, almost inevitably male, mostly solitary, and self-effacing (but not Eric Gill), giving birth to a new design after a long and sometimes painful gestation. New-style type designers: young and smart, almost inevitably male, mostly self-possessed, and some—like the Test Pilot Collective—firmly clannish, spinning off new designs in good time for lunch. Their wares are on offer at **www.testpilotcollective.com**.

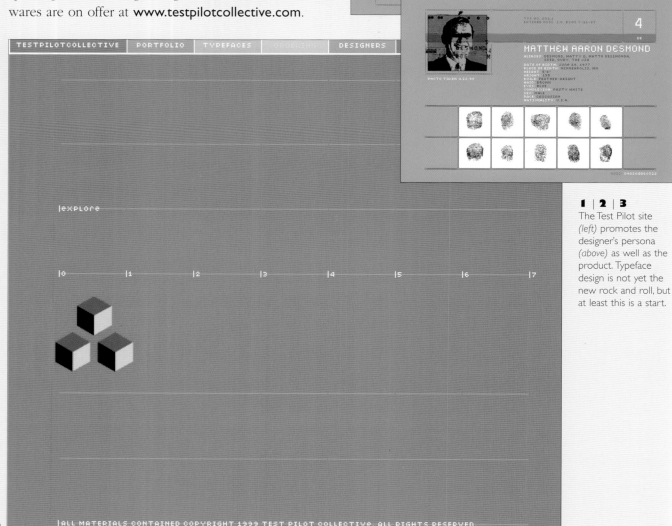

**1 | 2 | 3**
The Test Pilot site *(left)* promotes the designer's persona *(above)* as well as the product. Typeface design is not yet the new rock and roll, but at least this is a start.

150

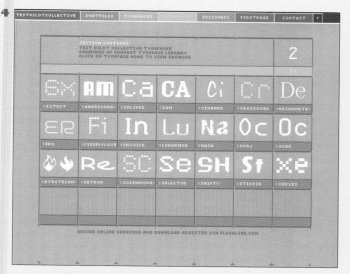

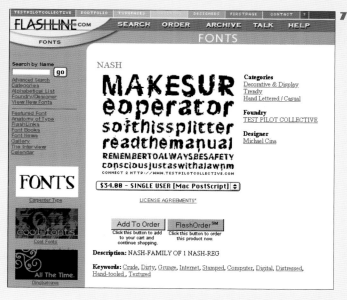

**4 | 5 | 6 | 7**

The fainthearted should not expect any concessions. Select your face *(top)* from a two-character specimen, and choose a weight from a nightmare showing *(above)*. Rest your retinas for a moment on the review of costs *(above right)*, and click on your choice. Relief is at hand, as the familiar shopping cart appears *(right)*.

★ SHOWCASE

# BUFFALO STYLE

Here are clocks, window blinds, picture frames, and garbage cans made by a former graphic designer and his industrial-designer partner, which evoke a brightly lit golden age in Middle America. The Umbra Company of Buffalo, N.Y. **www.umbra.com** has made a market all its own out of real or perceived nostalgia for an era that has hardly been laid to rest.

Does anyone recall colored plastic clip-on letters that could be fitted over fluorescent tubes? Umbra does, and also remembers overtracked and underleaded Univers Condensed (below) from a previous life.

a clock that makes time stand still

**U**
**umbra**
Find out what
you really want.
Visit The Room.

# C L O
# C K S

**umbra**

Zone Wall Clock

Rhythm Wall Clock

Fusion Wall Clock

Gyro Wall Clock

Roman Wall Clock

Spin Wall Clock

**2 | 3**
Carefully chosen colors and well-made GIFs show the **C L O C K S** to best advantage *(left)*. One day soon, the ugly pop-ups *(below)* will be replaced by glowing plug-in letters from a diner menu.

**153**

**rhythm wall clock**
**118450**

10" dia (25.4 cm dia)

Molded polypropylene with polished finish and molded lens

**$12.00**(US)

| -041 metallic black  ⬍ |

| **Add Item to my Cart** |

You can always add, remove or change your selections at the checkout.

Switch to Canadian Pricing

3

# FEATS OF ORGANIZATION

Lonely Planet **www.lonelyplanet.com** has a hard-won knowledge base. The starting point was a homemade guide book about traveling through Asia. Now there are 200 books in print; and all points of the compass, including Antarctica, are covered. The information database is augmented by grateful travelers.

Railtrack is Britain's statutory authority for railway infrastructure. It has a special place in the nation's affection, along with taxation and the common cold. The timetable site at **www.railtrack.co.uk** is a part of an attempt to reverse the massive weight of negative opinion that has accrued in recent years.

**1 | 2**
A ramble through the home page *(left)* offers many destinations. Choose Antarctica; change your mind, go to Tahiti; the system patiently responds with maps *(right)* and a link to a frantic local source *(opposite, top)*.

**3**

3

The stuff of dreams *(above)*. The Tahitians are a generous people. The right response to the qualities of their Web site design is a benign silence.

**4 | 5 | 6**

A voyage of discovery. Railtrack has a rather spartan look, with Gill and arbitrary rules *(right)*; but the curious rail traveler gets a quick and clear answer *(below and bottom)*. Railtrack, it must be remembered, is in charge of the track and not the trains.

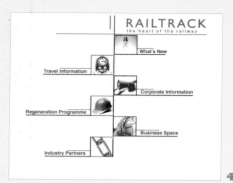

4

(155)

RAILTRACK
*Travel Information*

**Personalise** — My Timetable

**Feedback**

Regeneration Programme

Passenger News

Home

1 Enter your starting station: brighton
& your destination station: edinburgh
Via station (optional):

2 Date of Travel (dd/mm): 08/03
Time of Travel (hh mm): 16.00    Depart after ●    Arrive by ○

3 Maximum changes: [ Unlimited ⬍ ]
Avoiding London?: ○ Yes  ● No

[ Submit ]   [ Help ]

Site developers

5

6

leaves on the line... ice... snow

# RAILTRACK

Date service runs: Monday, 8th March 1999 with 3 legs. Journey Time 6:23

| From | Depart | To | Arrive | By | Class | Rsvns | Catering | Sleeper | Operator |
|---|---|---|---|---|---|---|---|---|---|
| BRIGHTON | 15:50 | LONDON VICTORIA | 16:41 | Train | First and standard class seats | | Trolley service | | Connex |
| LONDON VICTORIA | 16:56 | LONDON KINGS CROSS | 17:13 | Tube | | | | | London Underground |
| LONDON KINGS CROSS | 17:30 | EDINBURGH | 22:13 | Train | First and standard class seats | Reservations recommended | Restaurant | | Great North Eastern Railway Ltd. |

Earlier Journey    ◀ ▶    Later Journey    Return Journey    Revise Journey    New Enquiry

[ Booking Information ]

The answer to your timetable query shows the quickest journey within your chosen parameters - irrespective of cost.
Other services may operate along your route but may not suitably connect.
**Fares**. From the UK ring 0345-48-49-50. (charged at local rates)
**Booking** From UK and Overseas Click on "Booking Information" icon (in the left hand margin alongside this text) for full listing.

When booking you are advised to check that your service is unaffected by any short term alterations. Clearly state the **route** of your outward and return journey and make sure you have the correct fare for that route under the conditions of carriage. Remember the system shows the fastest - and not necessarily the cheapest route.

Please note that it is not possible to guarantee connections.

The Timetable is updated twice weekly.

Home

# ONE HAND CLAPPING

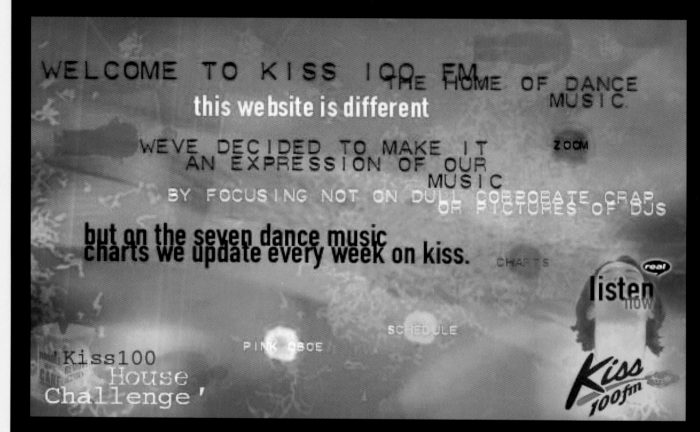

Young music enthusiasts grow middle-aged waiting for their sound clips to download—the best they can hope for is a cool screen to while away the minutes. In Britain, Kiss100's **www.kiss100.com** offers at least a live feed to the broadcast program. Peter Gabriel's Radio Real World **www.realworld.on.net** is not a radio station at all and has a different agenda. The screens are an encyclopedic tour of influences, but could use some music.

**3**

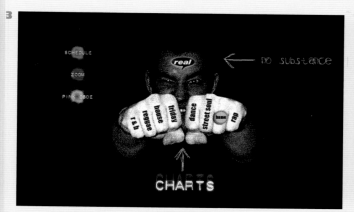

**5**

**4**

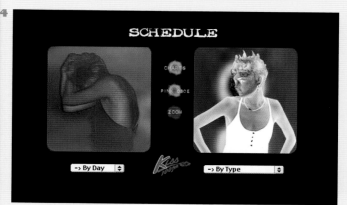

**6**

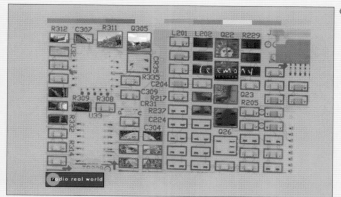

**1 | 2 | 3 | 4**

A fiery statement of intent *(opposite)*, including embossed tape and Folio Condensed. Listen to the live feed while contemplating the navigation system. A forbidding mixture of Stanley Kubrick and the Sex Pistols *(top)* symbolizes the charts. Schedules are fronted by heavily Photo-shopped women.

**5 | 6 | 7**

Radio Real World has a mixture of nature and technology for its home page *(top right)* and multimedia section *(above right)*. There is a promise of real music at **www.bathaser.com** *(right)*, but it's a long time coming.

**7**

# SEARCH, AND YE SHALL EVENTUALLY FIND

There's no entry to the Web, almost, without passing these grim portals. With a few honorable exceptions, the appearance of the average search engine has been set in stone for years. Yahoo! is beyond doubt the worst-looking. AltaVista and Infoseek show signs of a logical design process. We deserve better.

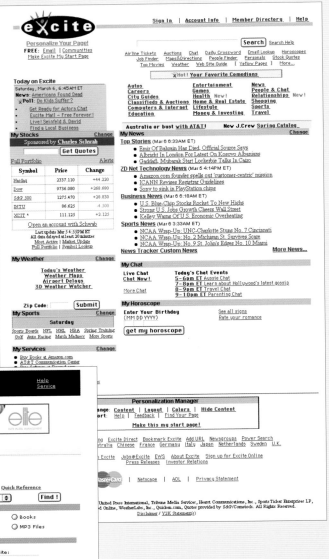

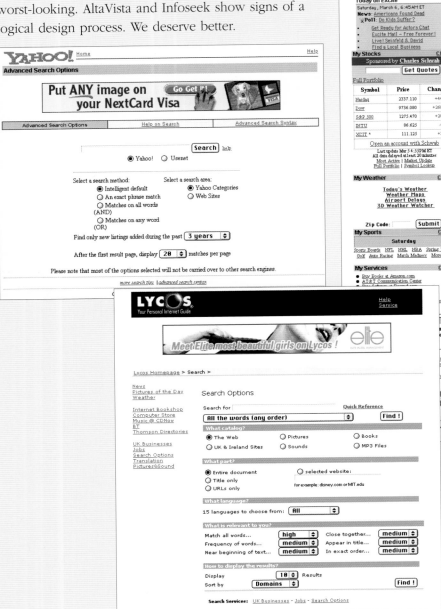

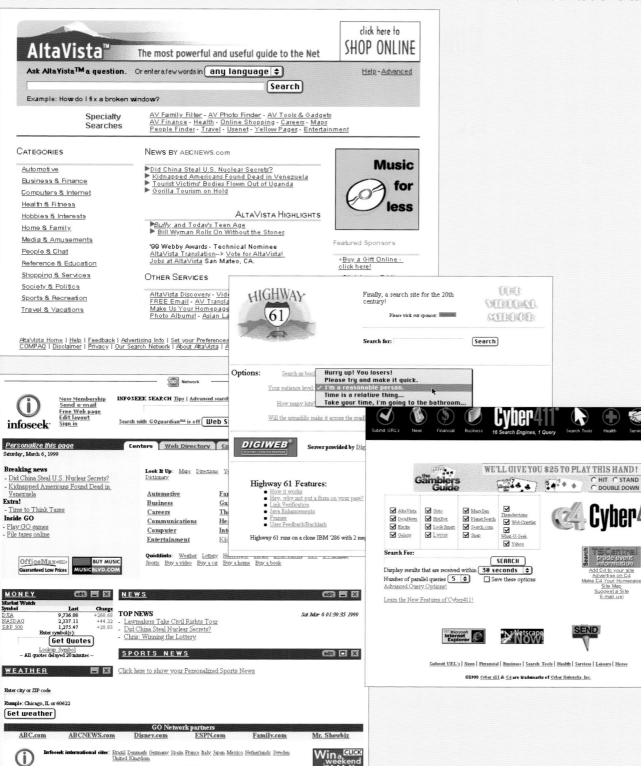

# STILL SMALL VOICE OF CALM

## This Page is Interactive Haiku Home Page

about this page :Workpaper on Lecture "InfomationMedia" by Ted Nelson

**Input your Haiku (Renga).**

NAME(Nick name):

E-mail address:

HAIKU:

After you finish putting down your message,

push this button: **WRITE**

Take the opportunity to make your own contribution to the culture of the Net. The rules are simple (and largely disregarded)—three lines only, of five, seven, and five syllables respectively. In a pinch, raw HTML code might accidentally suffice. Try **www.sfc.keio.ac.jp/~yukihiko/haiku.shtml** (the site shown here) or **sherrard@mindspring.com**, or just look for "haiku."

- Example <t93502yy@sfc.keio.ac.jp>
  "from Makoto.Ohka,"Rensi no Tanoshimi",Iwanami ,1991 "Poetry " sink

  don't sing.

  be simply

  silent.

  be simple:

  a string

  to world around

  autumn.

- Kei <keitoy@oslonett.no>
  "eating sashimi; waiting for seat Kyushu-guy."
- Yuki (Yukihiko Yoshdia) <t93502yy@sfc.keio.ac.jp>
  "Light But Not Electonic With A Sun I stand on Bridge."
- Dhugal <dhugal@ori..u-tokyo.ac.jp>
  "□$@K:$1$?$j3+$/2V2P$r8+$k$"$R$@□(J - Dhugal wasure-tari hiraku hanabi-o miru aida forgetting... for the time the fireworks blossom overhead - Dhugal (fireworks=summer) "
- stephen <sbaker@umassmed.ummed.edu>
  "the coffee brews yet unfinished the rain falls, my glasses break i am annoyed "
- max <max@vmedia.com>
  "Mount Fugi is very old. Older than very old dirt. It will erupt. Today or maybe tommorow."
- max <max@vmedia.com>
  "Handsome, attractive and Cavalier. I wept to find my new shirt."
- david <dnewman@onramp.net>
  "Dry grass locust sound Cloudless sky Too long the summer."
- greg <heflin@cs.utah.edu>
  "brite purple lites of hazy nights"
- Nuklar <ddsy60d@prodigy.com>
  "Death and Destruction I love the smell of Napalm It makes me Happy"
- meteor man <anon>
  "Far in the future an ape figure on his toes when the bomb went off "
- Jenna Lasich <plasich@ilhawaii.net>
  "Hi! I'm Jenna Lasich. I live in Kailua-Kona HI. I Like to Tap dance and am going to a big compation this summer. I have a dog named Mitzi. Here's a Haiku about her: Mitzi is my dog She likes to chew on bones Her sister's Penny"
- Jenna Lasich <plasich@ilhawaii.net>
  "Hi! I'm Jenna Lasich. I'm 11 years old. Here's a Hiku I'd like to share with you: Colors are lovely My favorit one's Purple How about your's? "
- Craizin <craizin@sirius.com>
  "The pond under stars; A bag of M&Ms floats With a dead goldfish. Evening thunderstorm; A house on a hill□□ Where are the keys? I wake up! A dog is barking In

160

# LEMON STEW

The speed and ease with which a site can be uploaded to the Net makes it an especially fertile field for foul-ups. There is a rich harvest hanging from overladen branches all over the Web. Some induce a wry smile, others—very narrow measure setting, for example—bring foam to the mouth. We all make mistakes.

## FishPager

### Fishing Reports, Wind Reports from 15 Bay locations, Bouy wind & Swell

### Tides & Fishing News via Pager

Think how often your have heard about fantastic fishing conditions AFTER they are over. By the time the news hits the magazines or the newspapers it is often too late. True, if you hang around the bait shops you get the word early, but most of us don't have that luxury.

#### Instant Reports

The FishPager is the answer for the avid fisherperson. Our crew at USAfishing will call in fishing reports directly to our pager company whenever good conditions develop. Within seconds you will receive the report via pager and can start planning your fishing trip. If suddenly the salmon are hitting or if there is heavy sturgeon action you will be among the first to know.

**GG report: Salmon 10-22 lbs. Late limits Farallons on threaded bait. Early limit on rockfish. Many small bass inside Bay. Abalone tide Sat -1.2**

**Actual size is smaller!**

#### Tiny Size

The Fish Pager uses an revolutionary new pager technology developed by Call of the Wind. The pager is so small it can fit on your keychain yet it can display up to 8 lines of razor sharp text.

#### Wind Reports

Weathger forecast

Windreports are updated every 15 minutes on your pager from: Crissy Field, Berkeley Marina, Pt. Richmond, Sherman Island/Delta, Candlestick Park, Coyote Point, Pt. San Quientin, Alameda, Santa Cruz,Bodega Bay, Tomales Bay and next season the offshore buoys.

#### More Features:

- Friends can send you lengthy personal pages in **plain english**
- Optional **nation-wide** service for personal pages
- Automatically learns **your favorite fishing areas** and puts them at the top of the list
- Plots out **histograms** of the wind speeds for each site as the reports come in.
- You can pick a distinctive alarm **sound for each wind sensor**.
- Up to **8 lines of text** can fit on a screen at a time and up to 1000 characters per page
- You can vary the **font size**...smaller for more reports at a glance or larger for legibility.

#### The Bottom Line

The cost for fishing reports will be only $12/month plus $11/month for your personal pages
To receive the pages you will need a Genius pager. We sell them at cost for $260

If your are interested in the FishPager call 707-762-9776 or e-mail

Catch of the day. Rod-caught typos all over, even a rare animated banner example. These fishermen know their typography, too. With your FishPager, you will be able to "vary the font size ... smaller for more reports at a glance or larger for legibilty." Or was that readabilty?

**2 | 3 | 4 | 5**
Lewis Baumgartner
*(left)* should stick to
farming, even so.
Others who know
better, like the Getty
Museum *(below left)*,
start in elegant style
then whack the
browser with 41 GIFs
to download. And for
what? Pale and not-
quite-circular chintz.

**6**
Magazine designers
who miss their usual
extra couple of
hundred millimeters
of page depth would
prefer us to scroll up
and down *(below)* to
avoid modifying their
concept. Neckbraces
will definitely be
needed; and probably
straitjackets, too.

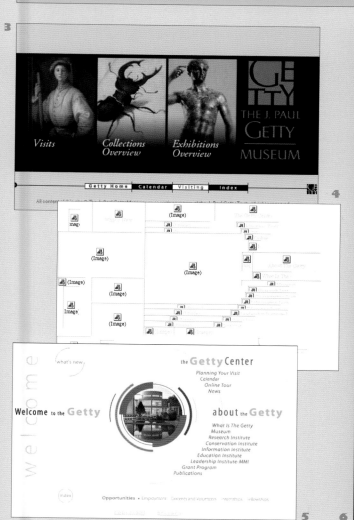

# SOMETHING NASTY IN THE BACKGROUND

Oddbins' site, is under construction so this page is just a taste of great things to come. No vine will remain untended or wine untasted as we bring you the best wine site on the Web! We know what we want, but in true Oddbins fashion, we'd like your help in getting there - we wouldn't want to get lost along the way! Please take a few moments to let us know your idea of the perfect wine web site - is it bells and whistles or facts and figures that will point your browser our way?

To whet your appetite, here's a fine selection of some of the many attractions you will find along the Sipper-Highway. These fabulous wines are our recommendations to help you enjoy the best year ever!

Click and hold to control the scrolling. If wine details do not appear in the box below, please click here for static version.

1998/9

WINE MAGAZINE
INTERNATIONAL
WINE
CHALLENGE
1998/9
WINE MERCHANT
OF THE YEAR
1998·1997·1996·1995
1992·1991·1990·1989·1988

### Coteaux du Layon Château de la Genaiserie 1997 Soulez
*Loire* £7.99

Since 1989 and 1990, two of the Loire's best vintages EVER, the face of Coteaux du Layon has been changing. Traditionally wines for keeping, today they are more wines to drink in the vivacity of their youth. These guys have been doing the Coteaux "thang" for ages and this is a really fine expression of the style (at a great price too) - sweet and minerally, with loads of exotic fruit and a lengthy finish.

Prices are here for your guidance. Full e-commerce will be heading down the Sipper-Highway soon!

**Give us a hand**

What could be nicer than a background image that repeats itself unattended, as required, while imposing no download penalties? Almost anything. The urge to fill up the background is a primordial one in computing terms. Once, screensavers were more highly regarded than word processors, and these cozily carpeted screens are tragic reminders of those days.

One of Britain's most esteemed wine and spirit merchants starts out unsteadily on the "sipper highway" *(above)*. Wiser counsels must have insisted on the plaintive "give us a hand" request. It is kinder to pass quietly by on the other side, leaving Oddbins to do their "thang."

## 5

### Jeff's flat tire page!

I have a mountain bike. To be specific, I have a red and black Univega Rover Sport. I love my bike, but for some reason I seem to get a LOT of flat tires. I would really like to know why I was chosen to run over every sharp object humanity has ever created. Just for fun, here is a list of why I have had so many flats.

Various objects that have embedded themselves in my bike tires:

1. Small thumbtack, white

2. Rusty nail, about 1/2 inch long

3. Safety pin, really not that safe at all...

4. Shard of clear glass

5. Large, sharp, jagged rock on Olentangy River Road

6. Long, slow leak. Cause: unknown.

7. Sharp Concrete street curb

8. This isn't really an object, but I had a really interesting flat when I went biking with Elaine. When we were on our way home, somehow my bike came halfway off the bike rack on the trunk of the car and the tire started dragging on the road. Well, you can sorta imagine what happened. When we got home I found a nice 3 inch gash in the tire and the tube. Lovely.

Well, thats about it so far, but I'm sure I'll run over more sharp stuff in the near future. Check back for updates!

## 5

"They laughed when I sat down at the keyboard." Can it really be true that there are sites constructed solely for inclusion in anthologies of bad design? Jeff's flat tire page *(left)* suggests that it might well be so.

## 6

Apostrophes from the word processor, backgrounds from hell. And Greg *(below)* has many more like these.

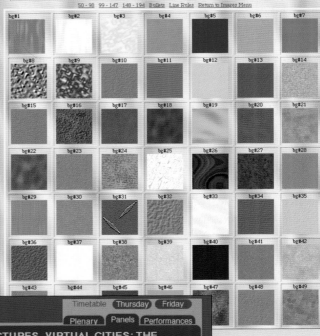

### Greg's WebWorx

### BACKGROUNDS 1 - 49

Below are #1 - #49 background images displayed 75 X 75 to use in your web pages. To see a background displayed in full with a selection of different font colored text, click desired background image. If your having Greg's WebWorx design your web site then write down the image # for later reference.

To copy any image below using Microsoft Internet Explorer or Netscape Navigator browser:
1. Place your cursor over the image you want to save on your hard drive.
2. For PC or UNIX-based users, right-click the mouse button. For Macintosh users, click and hold the mouse button. A small pop-up menu appears.
3. Choose the "Save image as" or "Download image" option from this menu. Choose where to save a copy of the image on your hard drive.

After you download the graphic to your computer, if your creating your own web pages then you will need to upload it to your Internet Service Provider (ISP) to have it appear on your site. Please contact your ISP for instructions on uploading HTML files and graphics.

50 - 98   99 - 147   148 - 194  Bullets   Line Rules   Return to Images Menu

## 2

With increasing use of high technology, the design and print business is ever more careless of its history. The St. Bride Printing Library *(below)* has struggled for years for friends and finance.

## 3 | 4

It's not just the shape and color of the words, it's what they say. If you've ever been patinated in Liverpool, you'll be an expert on cyclic completion and severance. However, you're already too late for the pleasures of the ISEA 98 Revolution *(below)*.

If you care at all about punch-cutters, dragon's blood, and litho stones, it's time to show some solidarity. Join in, take out a subscription, and make them change the diseased-lung-section background.

## 2

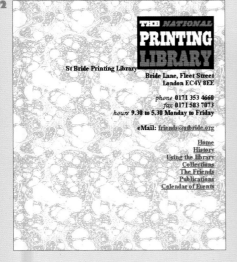

### THE NATIONAL PRINTING LIBRARY

**St Bride Printing Library**

**Bride Lane, Fleet Street**
**London EC4Y 8EE**

*phone* **0171 353 4660**
*fax* **0171 583 7073**
*hours* **9.30 to 5.30 Monday to Friday**

eMail: friends@stbride.org

Home
History
Using the Library
Collections
The Friends
Publications
Calendar of Events

## 3

# NEVER GO WITH STRANGERS

**1**

## Web site and page design for people who hate ugly sites...

If you want help and don't know where to go, this is where you should start.

**TOUR BAD BLOOD DESIGN STUDIO**

**TOUR THE TECHNICAL SIDE**

Some people like to browse by topic...so these are for you.

**Web Site Design**

Do your research
Site requirements
Hiring us
Design Process
Pricing
Finishing up
**Get Technical**

Online Documents
Put all those manuals on the web or CD.

Technical Writing
Some of the best are staffed right here. Specializing in telecommunications.

Technical Illustration
Help your readers understand the tech-talk. More graphics equals better comprehension!

BAD BLOOD
DESIGN STUDIO

Web World
we ask.
we research.
we design.

Tech World
we ask. we research.
we write.

Our World
subscribe now. tips. tricks.
professional help, without the cost

Have questions? We have answers! If you can't find it here, email us.
We'll find the information for you and post it in one of the forums in Our World!

BADazine. Get updated information about the industry...web and more.
Xspurt. Insider tips on Framemaker, Adobe PDF, Quark and others.

**2**

### Technical Writing - Technical Illustration - Telecommunications - Online Documentation
**Support for your Publications Group**

The techncial support group at Bad Blood Design Studio specializes in technical documentation for Telecommunication firms. By out sourcing the technical documentation to Bad Blood Design, telecommunication firms can get back to researching, developing, and building the state-of-the-art equipment that makes this industry so dynamic. We provide experienced technical writers with extensive of knowledge in telecommunications, the industry, the equipment, and most of all, the documentation that supports it.

**1 | 2**

Equipped with a heliotrope home page *(left)*, these technicians are so eager to please that they have at least two ways of spelling technical *(bottom)*.

**3 | 4**

Frightened by a roman character at an early age, the folks at Mardair *(right)* have got it all buttoned up. What a day it must have been when they realized that slopy type could be slanted backwards to make it look groovy! Nearly as good as the time they discovered initial caps and vaguely hanging subheads *(far right)*.

**3**

Technical & Commercial Illustration

Exhibit / Display Design and Detailing

Website Design and Management

Documentation & Charting

Caricatures and Custom Cartoons

Old folk art has kind and venerable grandmothers who can show you how to carve filigree eggshells and make table mats out of dog's hair. The new folk art of the Internet is the preserve of competing witch-doctors with miraculous design touchstones. So, join up either with Mardair's postmodernist slanty-shadowed button school, or arrange your trophies on Chris Miller's brown italic shelves. Click to begin.

**5**

Chris Miller
PSU - FIPSE

*Website Design*
## INTRODUCTION

Website_Design
Organization
Style Guide
Audience
Page Size
Layout

Web Images

Related_Tutorial
Scanning
Images

Chris's Home

Introduction — If you've spent much time exploring, or surfing the World Wide Web, you've almost certainly encountered some badly designed Web sites. Since almost anyone can create Web pages, it's not surprising that many sites are confusing, overwhelming, ugly, or incredibly slo-o-o-ow. Tantalizing content can be hidden forever from the world when a site is poorly designed.

Web imposes its own design limitations— While it's not easy to create a well-designed site, following a few rules can help. These are not rigid commandments, but rather suggestions to assist you in the process of creating a site. At the same time, though, Web technology imposes its own set of design limitations—in many ways more confusing than print.

# Presents a Superior image of your Company and your Products and Services

**Mardair Design Studio** places your company, your product or your service image to achieve maximum appeal for your current and potential clients.

Whether your needs are on the sales front or on the production line, Mardair can integrate a comprehensive package of sales and technical materials into your direct mail and your Internet website presence.

Serving the Exhibit, Cabinetry and Construction industries, Mardair provides design solutions and accurate drawings. These technical drawings and renderings enhance sales presentations and enable cost effective fabrication and installation. Mardair can be a valuable asset to your company's production team.

A diverse range of illustration services allows Mardair to provide enhancements for your sales and production capabilities.

Who we are    Contact Us

Technical Illustration | Exhibit Design & Detailing | Website Design & Management
Documentation & Charting | Caricatures & Cartoon Art | Contact Us

©1998 Mardair Design. All Rights Reserved.
Questions or Comments about our website? Contact Webmaster.

**7**

StudioDave *(right)* has it all in full measure, and he wants you to have it too. A generous soul, and way above cheap criticism.

**4**

**A New Age in Marketing**

**Getting and Keeping your audience**

**Maintaining your Web Presence**

**Are you baffled by the technology or terminology?**

Now that it seems that everybody and their mother has a web site, the savvy marketing exec has to wonder if the World Wide Web is really the best place to invest their advertising dollars. We have strategies to stage a site that targets the right demographic groups and commands their attention.

After the eye-catching images have convinced your visitor to check out your web site, it's time for the interactive features to come alive. We can make your web site ask to be explored with innovative graphics and enticing text.

Continuing to nourish your audience with new product highlights and current affairs can absorb hours of your precious time. We can track and report to you on the volume of visitors and tweak your site to assure it remains a consistently effective marketing tool .

The Web Wonder answer page is just one click away…ask us any internet question here.

**5 | 6**

There's little traditional heraldry on the Web, so it's a pleasure to collect Chris Miller's emblem *(opposite, below)*—two pizza shovels crossed with a chipboard pipe-rack. And he takes his own advice *(below)* when designing his faculty's psyc(h)ology pages.

---

## Welcome To StudioDave

Scroll Down the Page to See What's Here, or Highlight a Selection and Click Go! to Navigate StudioDave

[ StudioDave Home ] [Go!]
There is also a Navigation Table at the bottom of every page

If you're looking for Web or Graphics Design, Free Web Page and HTML help, Free Graphics and Images, Original Artwork, Midi files, Resources, Ideas, Answers, Entertainment, Games, You might as well Bookmark this page right now

### A little about myself?

I'm an Award Winning Artist and Sign Contractor in Beautiful South Texas. I live six blocks from the Beach. Ever hear the song "Margaritaville" by Jimmy Buffet? You get the idea... Anyway, I saw Web Design as a logical extention of my talents and interests. What initially began as a hobby is now a growing business and one of my *favorite* things to do. In the process I've accumulated a wealth of info, resources and knowledge that I'm more than willing to share with "Personal Homepage Builders" *free of charge.*

### Contents of StudioDave

**MIDI JUKEBOX** – While you're here, stop by my Midi Page and click on a song to listen to while you surf.

**WEB DESIGN** – Basic Price guide. I also do Custom Computer Graphics, Images and Desktop Publishing.

...

**GAMES/PUZZLES** – Okay, so you're bored. Take a break! Have some *fun!*

**HOW TO KEEP AN IDIOT BUSY** … at *least* for a couple of minutes. Okay, so maybe this page belongs on the java page.. but we don't want to crash your browser by stuffing too many applets down it's throat at once.

**JAVA/JAVASCRIPT** – This is my Java and Javascript playground. Some cool effects and gadgets, and some neat interactive scripts for you to play with. And lots more on the way.

**LINKS PAGE** – If you can't find it at StudioDave I suggest you check out my Huge Categorized Links Page. Something for everybody. I promise! Want to Suggest a link? Please do.

**SEARCH** – All the Major Search Engines on one page! Easily Search the Internet from StudioDave.

**FAMILY & FRIENDS** – I hear you're not supposed to put a personal page up on a Commercial Website. Doesn't look "professional." Oh well. I did it anyway, and added a little bit of South Texas for flavor.

**FREE TAROT** – Want to explore the Esoteric side of life? Welcome to one of most popular "Parlor Games" in the Twentieth Century…or *is* it a game…

**GUESTBOOK** – You *weren't* going to leave without signing my guestbook, were you? I didn't *think* so…

*Can't find what you want at StudioDave?*
I will be updating all StudioDave pages and adding new content on a regular basis so keep checking back.
*A very good reason to BOOKMARK STUDIODAVE right now!*
Or just Email me and, if I can, I'll share what I've got or point you in the right direction.

Questions? Comments?    Suggestions? Requests?

I am a member of

THE HTML WRITERS GUILD

---

## Psycology 523 Course Page

### ψ PSYCHOLOGY 523 / 623
### COURSE PAGE
### PORTLAND STATE UNIVERSITY

PSY 523
Syllabus
Course
Homework
Resources
Grades
Site Map

Perrin's Home

PSU
PSY Dept.

Click Here to get back to the style Guide

**Course Information:**
- **Course:** PSY 523/623, Spring Term
- **Class Time:** TTh 12:00 - 1:50
- **Class Location:** NH 366

**Instructor:**
- **Nancy Perrin**
- **Office:** 103 Systems Science Building
- **Office Hours:**
  - 2 -3 Thursday,
  - or by appointment, call 725-5060
- **Phone:** 725-5058

167

# FADE TO BLACK

**W**hile patient and constructive criticism might sometimes restrain the more ardent enthusiasts of cyberrhea, others might respond more positively to hammer-blow instruction like this extremely melancholic European view of the whole design process.

¹gräBBing them by          their eyeballs

aND rhytmically hammering nail of visual knowledge into undeveloped craniis, by exposing to imagery beyond comprehension, with imploding cohesiveness of anti-climactic multilayers, developing unique experience, simulating n-dimentional field in the context of the one[1]-dimentional cortex, randomly supressing or stimulation urge to operate "back" button either by applying pointy-ing device with certain level of clickability, or leveraging knowledge of implicit k-level vocabulary which+++++

⁰dÊÊ>>>generÄtion zeite

¹gräBBing them by          their eyeballs

²pound down on          your BRAIN

³of impeNëTrable PSYchic          VÅCÜÜM

⁴tötâl visual          (æ)ññihïlÆtiöñ

**1 | 2**
The lesson begins *(above)* with fiercely anatomical proposals. Such panels continue until the whole philosophy has been neatly summarized *(left)*.

# COLOR MECHANICS

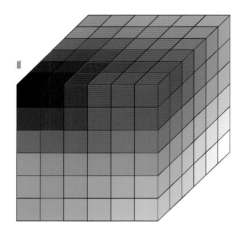

**1**
The 216-color cube
shows seven of its
eight corners (left).
Yellow (red and green
mixed at full strength)
is hidden at the back
left corner.

The tiny rosette of dots that is the basis of the four-color print process makes a dull bouquet alongside the monitor's glowing phosphors. Although the printed page has a fundamental resolution about four times finer than the screen, its apparent superiority is more than negated by the screen's much greater contrast range and highly saturated color values. The typical user, moreover, sits at least twice as far away from the screen as from a book, adding more apparent sharpness to the screen image.

With sufficient processing power, current monitors can deliver more than 16 million different colors. This is as near "true" color as makes no practical difference. Prehistoric monitors could only turn pixels on and off —screens were black-and-white (or, variously, black and green or orange). This was "one-bit" color depth, and great was the joy in the land when the frontiers were gradually pushed back through four-bit, giving 16 ($2^4$) colors, and then the eight-bit 256 ($2^8$) games standard, right up to 24-bit ($2^{24}$) with 16,777,216 colors.

Large numbers of this order won't work reliably on the Web. A handy compromise for now is a 256-color range. Subtract the 40 colors demanded for its own purposes by the computer's operating system, and you are left with 216. This offers an elegant cube with six units per edge. Another sum: 6 x 6 x 6 = 216. A cube has eight convenient corners—and the red, green, and blue electron guns at the back of the screen, when either full on or off, can produce eight combinations

of color. Put these extremes at the corners of the cube and string the intermediate colors along each edge to give a 20% difference between each color. In other words, the guns have a six-step range between 0 (completely off) and 255 (full on).

**2**

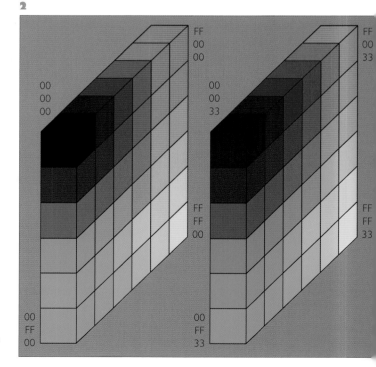

**2**
Filleted out, the cube reveals all 216 colors (right). Black (no signal at all) and white (all three guns full on) are found at diagonally opposite corners.

Only one hurdle remains. The computer needs a single character to represent numeric values. Hexadecimal comes to the rescue. In hexadecimal there are 16 values, represented by the numerals 0–9 followed by the characters A–F. Only six of these values concern us here, because of the 20% gap between one value and the next. In HTML code, colors are represented by settings for the red/green/blue guns in the paired form *rrggbb*. Since it's difficult to visualize a color labeled CC0033, Web-design software conceals the mathematics and calls it "pinkish red." Such programs will accept intermediate colors (like B0C4DE, "light steel blue"), but they will appear dithered on 256-color screens.

The flattened cube is shown (within the limitations of the four-color process) on the following two pages. The two subsequent pages then show patches of 18 selected colors overlaid with 12 different shades.

**3**

| Value | % | Hex |
|---|---|---|
| 0 = | 0% = | 00 |
| 51 = | 20% = | 33 |
| 102 = | 40% = | 66 |
| 153 = | 60% = | 99 |
| 204 = | 80% = | CC |
| 255 = | 100% = | FF |

**4**

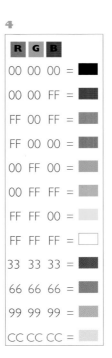

| R | G | B | |
|---|---|---|---|
| 00 | 00 | 00 = | |
| 00 | 00 | FF = | |
| FF | 00 | FF = | |
| FF | 00 | 00 = | |
| 00 | FF | 00 = | |
| 00 | FF | FF = | |
| FF | FF | 00 = | |
| FF | FF | FF = | |
| 33 | 33 | 33 = | |
| 66 | 66 | 66 = | |
| 99 | 99 | 99 = | |
| CC | CC | CC = | |

**3 | 4**
Numeric, percentage, and hexadecimal compared *(above)*. Only these values are "Web-safe" on 256-color screens. Hexadecimal settings of the three guns *(right)* show the cube's corner values, followed by the only four available grays.

171

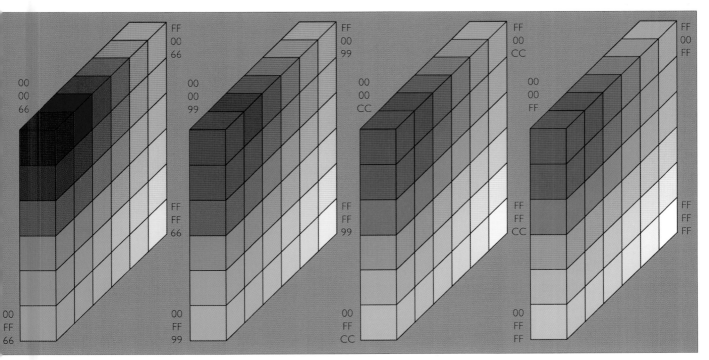

FF 00 66
00 00 66
FF FF 66
00 FF 66

FF 00 99
00 00 99
FF FF 99
00 FF 99

FF 00 CC
00 00 CC
FF FF CC
00 FF CC

FF 00 FF
00 00 FF
FF FF FF
00 FF FF

| | | | | | | | | |
|---|---|---|---|---|---|---|---|---|
| 330000 | 333300 | 336600 | 339900 | 33CC00 | 33FF00 | 66FF00 | 66CC00 | 669900 |
| 330033 | 333333 | 336633 | 339933 | 33CC33 | 33FF33 | 66FF33 | 66CC33 | 669933 |
| 330066 | 333366 | 336666 | 339966 | 33CC66 | 33FF66 | 66FF66 | 66CC66 | 669966 |
| 330099 | 333399 | 336699 | 339999 | 33CC99 | 33FF99 | 66FF99 | 66CC99 | 669999 |
| 3300CC | 3333CC | 3366CC | 3399CC | 33CCCC | 33FFCC | 66FFCC | 66CCCC | 6699CC |
| 3300FF | 3333FF | 3366FF | 3399FF | 33CCFF | 33FFFF | 66FFFF | 66CCFF | 6699FF |
| 0000FF | 0033FF | 0066FF | 0099FF | 00CCFF | 00FFFF | 99FFFF | 99CCFF | 9999FF |
| 0000CC | 0033CC | 0066CC | 0099CC | 00CCCC | 00FFCC | 99FFCC | 99CCCC | 9999CC |
| 000099 | 003399 | 006699 | 009999 | 00CC99 | 00FF99 | 99FF99 | 99CC99 | 999999 |
| 000066 | 003366 | 006666 | 009966 | 00CC66 | 00FF66 | 99FF66 | 99CC66 | 999966 |
| 000033 | 003333 | 006633 | 009933 | 00CC33 | 00FF33 | 99FF33 | 99CC33 | 999933 |
| 000000 | 003300 | 006600 | 009900 | 00CC00 | 00FF00 | 99FF00 | 99CC00 | 999900 |

172

| | | | | | | | | |
|---|---|---|---|---|---|---|---|---|
| 666600 | 663300 | 660000 | FF0000 | FF3300 | FF6600 | FF9900 | FFCC00 | FFFF00 |
| 666633 | 663333 | 660033 | FF0033 | FF3333 | FF6633 | FF9933 | FFCC33 | FFFF33 |
| 666666 | 663366 | 660066 | FF0066 | FF3366 | FF6666 | FF9966 | FFCC66 | FFFF66 |
| 666699 | 663399 | 660099 | FF0099 | FF3399 | FF6699 | FF9999 | FFCC99 | FFFF99 |
| 6666CC | 6633CC | 6600CC | FF00CC | FF33CC | FF66CC | FF99CC | FFCCCC | FFFFCC |
| 6666FF | 6633FF | 6600FF | FF00FF | FF33FF | FF66FF | FF99FF | FFCCFF | FFFFFF |
| 9966FF | 9933FF | 9900FF | CC00FF | CC33FF | CC66FF | CC99FF | CCCCFF | CCFFFF |
| 9966CC | 9933CC | 9900CC | CC00CC | CC33CC | CC66CC | CC99CC | CCCCCC | CCFFCC |
| 996699 | 993399 | 990099 | CC0099 | CC3399 | CC6699 | CC9999 | CCCC99 | CCFF99 |
| 996666 | 993366 | 990066 | CC0066 | CC3366 | CC6666 | CC9966 | CCCC66 | CCFF66 |
| 996633 | 993333 | 990033 | CC0033 | CC3333 | CC6633 | CC9933 | CCCC33 | CCFF33 |
| 996600 | 993300 | 990000 | CC0000 | CC3300 | CC6600 | CC9900 | CCCC00 | CCFF00 |

173

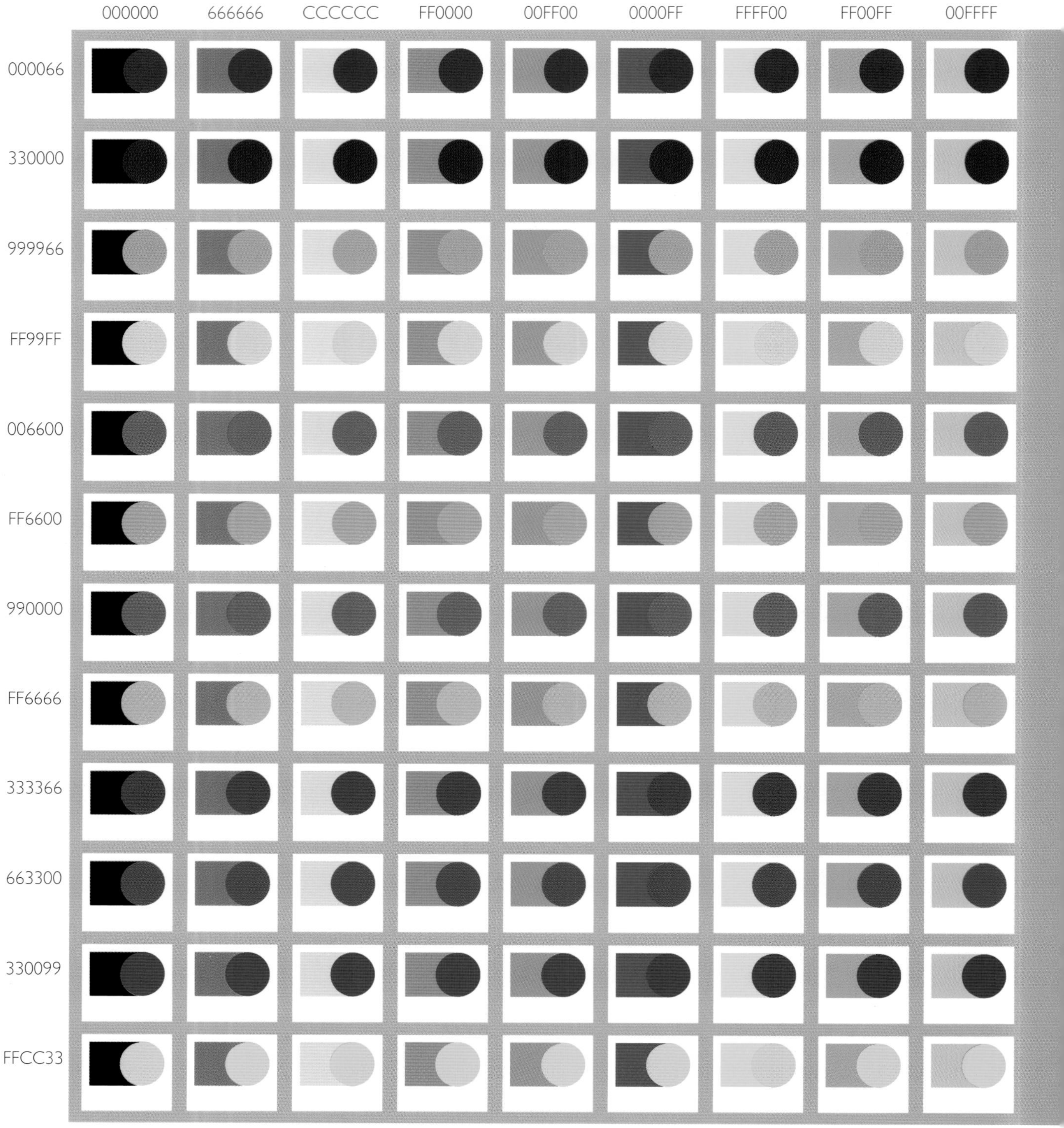
000000
666666
CCCCCC
FF0000
00FF00
0000FF
FFFF00
FF00FF
00FFFF
000066
330000
999966
FF99FF
006600
FF6600
990000
FF6666
333366
663300
330099
FFCC33

| CC0000 | CC00CC | 0000CC | 00CCCC | 00CC00 | CCCC00 | 336633 | 99CC99 | CCFF66 | |
|--------|--------|--------|--------|--------|--------|--------|--------|--------|--------|
| | | | | | | | | | 000066 |
| | | | | | | | | | 330000 |
| | | | | | | | | | 999966 |
| | | | | | | | | | FF99FF |
| | | | | | | | | | 006600 |
| | | | | | | | | | FF6600 |
| | | | | | | | | | 990000 |
| | | | | | | | | | FF6666 |
| | | | | | | | | | 333366 |
| | | | | | | | | | 663300 |
| | | | | | | | | | 330099 |
| | | | | | | | | | FFCC33 |

Can you imagine a world with only one typeface to serve as the vehicle for all communication? How content would you be to see the same face on your supermarket i.d. card as on a wedding invitation? Would you take the taxman seriously if he wrote to you in Hobo? The way computers work makes it easy to use the same group of faces over and over. In the interests of keeping typographic options open, here follows a symbolic and arbitrary selection of mostly improving quotations set in fonts widely available in both Macintosh and Windows environments. Opposite, a nod to the Windows/Macintosh size disparity issue.

**Where none admire, 'tis useless to excel; where none are beaux, 'tis vain to be a belle.**
GEORGE, LORD LYTTELTON
**IMPACT**

No more things should be presumed to exist than are absolutely necessary
WILLIAM OCCAM
DEL A ROBBIA

In the affluent society no useful distinction can be made between luxuries and necessaries.
K GALBRAITH, *The Affluent Society*
**SAND REGULAR**

All great truths begin as blasphemies.
GEORGE BERNARD SHAW
*Annajanska.*
COURIER

**No gentleman has soup for luncheon.**
LORI CURZON OF KEDLESTON
**VINETA**

All kings is mostly rapscallions.
MARK TWAIN *The Adventures of Huckleberry Finn*
TREBUCHET

The louder he talked of his honour, the faster we counted our spoons.
RALPH WALDO EMERSON *Worship.*
**WASHOUT THIN**

*Ah, what a dusty answer gets the soul When hot for certainties in this life.*
GEORGE MEREDITH.
**TEXTILE REGULAR**

IT TAKES A GREAT DEAL OF HISTORY TO PRODUCE A LITTLE LITERATURE
HENRY JAMES, *Life of Nathaniel Hawthorne*
EMPIRE

The important thing for Government is not to do things which individuals are doing already, and to do them a little better or a little worse; but to do those things which at present are not done at all.

J.M.KEYNES, *The End of Laisser-Faire*
**BAUER BODONI BOLD CONDENSED**

I am not so lost in lexicography, as to forget that words are the daughters of earth, and that things are the sons of heaven. Language is only the instrument of science, and words are but the signs of ideas: I wish, however, that the instrument might be less apt to decay, and that signs might be permanent, like the things which they denote.

Norway, too has wild prospects; and Lapland is remarkable for noble wild prospects. But Sir, let me tell you, the noblest prospect which a Scotchman ever sees, is the high road that leads him to England.

Shakespeare never had six lines together without a fault. Perhaps you may find seven, but this does not refute my general assertion.

# Remember that all tricks are either knavish or childish.

**1 | 2**

Five levels of HTML heading styles bring Samuel Johnson's spleen to a Windows browser *(left)*, and a Macintosh *(below)*.

177

**2**

There are two things which I am confident I can do very well: one is an introduction to any literary work, stating what it is to contain, and how it should be executed in the most perfect manner; the other is a conclusion, shewing from various causes why the execution has not been equal to what the author promised to himself and to the public.

I am not so lost in lexicography, as to forget that words are the daughters of earth, and that things are the sons of heaven. Language is only the instrument of science, and words are but the signs of ideas: I wish, however, that the instrument might be less apt to decay, and that signs might be permanent, like the things which they denote.

Norway, too has wild prospects; and Lapland is remarkable for noble wild prospects. But Sir, let me tell you, the noblest prospect which a Scotchman ever sees, is the high road that leads him to England.

Shakespeare never had six lines together without a fault. Perhaps you may find seven, but this does not refute my general assertion.

**Remember that all tricks are either knavish or childish.**

# USEFUL SOURCES

## BOOKS

**Cascading Style Sheets**
David Busch & J.W. Olsen
McGraw Hill, 1998

**Creating Killer Web Sites**
David Siegel
Hayden Books, 1997

**Effective Web Design**
Ann Navarro & Tabinda Khan
Sybex, 1998

**The Thames and Hudson Manual of Typography**
Ruari McLean
Thames & Hudson, 1980

**Typography**
Friedrich Friedl, Nicolaus Ott &
Bernard Stein
Könemann Verlagsgesellschaft, 1998

**Typography on the Web**
Joseph T. Sinclair
AP Professional, 1999

**Web Designer's Guide to Style Sheets**
Steven Mulder
Hayden Books, 1997

**Web Pages That Suck**
Vincent Flanders & Michael Willis
Sybex, 1998

**Web Style Guide**
Patrick J. Lynch & Sarah Horton
Yale University Press, 1999

## WEB SITES

### Commercial Foundries

www.adobe.com

www.bertholdtypes.com

www.bitstream.com

www.emigre.com

www.fontbureau.com

www.monotype.com

### Freeware foundries

www.orange.ne.jp

www.surface-type.com

### Type distributors

www.faces.co.uk

www.type.co.uk

www.intra.nl/wsfn

www.typeindex.com

### Typography magazines

www.graphic-design.com

www.baselinemagazine.com

www.will-harris.com

www.dol.com

www.type.co.uk

www.fontsite.com

www.quixote.com/serif

www.typ.nl

www.itcfonts.com/itc/ulc

### Typography-related Web sites

www.alphabytes.com/index.html/

www.ac4d.org

www.aiga.org

www.unicode.org

www.bno.nl

www.typeindex.com

www.spy.co.uk

www.concentric.net/~brandt58

www.rit.edu/~goudyctr/
   goudycenter.html/

www.fonts.com

www.cooper.edu/art/lubalin

www.truetype.demon.co.uk

www.tdc.org

www.typeright.org

www.typocircle.co.uk

# GLOSSARY

**A/UX** A version of the AT&T UNIX operating system that can be used on Macintosh computers.

**absolute leading** Lines of text spaced by a fixed amount, generally measured in points.

**absolute path** The path, or route, taken to locate a file by starting at the highest level and searching through each directory (or folder) until the file is found. The path is spelled out by listing each directory en route.

**absolute URL** A complete address, or "uniform resource locator" (URL), which takes you to a specific location in a Web site rather than to the home page of the site. An absolute URL will contain the full file path to the page document location on the host server, for example: http://yoursite.com/extrainfo/aboutyou/yourhouse.htm

**access path** The description of the route taken to access a file, created when it is opened.

**active hyperlink** A currently selected word or button that forms a link to another location, often differentiated from other links on the same page by a different color.

**ActiveX** Microsoft's proprietary technology for creating interactive Web pages. ActiveX controls are not platform-independent and are mainly supported only in Microsoft Windows environments.

**Adobe Acrobat** Proprietary software that lets you convert any document into a PDF (portable document format) file in which fonts and images are embedded, enabling it to be viewed on different computer systems.

**Afterburner** Proprietary file compression software for compressing and delivering Macromedia Director film strips on the Internet.

**aliasing** The term describing the jagged appearance of bitmapped images or fonts either when the resolution is insufficient or when they have been enlarged. This is caused by the pixels—which are square with straight sides—making up the image that becomes visible.

**alignment** The placement of type or images so that they line up according to an invisible line, either horizontally or vertically.

**alphabet length** The measure, in points, of the entire length of the 26 alphabet characters of a font of any one size set in lowercase.

**alphanumeric set** The complete set of alphabet characters, numbers, punctuation and associated symbols, and accents of a font.

**anchor** A text or graphic element that has an HTML tag that either links it to another location or acts as a destination for an incoming link.

**animation (1)** A process of creating a moving image by rapidly moving from one still image to the next. Traditionally, this was achieved through a laborious process of drawing or painting each "frame" manually onto cellulose acetate sheets ("cels," or "cells"). However, animations are now more usually created with specialized software that renders sequences in a variety of formats, typically QuickTime, AVI, and animated GIFs.

**Animation (2)** A "lossless" compression setting ("codec") used by QuickTime that will work with all bit depths. Since it is very sensitive to picture changes, the Animation codec works best for creating sequences in images that were rendered digitally.

**animation value** The value applied to a keyframe in an animation sequence that represents a change in the object's property, which, in turn, determines how the animation of a sequence is interpolated.

**anonymous FTP** A means of accessing files on a remote computer across the Internet using the File Transfer Protocol (FTP) service, but without having to provide, as is often the case, a predefined password or other "login" name. Access is achieved by logging in with a username of "anonymous" and using an e-mail address as the password.

**antialias/antialiasing** A technique of optically eliminating the jagged effect of bitmapped images or text reproduced on low-resolution devices such as monitors. This is achieved by adding pixels of an in-between tone—the edges of the object's color are blended with its background by averaging the density of the range of pixels involved. Antialiasing is also sometimes employed to filter texture maps, such as those used in 3D applications, to prevent moiré patterns.

**applet** Although a general term that can be applied to any small application that performs a specific task, such as the calculator, an applet is usually used to describe a small application written in the Java programming language, which is downloaded by an Internet browser to perform specific tasks.

**Archie** An Internet service that logs the whereabouts of files so that they can be located for downloading. Once found, files are downloading by using FTP.

**argument** Used to describe words or numbers entered as part of an HTML instruction to modify how that instruction operates.

**ascender** The part of a lowercase character which extends above its body ("x-height"), as in the letters b, d, f, h, k, l, t.

**ASCII** (*pron.*: asskee) Acronym for the American Standard Code for Information Interchange, a code that assigns a number to 256 letters, numbers, and symbols (including carriage returns and tabs) which can be typed on a keyboard. ASCII is the cross-platform, computer industry–standard, text-only file format.

**aspect ratio** The ratio of the width of an image to its height, expressed as x:y. For example, the aspect ratio of a image measuring 200 × 100 pixels is 2:1.

**asynchronous** A communications protocol in which data bits are transmitted one after the other, start-and-stop bits denoting the beginning and end of each character transmitted.

**asynchronous communication** A communications protocol in which a start/stop signal indicates the beginning and end of each character being transmitted, thus allowing data to move back and forth without being restricted to rigid timing signals.

**ATM** *abb.*: Adobe Type Manager, a utility for managing, displaying, and printing fonts. ATM improves the display of PostScript® Type 1 fonts by using the outlines contained within their corresponding printer files, rather than relying on the jagged, inelegant appearance of screen fonts.

**attachment** An external file such as an image or text document "attached" to an e-mail message for electronic transmission.

**attribute** (1) A characteristic of an HTML tag that is identified alongside the tag in order to describe it.

**attribute** (2) The specification applied to a character, box, or other item. Character attributes include font, size, style, color, shade, scaling, kerning, etc.

**authoring tool/application/program** Software that enables you to create interactive presentations such as those used in multimedia titles and Web sites. Authoring programs typically provide text, drawing, painting, animation, and audio features and combine these with a scripting language that determines how each element of page, or screen, behaves, such as an instruction contained within a button to tell the computer to display a different page or perform a specific task—playing a movie, for example.

**backbone** The main high-speed link between nodes linking networked devices.

**bandwidth** The measure of the speed at which information is passed between two points, which may be between modems, or across a "bus," or from memory to disk—the broader the bandwidth, the faster data flows.

**banner** An image on a Web page, usually at the top, which deliberately attracts attention, generally for advertising purposes.

**base alignment** The alignment of type characters of differing sizes or fonts along their baselines.

**baseline** The imaginary line, defined by the flat base of a lowercase letter such as "x," upon which the bases of all upper and lowercase letters apparently rest.

**batch mode/batch processing** The processing of data in automated batches, as distinct from data that is processed as you input it (interactive mode, or "realtime"). For example a spellchecker, when applied to a block of text, runs in batch mode, whereas it doesn't if applied to an individual word. An example of batch processing is when you apply a Photoshop "Action" to two or more files.

**baud** (pron.: bawd) In data transmission by modem, the number of signal changes transmitted per second.

**baud rate** The speed at which a modem transmits data, or the number of "events" it can handle per second. Often used to describe the transmission speed of data itself, but since a single event can contain two or more bits, data speed is more correctly expressed in "bits per second" (bps).

**BBS** abb.: bulletin board service—a facility, usually noncommercial, by which you can use a modem and telephone line to share information and exchange files on specialized subjects with other computer users of like mind.

**binary code** The computer code, using 1 or 0, which is used to represent a character or instruction. For example, the binary code 01100010 represents a lowercase "b."

**binary file** A file that is described in binary code rather than text. Binary files typically hold pictures, sounds, or a complete application program.

**binary system** Numbering system that uses two digits, 0 and 1, as distinct from the decimal system of 0–9.

**BinHex** An acronym for binary to hexadecimal, a file format that converts binary files to ASCII text for, usually, transmission via e-mail. This is the safest way of sending document files—particularly to and from Macintosh computers—since some computer systems along the e-mail route may accept only standard ASCII text characters. Encoding and decoding BinHex may be done automatically by some e-mail software, but otherwise it must be done manually, usually with a file compression utility.

**bit** Acronym for binary digit, the smallest piece of information a computer can use. A bit is expressed as one of two values, which can be a 1 or a 0, on or off, something or nothing, negative or positive, small or large, etc. Each alphabet character requires eight bits (called a "byte") to store it.

**bit density** The number of bits occupying a particular area or length—per inch of magnetic tape, for example.

**bit depth** Describes the number of bits assigned to each pixel on a monitor, scanner or image file. One-bit, for example, will only produce black and white (the bit is either on or off), whereas 8-bit will generate 256 grays or colors (256 is the maximum number of permutations of a string of eight 1s and 0s), and 24-bit will produce 16.7 million colors (256 × 256 × 256).

**bit map/bitmap** Strictly speaking, any text character or image composed of dots. A bit map is a "map" of "bits" that describes the complete collection of the bits that represent the location and binary state (on or off) of a corresponding set of items, such as pixels, which are required to form an image, such as on a display monitor.

**bit rate** The speed at which data is transmitted across communications channels, measured in bits per second (bps). Sometimes erroneously referred to as baud rate.

**bitmapped font** A font in which the characters are made up of dots, or pixels, as distinct from an outline font that is drawn from "vectors." Bitmapped fonts generally accompany PostScript® "Type 1" fonts and are used to render the font's shape on screen (they are sometimes called "screen" fonts). To draw the shape accurately onscreen, your computer must have a bitmap installed for each size (they are also called "fixed-size" fonts), although this is not necessary if you have ATM installed, since this uses the outline, or "printer" version of the font (the file that your printer uses in order to print it). TrueType® fonts are "outline" and thus do not require a bitmapped version.

**bitmapped graphic** An image made up of dots, or pixels, and usually generated by "paint" or "image-editing" applications, as distinct from the "vector" images of "object-oriented" drawing applications.

**block** A place, or area, regarded as a single unit, where data is stored either temporarily in memory or on a storage medium such as a hard disk.

**body** One of the main structures of an HTML document, falling between the header and the footer.

**Boolean** Named after G. Boole, a 19th-century English mathematician, Boolean is used to describe a shorthand for logical computer operations, such as those that link values ("and," "or," "not," "nor," etc., called "Boolean operators"). For example, the search of a database could be refined using Boolean operators such as in "book *and* recent *or* new *but not* published." "Boolean expressions" compare two values and come up with the result ("return") of either "true" or "false," which are each represented by 1 and 0. In 3D applications, Boolean describes the joining or removing of one shape from another.

**browser** An application enabling you to view, or "browse," World Wide Web pages across the Internet.

**buffer** An area of computer memory set aside for the storage or processing of data while it is in transit. The buffer can either be in RAM or on a hard disk—within your computer the buffer is called the "cache." Buffers are commonly used by output devices such as modems and printers, which are then able to process data more quickly while at the same time freeing up your computer so that you can keep on working.

**burn** To convert a file from an uncompressed to a compressed format specifically for use with Internet Web browsers.

**bus** A path along which information, or data, is passed in a computer or between one device and another.

**button** An interface control, usually appearing in dialog boxes, which you click to designate, confirm, or cancel an action. Default buttons are those that are usually emphasized by a heavy border and can be activated by the "enter" or "return" keys.

**byte** A single group made up of eight bits (0s and 1s) that is processed as one unit. It is possible to configure eight 0s and 1s in only 256 different permutations; thus a byte can represent any value between 0 and 255—the maximum number of ASCII characters for example, one byte being required for each.

**cache** (*pron.*: cash) A small area of memory (RAM) set aside for the temporary storage of frequently accessed data. This has the effect of speeding up some computer operations—accessing font information, for example—since data accessed from RAM is processed much faster than that from disk. Cache can

also be stored in a separate hardware chip, which comes soldered onto the motherboard of some computers and on some add-on circuit boards.

**canceled numeral** A numerical character, used in mathematics, crossed through with a diagonal stroke.

**cap height** The height of a capital letter, measured from its baseline.

**cascading style sheet** *see* **CSS**

**case-sensitive** The term used to indicate that upper- or lowercase characters input into a field, such as in a "Find" dialog or e-mail address, are significant and will determine the outcome of the request.

**CCITT** *abb.*: Comité Consultatif Internationale Téléphonique et Télégraphique (Consultative Committee on International Telephony and Telegraphy), an organization sponsored by the United Nations that sets worldwide communications standards, especially with regard to data and voice transmission and compression.

**cel** In conventional, hand-drawn animation the individual animated stages of a sequence, drawn on transparent acetate sheets, which are overlayed onto a static background. Each cel forms a "frame" in the animation.

**cell** A space containing information in the rows or columns of a table.

**cell padding** The space between cells in a table.

**cell spacing** The number of pixels between cells in a table.

**centered** Type that is centered in its measure, as distinct from ranged (aligned) left or right.

**CGI** *abb.*: common gateway interface, a specification for passing information between Web browsers and servers.

**character** On a computer any single letter, number, punctuation mark, or symbol represented by 8 bits (1 byte), including invisible characters such as "space," "return," and "tab."

**Character Shape Player** (**CSP**) Software contained within a Web browser that plays back the shape of characters in a Web page.

**character space** The distance between each character as determined by the font designer, as distinct from "kerning" and "tracking," which are modifications of that distance.

**character/text mode** Of Web browsers, those that can display text data only and cannot display graphics without the assistance of a "helper" application. Even graphics-savvy browsers allow a preference for operating in character mode, which many users prefer because of the increased speed—although they inevitably miss out, since it is now common for much of the text on Web pages to be transmitted as images.

**chatterbots** The term given to software "helpers" that give advice and explain local etiquette in interactive environments—such as chat rooms—on the Web.

**child** (**object**) An object linked hierarchically to another object (its "parent"). For example, when a "child" box is placed within—or linked to—a "parent" box, then when the latter is moved, the child—and all its "grand-children"!—move with it, retaining their relative positions and orientation. This enables manipulation of complex structures, particularly in 3D applications.

**chroma** The intensity, or purity, of a color, thus its degree of saturation.

**Cinepak** A compression setting ("codec") used by QuickTime, which is best suited for sequences to be played from multimedia CD-ROM presentations, especially when slower computers or slower CD-ROM drives (such as 2x speed) may be used. However, Cinepak does not produce good results at Web data rates (below 30Kbps), or at the other end of the scale at higher data rates such as with 4x CD-ROM drives or faster.

**CIX** Acronym (*pron.*: kicks) for Commercial Internet Exchange, an alliance of Internet Service Providers (ISPs).

**clickable map/image** An invisible shape surrounding a graphic on a Web page that serves as a "button" that, when clicked, will take you to another page or Web site.

**client** In a "client/server" arrangement, such as on a network or on the Web, the client is the end-user's computer—yours, in other words.

On the Web, your browser is a "client program" that talks to Web servers.

**client/server** An arrangement that divides computing into two separate functions, connected by a network. The "client" is the end-user (your computer), while the server is a centralized computer that holds and manages information or shared activities that your computer, and other computers, access when necessary.

**clip art/clip media** Collections of (usually) royalty-free photographs, illustrations, design devices, and other precreated items such as movies, sounds, and 3D wireframes. Clip art is available in three forms—on paper that is cut out and pasted onto camera-ready art, on computer disk, or, increasingly, via the Web.

**closed file** A file that does not have an access path, thus preventing you from reading from or writing to it.

**closed h** An italic "h" in which the shorter stroke curves inward, as in "*h*."

**CLUT** Acronym for color lookup table, a preset table of colors (to a maximum of 256 colors) that the operating system uses when in 8-bit mode. CLUTs are also attached to individual images saved in 8-bit "indexed" mode—that is, when an application converts a 24-bit image (one with millions of colors) to 8-bit, it draws up a table ("index") of up to 256 colors (the total number of colors depends on where the image will be viewed—Mac, Windows, or Web, for example) of the most frequently used colors in the image, so if a color in the original image does not appear in the table, the application chooses the closest one or simulates it by "dithering" available colors in the table.

**codec** Acronym for compressor/decompressor, which describes the technique used to rapidly compress and decompress sequences of images, such as those used for QuickTime and AVI movies.

**color depth** The number of bits required to define the color of each pixel. For example, only one bit is required to display a black-and-white image (it is either on or off), whereas an 8-bit image can display either 256 grays or 256 colors, and a 24-bit image displays 16.7 million colors—eight bits each for red, green, and blue (256 × 256 × 256).

**color library** An application support file that contains predefined colors. These may be the application's default colors, colors defined by you, or other predefined color palettes or tables.

**color picker** The term describing a color model when displayed on a computer monitor. Color pickers may be specific to an application such as Adobe Photoshop, a third-party color model such as PANTONE, or to the operating system running on your computer.

**comment** A note, marked with an exclamation point, written into an HTML page but ignored by Web browsers. This allows you to read or make notes about the markup of a page without their being visible when viewed with a browser.

**commercial a/at** The type character @ used as an abbreviation for "at," thus used in e-mail addresses to signify, for example, "you@your-domain."

**Common Ground** A "portable document format" (PDF) for creating material to be viewed across the World Wide Web. Common Ground DP ("DigitalPaper") format documents retain all the formatting of text and graphics and can be shared by Macintosh, Windows, and UNIX users. Like Adobe Acrobat PDF files, Common Ground DP documents can be indexed and searched, but, unlike Acrobat files, which require you to have viewing software already installed on your computer, Common Ground DP documents contain a "mini" viewer already embedded in the file.

**complementary colors** On a color wheel, two colors directly opposite each other that, when combined, form white or black depending on the color model (subtractive or additive).

**compression** The technique of rearranging data so that it either occupies less space on disk or transfers faster between devices or on communication lines. Different kinds of compression techniques are employed for different kinds of data—applications, for example, must not lose any data when compressed, whereas photographic images and movies can tolerate a certain amount of data loss. Compression methods that do not lose data are referred to as "lossless," whereas "lossy" is used to describe methods in which some data is lost. Movies and animations employ techniques called "codecs" (compression/decompression). There are many proprietary utilities for compressing data. Typical compression formats for images are LZW (lossless), JPEG, and GIF (both lossy), the latter two being used commonly for files transmitted across the Internet.

**CompuServe GIF** see **GIF**

**concatenate** To string together two or more units of information. For example "Quick" and "Time" becomes "QuickTime" when concatenated, or a split file becomes one.

**condensed** Of type designs, those faces whose height is greater than their width. Although a condensed style can be applied to computer-generated fonts by "horizontal scaling," specifically designed condensed typefaces retain the correct relative proportions, or "stress," between their horizontal and vertical strokes—a characteristic that is distorted and exaggerated by horizontal scaling.

**content-type** A MIME (Multipurpose Internet Mail Extensions) convention for identifying the type of data being transmitted over the Internet to such things as e-mail applications and Web browsers.

**cookie** A small piece of information deposited in your Web browser (thus on your hard disk) by a WWW site, storing such things as custom page settings or even personal information about you, such as your address or your password for that site.

**copyright** The term describing the right of a person who creates an original work to protect that work by controlling how and where it may be reproduced. While certain aspects of copyright are broadly controlled by international agreement as defined by the Universal Copyright Convention (UCC), there are some differences from country to country, particularly when it comes to the period, or "term," for which a work is protected (in most countries this is 50 years after its

183

184

creator's death). In the United States, the Pan American agreement decrees that ownership of an "intellectual property" (the legal description of copyright ownership) be established by registration, whereas in the United Kingdom it exists automatically by virtue of the creation of the work. There is often confusion between copyright in a work and the "right" to publish it—ownership of the right to publish a work in one country may not extend to other countries, nor does it necessarily signify ownership of copyright. Equally, ownership of copyright may be shared—the author of a book, for example, may own copyright in the text, whereas copyright in the design of the book may be owned by its publisher.

**copyright notice/line** The indication of ownership of copyright in a work ("form of notice"), particularly one that is reproduced, as required by the Universal Copyright Convention. This states that all the first and subsequent editions of a work bear the word "Copyright" or the symbol "©" (most publishers include both), the year of publication (or first publication if it is a straight reprint), and the name of the owner of the copyright in the work.

**copyright-free** A misnomer used to describe ready-made resources such as clip art. In fact, resources described as such are rarely "copyright free"—it is generally only the license to use the material that is granted by purchase. The correct description would normally be "royalty-free"—that is, material that you can use—under license—that is free from payment of further fees or royalties.

**cps** abb.: characters per second, the output speed of a printing machine such as an inkjet or dot-matrix printer, or the number of characters transmitted by a modem each second.

**cross-platform** The term applied to software, multimedia titles, or anything else (such as floppy disks) that will work on more than one computer platform—that is, those that run different operating systems, such as the Macintosh OS or Microsoft Windows.

**CSS** abb.: Cascading Style Sheets, the name for a specification sponsored by the World Wide Web Consortium for overcoming the limita-

tions imposed by "classic HTML." Web designers ("authors") have increasingly sought tools which would enable them to control every element of page design more tightly, with the result that the Web authoring community has developed unwieldy workarounds (such as using single-pixel GIF images to add character spacing), generating bulky HTML code, which, in turn, resulted in longer downloads and browser incompatibilities. CSS allows the designer to exercise greater control over typography and layout in much the same way as he or she would expect in, say, a page-layout application, and provides the means of applying attributes such as font formats to paragraphs, parts of pages, or entire pages. Several style sheets can be applied to a single page, thus "cascading."

**cursor** The name for the blinking marker that indicates the current working position in a document. For example, the point in a line of text at which the next character will appear when you strike a key on the keyboard. The cursor may be represented by a small vertical line or block and is not to be confused with the "pointer"—the marker that indicates the current position of the mouse.

**daemon** Special networking software, used mostly on computers running the UNIX operating system, which handles requests from users, such as e-mail, the Web, and other Internet services.

**dash** Strictly speaking a dash can be any short rule, plain or decorative, but is usually used to describe an em dash (—) or en dash (–), as distinct from a hyphen (-).

**data** Although strictly speaking the plural of "datum," meaning a piece of information, "data" is now used as a singular noun to describe—particularly in the context of computers—more or less anything that can be stored or processed, for example a single bit, a chunk of text, or an image.

**data bits** A term used in data transmission to distinguish bits that contain the data being transmitted from bits that give instructions on how the data is to be transmitted.

**database** Information stored on a computer in a systematic fashion and thus retrievable. This generally means files where you store any

amount of data in separate but consistent categories (called "fields") for each type of information such as names, addresses, and telephone numbers. The electronic version of a card index system (each card is called a "record"), databases are constructed with applications called "database managers," which allow you to organize information any way you like.

**DDES** abb.: Digital Data Exchange Standards, an ANSI/ISO approved standard that allows equipment produced by different manufacturers to communicate ("interface").

**decryption** The process of removing the protection given to data or a document by encryption. Usually, the same software used to encrypt data must be used to decrypt it.

**default** The settings of a hardware device or software program that are determined at the time of manufacture or release. These settings remain in effect until you change them, and your changes are stored—when applied to software—in a "preferences" file. Also called "presets" and "factory settings."

**delimit** To separate items of information, such as words, lines of text, or—in databases, for example—fields and records. This is done by placing a character ("delimiter") at the end (limit) of each item. Commonly used characters are generated by the "tab" and "comma" keys (to separate fields) and the "return" key (to separate records). Files that are formatted thus are described as "delimited."

**descender** The part of a lowercase character that extends below the baseline of the x-height, as in the letters p, q, j, g, y.

**DHTML** see **Dynamic HTML**

**dial-up** The term describing a connection to the Internet or to a network that is made by dialing a telephone number for access.

**differential letterspacing** The spacing of each letter according to its individual width.

**digit (1)** Any numeral from 0 to 9.

**digit (2)** A printer's symbol ("ornament") depicting a hand with a pointing finger. Also known as a "hand," "fist", or "index."

**digital** Anything operated by or created from information or signals represented by binary digits—such as in a digital recording—as distinct from analog, in which information is represented by a physical variable (in a recording this may be via the grooves in a vinyl platter).

**digital data** Information stored or transmitted as a series of 1s and 0s ("bits"). Because values are fixed (so-called "discrete values"), digital data is more reliable than analog, because the latter is susceptible to sometimes uncontrollable physical variations.

**digitize, digitalize** To convert anything, such as text, images, or sound, into binary form so that it can be digitally processed, manipulated, stored, and reconstructed.

**DIN** abb.: Deutsche Industrie-Norm, a code of standards established in Germany and used throughout the world to standardize properties of particular materials and manufactured items—computer connectors and photographic film speed, for example—so that they are universally compatible.

**dither**(**ing**) The term describing a technique of "interpolation" that calculates the average value of adjacent pixels. This technique is used either to add extra pixels to an image—to smooth an edge, for example, as in "antialiasing"—or to reduce the number of colors or grays in an image by replacing them with average values that conform to a predetermined palette of colors, such as when an image containing millions of colors is converted ("resampled") to a fixed palette ("index") of, say, 256 colors—in Web use, for example. A color monitor operating in 8-bit color mode (256 colors) will automatically create a dithered pattern of pixels. Dithering is also used by some printing devices to simulate colors or tones.

**DNS** see **domain name service**

**document** The term describing the entire contents of a single HTML file. HTML documents are generally referred to as "Web pages," since this is how they are rendered for display by browsers.

**document heading** An HTML style ("tag") that defines text headings in a range of predetermined sizes and weights (levels 1 through 6), so that you can add emphasis to a line of text.

**document root** The term describing the place on a Web server where all the HTML files, images, and other components for a particular Web site are located.

**document transfer rate** The speed, measured in documents per minute, at which Web pages are transmitted to your computer once you have requested them.

**document-based queries** The term describing a method of sending information from your browser to a Web server, such as when you click on a "search" button to look something up.

**domain name** (**service**) (DNS) The description of a Web site's "address"—the means by which you find or identify a particular Web site, much like a brand name or trademark. A Web site address is actually a number that conforms to the numerical Internet protocol (IP) addresses that computers use for information exchange—but names are far easier for us mortals to remember. Domain names are administered by the InterNIC organization and include at least two parts: the "subdomain," typically a company or organization, and the "high-level domain," which is the part after the first dot, such as in ".com" for commercial sites, ".org" for nonprofit sites, ".gov" for governmental sites, ".edu" for educational sites, and so on. The high-level domain name may also indicate a country code for sites outside the United States (although a site without a country code does not necessarily mean it is inside the U.S.), such as ".uk" for the United Kingdom, ".de" for Germany, ".fr" for France, and so on.

**DTD** abb.: Document Type Definition, a formal SGML specification for a document that lays out structural elements and markup definitions.

**Dynamic HTML, DHTML** abb.: dynamic hypertext markup language, a development of basic HTML code that enables you to add such features as simple animations and highlighted buttons to Web pages without relying on browser "plug-ins."

**e-commerce** Commercial transactions conducted electronically over a network or the Internet.

**e-mail** Acronym for electronic mail, messages you send from your computer to someone else with a computer either locally through a network, or using a modem to transmit over telephone lines, usually via a central computer ("server") that stores messages in the recipient's "mailbox" until they are collected.

**Envoy** A "portable document format" (PDF) created by Novell for the exchange of formatted documents across the Internet.

**error-checking** A means of ensuring the integrity of data. This can occur either when the data is input—via a keyboard, for example (a spellchecker is a type of error-check)—or when it is transmitted via a device such as a modem.

**Ethernet** A hardware connection standard used on local area networks (LAN) that offers fast data transfer.

**external reference** A resource that resides in a location outside of the application using it.

**FAQ** abb.: frequently asked questions, a list, often posted on Web pages or in promotional literature, of answers to the most common questions that purchasers of software or hardware or users of Internet services ask.

**file dependency** Condition where a file depends upon the contents of another in order that it may function.

**file extension** The term describing the abbreviated suffix at the end of a filename that describes either its type (such as EPS or JPG) or origin (the application that created it, such as QXP for QuarkXPress files). A file extension is usually comprised of three letters (although Macintosh and UNIX systems may use more) and is separated from the filename by a period.

**footer** (**1**) The facility in some applications, particularly word processing programs, to automatically place text and numbers at the foot of each page.

**footer** (**2**) In an HTML document, the concluding part, containing information such as the date, version, etc.

**form** A term describing fillable spaces (fields) on a Web page that provide a means of collecting information and receiving feedback

185

from people who visit a Web site. They can be used, for example, to buy an item, answer a questionnaire or access a database.

**frame** On the Web, a means of displaying more than one page at a time within a single window—the window is divided into separate areas ("frames"), each one displaying a separate page. Confusingly, although a window displaying frames may contain several pages, it is nevertheless described as a singular page. A common use of frames is to display a menu that remains static while other parts of the Web page—displayed in the same window—contain information that can, for example, be "scrolled."

**front end** In a networked system where your computer is connected to a server, "front end" describes the software that you use to gain access and interact with the server (the "back end"). A Web browser is one such front end.

**full-text indexing** The facility to search and find a "string" (contiguously connected text characters) that may occur within an entire text file.

**gateway** A device or program used to connect disparate computer networks.

**GIF** *abb.*: Graphic Interchange Format, a bitmapped graphics format devised by CompuServe, an Internet service provider (now part of AOL), and thus sometimes referred to as "CompuServe GIF." There are two specifications, GIF87a and, more recently, GIF89a, the latter providing additional features such as transparent backgrounds. The GIF format uses a "lossless" compression technique, or "algorithm," and thus does not squeeze files as much as does the JPEG format, which is "lossy" (some data is discarded). For use in Web browsers JPEG is the format of choice for tone images such as photographs, whereas GIF is more suitable for line images and other graphics such as text.

**GIF89a** see **transparent GIF**

**global renaming** Software that updates all occurrences of a name throughout a Web site when one instance of that name is altered.

**gopher** A software "protocol" developed at the University of Minnesota that provides a means of accessing information across the Internet using services such as WAIS and Telnet.

**Gzip** File compression technology used mainly on UNIX computers.

**header file** File that contains information identifying incoming data transmitted via the Internet.

**heading** A formatting term used in HTML that determines the size at which text will be displayed in a WWW browser. There are six sizes available, usually referred to as H1, H2, H3, H4, H5, and H6.

**helper application** Application that assists Web browsers in delivering or displaying information such as movie or sound files.

**hierarchical structure** The term describing a technique of arranging information in a graded order, which establishes priorities and therefore helps the user find a path that leads them to what they want. Used extensively in networking and databases.

**history (list)** The term used to describe a list of visited Web pages your browser logs during a session on the Web. The history provides a means of speedy access to pages already visited during that session.

**host** A networked computer that provides services to anyone who can access it, such as for e-mail, file transfer, and access to the Web.

**HotJava** A Web browser developed by Sun Microsystems that is written in the Java programming language.

**hotlist** A theme-related list on a Web page that provides links to other pages or sites dedicated to that theme.

**HTML** *abb.*: Hypertext Markup Language, a text-based "page description language" (PDL) used to format documents published on the World Wide Web and which can be viewed with Web browsers.

**http** *abb.*: Hypertext Transfer Protocol, a text-based set of rules by which files on the World Wide Web are transferred, defining the commands that Web browsers use to communicate with Web servers. The vast majority of World Wide Web addresses, or "URLs," are prefixed with "http://."

**httpd** *abb.*: Hypertext Transfer Protocol Daemon, a collection of programs on a Web server that provides Web services, such as handling requests.

**https** *abb.*: Hypertext Transfer Protocol Secure, synonymous with "http" but providing a secure link for such things as commercial transactions—online shopping with credit cards, for example—or when accessing password-protected information.

**hyperlink** A contraction of "hypertext link," an embedded link to other documents, which is usually identified by being underlined or highlighted in a different color. Clicking on or selecting a hyperlink takes you to another document, part of a document, or Web site.

**hypermedia** The combination of graphics, text, movies, sound, and other elements accessible via hypertext links in an online document or Web page.

**hypertext** A programming concept that links any single word or group of words to an unlimited number of others, typically text on a Web page that has an embedded link to other documents or Web sites. Hypertext links are usually underlined and/or in a different color from the rest of the text and are activated by clicking on them.

**hypertext link** see **hyperlink**

**I/O** *abb.*: input/output, referring to the hardware interactions between a computer and other devices such as the keyboard and disk drives.

**IAB** *abb.*: Internet Architecture Board, a ruling council that makes decisions about Internet standards and related topics.

**IETF** *abb.*: Internet Engineering Task Force, a suborganization of the Internet Architecture Board (IAB) that comprises a group of volunteers that investigates and helps solve Internet-related problems and makes recommendations to appropriate Internet committees.

**image map** An image that contains a series of embedded links to other documents or Web sites. These links are activated when clicked on in the appropriate area of the image. For example, an image of a globe may incorporate an embedded link for each visible country which, when clicked, will take the user to a document giving more information about that country.

**inheritance** The description of the hierarchical relationship between objects in object-oriented programming.

**interleaved, interleaving** The technique of displaying an image onscreen—using a Web browser, for example—so that it is revealed as a whole in increasing layers of detail rather than bit by bit from the top down. The image appears gradually, starting with slices, which are eventually filled in when all the pixels appear.

**intermediate code** A representation of computer code that lies somewhere between code that can be read by you or me (such as HTML source code) and machine-readable binary code (1s and 0s). Java bytecode is one such example.

**Internet** The entire collection of connected worldwide networks, including those used solely for the Web. The Internet was originally funded by the U.S. Defense Department.

**intranet** A network of computers similar to the Internet but to which the general public does not have access. A sort of "in-house" Internet service, intranets are used mainly by large corporations, governments, and educational institutions.

**IP** abb.: Internet Protocol, the networking rules that are applied to tie computers together across the Internet.

**IP address** abb.: Internet Protocol address, the unique numeric address of a particular computer or server on the Internet (or any TCP/IP network). Each one is unique and consists of a dotted decimal notation, e.g., 194.152.64.68.

**IPnG** abb.: IP next generation, a new generation of Internet protocols that will expand the number of available Internet addresses.

**IRC** abb.: Internet Relay Chat, an Internet facility provided by some ISPs that allows multiple users to type messages to each other in real time on different "channels," sometimes referred to as "rooms."

**ISDN** abb.: Integrated Services Digital Network. A telecommunication technology that transmits data on special digital lines rather than on old-fashioned analog lines and is thus much faster.

**ISO** abb.: International Standards Organization, a Swiss-based body that is responsible for defining many elements common to design, photography, and publishing, such as paper sizes, film speed ratings, and network protocols ("ISO/OSI" protocols).

**ISOC** Acronym for the Internet Society, a governing body to which the Internet Architecture Board (IAB) reports.

**ISP** abb.: Internet service provider, any organization that provides access to the Internet. At its most basic this may merely be a telephone number for connection, but most ISPs also provide e-mail addresses and capacity for your own Web pages.

**Java** A programming language devised for creating small applications ("applets") that can be downloaded from a Web server and used, typically in conjunction with a Web browser, to add dynamic effects such as animations.

**JavaScript** A "scripting" language that provides a simplified method of applying dynamic effects to Web pages.

**JPEG** abb.: Joint Photographics Experts Group, JPEG (pronounced "jay-peg") is a file format for compressing bitmapped images. The degree of compression (from high compression/low quality to low compression/high quality) can be defined by the user, which makes the format doubly suitable for images that are to be used either for print reproduction or for transmitting over the Internet—for viewing in Web browsers, for example.

**Kbps** abb.: kilobits per second, a measurement of the speed at which data is transferred across a network, a kilobit being 1,024 bits, or characters.

**layout element** The description of any component in the layout of an HTML document—a Web page, for example—such as a graphic, list, rule, paragraph, and so on.

**link** A pointer, such as a highlighted piece of text, in an HTML document (a Web page, for example) or multimedia presentation that takes the user to another location, page, or screen just by clicking on it.

**list element** Text in a Web page that is displayed as a list and is defined by the HTML tag <LI> (list item).

**list tag** The name describing the HTML coding ("tags") that tells a Web browser how to display text in a variety of list styles, such as ordered lists <OL>, menus <MENU>, and glossary lists <DL>.

**listserv** An automated mailing list distribution system, typically based on UNIX servers.

**Lynx** A UNIX-based Web browser that runs in character, or text, mode.

**majordomo** A system of automated multiple electronic mailing lists that users can subscribe to or unsubscribe from at will.

**map file** see **image map**

**markup** The technique of embedding "tags" (HTML instructions) within special characters ("metacharacters") that tell a program such as a Web browser how to display a page.

**markup language** A defined set of rules for describing the way files are displayed by any particular method. HTML is one such language, used for creating Web pages.

**Mbps** abb.: megabits per second, a measure of data transfer speeds.

**metacharacter** Character within text that indicates formatting, such as the "tags" in an HTML file. Angle brackets (< >) and ampersands (&) are typical metacharacters.

**MIME** abb.: Multipurpose Internet Mail Extension, a format for conveying Web documents and related files across the Internet, typically with e-mail.

**MOTD** abb.: message of the day. A message posted by an ISP (Internet Service Provider) on its server to inform its users of any known problems that may be affecting the network for that day. An MOTD is usually read either by using special software that "fingers" the server or by using a Web browser.

**navigate** The process of finding your way around a multimedia presentation or Web site by clicking on words or buttons.

187

**navigation bar** A special bar in a Web browser, Web page, or multimedia presentation that helps you to "navigate" through pages by clicking on buttons or text.

**navigation button** A button in a Web browser, Web page, or multimedia presentation that links you to a particular location or page.

**NCSA** *abb.*: National Center for Supercomputing Applications, a group of programmers at the University of Illinois who developed the first Web browser and produces software such as NCSA Telnet for the scientific community.

**network link** The part of the network that forms the link between your computer and the network itself, such as a telephone line or Ethernet cable.

**node (1)** A basic object, such as a graphic within a scene, used in the VRML environment.

**node (2)** Any device connected to a network, such as a computer, printer, or server.

**online** Any activity taking place on a computer or device while it is connected to a network such as the Internet. The opposite of offline.

**orphan file** A file on a Web site that is not referred to by any link or button and thus cannot be reached by any means other than through its absolute URL—in other words, to find it you must know its exact pathname.

**packet** A bundle of data—the basic unit transmitted across networks. When data is sent over a network such as the Internet it is broken up into small chunks called packets, which are sent independently of each other.

**page** An HTML document (text structured with HTML tags) viewed with a Web browser.

**paragraph** In an HTML document, a markup tag <P> used to define a new paragraph in text.

**Perl** A programming language much favored for creating CGI programs.

**pipe** The term describing the bandwidth of the actual connection being used between your computer and a server on the Internet.

**plug-in** Software, usually developed by a third party, which extends the capabilities of a particular program. Plug-ins are common in image-editing and page-layout applications for such things as special-effect filters. Plug-ins are also common in Web browsers for such things as playing movies and audio, although these often come as complete applications ("helper applications") that can be used with a number of browsers rather than any specific one.

**port address** The precise address (the program on the receiving end) to which data is delivered by a remote computer on a network.

**POTS** Acronym for plain old telephone system, a standard analog telephone system.

**PPP** *abb.*: Point-to-Point Protocol, the most common form of establishing dial-up connections to the Internet. It provides a method for transmitting packets over serial point-to-point links. It also allows you to use other standard protocols (such as IPX and TCP/IP) over a standard telephone connection and can also be used for local area network (LAN) connections.

**provider** *see* **ISP**

**Push (technology)** A Web-based technology by which information, distributed to designated groups of users, can be updated immediately whenever changes are made.

**RealAudio** A proprietary helper application that enables audio playback in Web browsers.

**request** The term describing the act of clicking on a button or link in a Web browser—you are, in fact, making a request to a remote server for an HTML document.

**response** On a network, the server's reply to a user's request for information.

**robot** Colloquially called a "'bot," a robot is a program that roams the World Wide Web, gathering and cataloging information, usually for use by various Web search engines such as Yahoo and Alta Vista.

**router** *see* **gateway**

**search engine** The part of a program such as a database that seeks out information in response to requests made by you. On the Web, search engines such as Yahoo, HotBot, and Alta Vista provide sophisticated criteria for searching, and provide summaries of each result as well as the Web site addresses for retrieving more information.

**search tool** A program that enables specific Web pages to be searchable.

**secure area** The part of a Web site where personal or sensitive information can be filled in by users. Secure areas are usually identified by the prefix "https" in the URL and are particularly important for commercial transactions made via the Web.

**server** A networked computer that serves client computers, providing a central location for files and services, and typically handling such things as e-mail and Web access.

**SGML** *abb.*: Standard Generalized Markup Language, an ISO markup standard for defining documents that can be used by any computer, regardless of platform.

**Shocked** The term applied to Web pages that contain material prepared with Macromedia's Shockwave technology, and thus require the Shockwave plug-in in order to be viewed.

**Shockwave** A technology developed by Macromedia for creating Director presentations that can be delivered across the Internet and viewed with a Web browser.

**singleton** An HTML "tag" without a corresponding closing tag.

**SLIP** *abb.*: Serial Line Internet Protocol, a communications protocol that supports an Internet connection over a dial-up line. Now superseded by PPP.

**spider** A program that tirelessly roams the World Wide Web, gathering and cataloging information, typically for use by Web search engines.

**SSL** *abb.*: Secure Sockets Library, a programming "library" devised by Netscape for helping programmers add secure areas to Web sites.

**syntax** The arrangement of words, showing their grammatical relationship. In programming languages such as those used for creating multimedia presentations and HTML documents for the Web, syntax describes the correct use of the programming according to a given set of rules.

**syntax checker** A program that checks a programmer's use of a particular programming language against the rules set for that language.

**table** In a Web page, the arrangement of information in "cells," which are organized in rows and columns, similar to a spreadsheet.

**tag** The formal name for a markup language formatting command. A tag is switched on by placing a command inside angle brackets "< >" and switched off again by repeating the same thing but additionally inserting a forward slash before the command. Thus, for example, "<bold>" makes text that follows appear in bold and "</bold>" switches bold text off.

**tenant** People who administrate a Web site that is located on another person's server, typically one belonging to an Internet Service Provider (ISP).

**terminal emulation** Software that allows your computer to mimic another, remote, computer by acting as a terminal for the other—in other words, it is as though you are actually working on that remote computer.

**text mode** see **character mode**

**throughput** (1) A unit of time measured as the period elapsing between the start and finish of a particular activity. For example, the amount of data that is passed along a communications line in a given period of time.

**tile, tiling** (1) The term used for repeating a graphic item and placing the repetitions side-by-side in all directions so that they form a pattern—just like tiles.

**title** In a Web page, text that appears on that page's title bar.

**transparent background** see **transparent GIF**

**transparent GIF** A feature of the GIF file format that lets you place a nonrectangular image on the background color of a Web page.

**troll, trolling** A newsgroup posting designed to exasperate, annoy, or enrage its readers—the purpose being to create as much argument as possible.

**UNIX** An operating system developed by AT&T, devised to be multitasking and portable from one machine to another. UNIX is used widely on Web servers.

**URI** *abb.*: Uniform Resource Identifier, something that identifies resources available to the Web, such as a URL.

**URL** *abb.*: Uniform Resource Locator, the unique address of a page on the Web, comprising three elements: the protocol to be used (such as http), the domain name ("host"), and the directory name followed by pathnames to any particular file.

**URL-encoded text** A method of encoding text for passing requests from your Web browser to a server.

**URN** *abb.*: Uniform Resource Name, a permanent name for a Web resource.

**USB** *abb.*: Universal Serial Bus. A port (socket) for connecting peripheral devices to your computer, which can be daisy-chained together. These can include devices such as scanners, printers, keyboards, hard drives.

**Usenet** Acronym for user's network, in which a vast number of articles, categorized into newsgroups, are posted by individuals on every conceivable subject. These are hosted on servers throughout the world in which you can post your own articles to people who subscribe to those newsgroups. Special "newsreader" software is required to view the articles.

**videoconferencing** The facility to conduct conferences over a computer network using sound and video pictures.

**ViewMovie** A Netscape plug-in for viewing animations.

**virtual shopping cart** A method of providing Web shoppers with a means of selecting items for purchase as they browse a site, paying for them all at once when done—just as you would in any store.

**VRML** *abb.*: Virtual Reality Modeling Language, an HTML-type programming language designed to create 3D scenes called "virtual worlds."

**W3** see **World Wide Web**

**W3C** see **World Wide Web Consortium**

**WAIS** *abb.*: Wide Area Information Service. A system developed to access information in indexed databases across the Internet.

**wanderer** see **robot**; **spider**

**watermark** The technique of applying a tiled graphic to the background of a Web page that remains fixed, no matter what foreground materials scroll across it.

**Web** see **World Wide Web**

**Web page** A published HTML document on the World Wide Web.

**Web server** A computer ("host") that is dedicated to Web services.

**Web site** The address, location (on a server), and collection of documents and resources for any particular interlinked set of Web pages.

**World Wide Web** (**WWW**) The term given to describe the entire collection of Web servers all over the world that are connected to the Internet. The term also describes the particular type of Internet access architecture that uses a combination of HTML and various graphic formats, such as GIF and JPEG, to publish formatted text that can be read by Web browsers. Also called "The Web" or "W3".

**World Wide Web Consortium** (**W3C**) The organization that is jointly responsible with the IETF for maintaining and managing standards across the Web.

**X Windows** A GUI (Graphical User Interface) used on UNIX computers.

**X-face** An encoded 48 x 48 bitmap image used by e-mail and news users to contain a picture of their face or company logo.

**Xobject** External objects, such as sounds and movies, which are used in Macromedia Director presentations.

# INDEX

**A**

ActiveX control 30
Adobe
  online type shop 132
  OpenType 13
  Page Description Language 12
  Première 54–5
advertising, banners 115
advertising agencies, Web pages 74–5, 126
airlines, Web pages 110–11
ancient letterforms 142–3
animation 52–9, 96–7, 126
annual reports, online 116
antialiasing 12, 34
architecture, Web pages 138–9
art, Web pages 72–3, 80, 93, 96–7, 100–1, 127
Audi, Web pages 76–7

**B**

backgrounds
  black 74–5, 93, 104, 123, 148–9
  dark 82, 85
  images 64, 137, 164–5
  legibility 9, 14
  plain 90
  white 68, 84–5, 88–9, 90–1, 103
bad design, Web pages 75, 137, 162–8
banking, Web pages 70–1, 122
banners 97, 115
BBC, Web pages 78
bitmapped fonts 12
Bitstream, TrueDoc 13, 30
Bombsite, Web pages 100
bookselling, Web pages 140–1
brand identity 64, 70, 104–5, 108, 118–19
brewing industry, Web pages 94–5
browsers
  comparing results 9, 19
  CSS handling 28
  default fonts 20–1
  problems 71
buttons 62, 85, 88, 98, 134, 147
  see also navigation

**C**

Cable & Wireless, Web pages 66
Cadbury Schweppes, Web pages 147
cars, Web pages 63, 76–7
Cascading Style Sheets (CSS) 13, 28–9
channels, Photoshop 40–3
character group recognition 15
chemical industry, Web pages 102–3, 116
cinema, Web pages 82–5
circular themes 66–7
clocks, Web pages 152–3
CNN, Web pages 78–9
color
  combinations 174–5
  control 14
  cube 170–3
  depth 170
  legibility 9, 14
  mechanics 170–5
  page design 98–9
  rendered images 34–6
  site navigation 80, 111, 134
computer industry, Web pages 86–7
consumer durables, Web pages 148–9
corporate identity 64, 70, 104–5, 108, 118–19
CSS see Cascading Style Sheets
culture, Web pages 80–1, 97, 100, 160

**D**

default fonts 12, 20–1
  see also user preferences
design, print-based 8–10
design industry, Web pages 88–9, 96, 98–9, 130–1, 152–3, 165–8
designers, of Web sites 136–7, 166–7
displacement maps 44–5
dithering, color 34
download problems 87
download time
  enclosed fonts 30

images 36–7
long 67, 76, 103
short 119
drinks industry, Web pages 64–5, 94–5, 164
Dynamic HTML 144–5

**E**

electron guns 170
embedded fonts 30–1
embedded style sheets 28
enclosed fonts 30
external style sheets 28

**F**

farming, Web pages 163
fashion, Web pages 68–9, 90–1, 120–1, 128–9
file size
  enclosed fonts 30
  images 36–7
film industry, Web pages 82–5
filters
  Andromeda 3D 50–1
  animation 54–5
  KPT 46–7, 48–9
  Photoshop 46–7, 48–9
finance, Web pages 70–1, 108–9, 116–17
  see also banking
fishing reports, Web pages 162
Flash animation
  examples 67, 72, 76–7, 82, 94, 96, 138, 143
  using software 56–9
flashing devices 79
fonts
  default 12, 20–1
  downloadable 142
  enclosed 30–1
  intellectual property 30
  online selling 106–7, 132, 150–1
  overriding 27
  scaleable outline 12
  screen display 12–15
  tags 26–7, 29
  user preferences 12, 27
  see also typefaces

food industry, Web pages 132–3, 147
frame-based construction 80, 137
Freehand 38–9, 64
freely embeddable typefaces 31

**G**

Gamelan, Web pages 60
GIF
  animation 52–3, 54
  backgrounds 64
  color encoding 35, 36
  dithering 35, 36
  file format 32
  spacers 22
  standing type 16
  transparency 37
GifBuilder 52–3, 54
Gill, Eric 138
government, Web pages 74
Gradient Designer, KPT plug-ins 46–7
graduated fills, color 35
graphics see images
Graphics Interchange File see GIF
Green Party, Web pages 112–13
Guinness, Web pages 94–5

**H**

haiku, Web pages 160
heading tags 18–19
hexadecimal color codes 171–5
hinting, typeface integrity 31
HTML
  browser problems 71
  cascading style sheets 28–9
  color codes 171–5
  fonts 12–13, 26–7, 29, 30–1
  heading tags 18–19
  legibility 14–15
  line length 20–1
  lists 25
  paragraph breaks 22
  rules 23
  spaces 23
  tables 23–4
  type style tags 19
  typographic control 26–9

## Copyright Notice